D103 SOCIETY AND SOCIAL SCIENCE : A FOUNDATION COURSE

BLOCK I
FOOD FOR THOUGHT

THE OPEN UNIVERSITY

D103 PRODUCTION TEAM

John Allen
James Anderson (Chairperson)
Robert Bocock
Peter Bradshaw
Vivienne Brown
Linda Clark (Course Secretary)
David Coates
Allan Cochrane
Jeremy Cooper (BBC)
Neil Costello
Clare Falkner (BBC)
Stuart Hall
Susan Himmelweit
Jack Leathem (BBC)
Richard Maidment
Doreen Massey
Gregor McLennan
Andrew Northedge
Kay Pole
Marilyn Ricci (Course Manager)
Paul Smith
Richard Stevens
Elaine Storkey
Kenneth Thompson
Diane Watson
Margaret Wetherell

External Consultants
Tom Burden
David Deacon
David Denver
Caroline Dumonteil
Owen Hartley
Tom Hulley
Robert Looker
Angela Phillips
Colm Regan
Richard Sanders
Neil Thompson
Patrick Wright

Tutor Assessors
Alan Brown
Lyn Brennan
Mona Clark
Ian Crosher
Donna Dickenson
Brian Graham
Philip Markey
Norma Sherratt
Jan Vance

Tom Hunter, Chris Wooldridge, David Wilson, Robert Cookson, Nigel Draper, David Scott-Macnab (Editors); Paul Smith (Librarian); Alison George (Graphic Artist); Jane Sheppard (Designer); Sue Rippon (Project Control); Robin Thornton (Summer School Manager); John Hunt (Summer School IT); John Bennett; and others.

External Academic Assessors

Professor Anthony Giddens, Cambridge University (Overall Assessor)
Dr Geoffrey Harcourt, Cambridge University (Block III)
Dr Patrick Dunleavy, London School of Economics (Block IV)
Dr Halla Beloff, Edinburgh University (Block V)
Professor Brian Robson, Manchester University (Block VI)

The Open University,
Walton Hall, Milton Keynes,
MK7 6AA

First published 1991. Reprinted 1993, 1994, 1995. Copyright © 1991 The Open University

Designed by the Graphic Design Group of the Open University.

Typeset by The Open University and printed in the United Kingdom by The Alden Press, Oxford.

ISBN 0 7492 0037 5

For general availability of supporting material referred to in this text, please write to Open University Educational Enterprises Limited, 12 Cofferidge Close, Stony Stratford, Milton Keynes, MK11 1BY, United Kingdom.

Further information on Open University Courses may be obtained from the Admissions Office, The Open University, P. O. Box 48, Walton Hall, Milton Keynes, MK7 6AB.
1.5

BLOCK INTRODUCTION AND STUDY GUIDE

Prepared for the Course Team by James Anderson

CONTENTS

1 STUDYING SOCIETY AND SOCIAL SCIENCE

Welcome to Block I of 'Society and Social Science'. The five weeks you will spend on 'Food for Thought' is a time for you to find your feet, to discover what the course is about and how to study it.

When starting a new course you're not sure what to expect, or what will be expected of you. What is social science anyway, you may be wondering, particularly if this is your first social science course? How does it differ from other subjects you may have studied — natural science, or literature, or history? What, you may ask, can social science tell you about society that you don't already know simply from living in it, working in it, bringing up children, reading the papers or watching television? What sorts of knowledge and understanding will it add to what you already have? If this is your first university course you may be wondering how you will cope, what are the 'tricks of the trade' needed to get through the course, what help and guidance can you expect? And, if you have been studying recently, how will D103 improve your study skills and enable you to use your study time more efficiently?

The *Course Guide* gives some general answers to these questions. As you may already have read, it tells you that D103:

- will give you challenging insights into familiar aspects of United Kingdom society, placing them in a wider international and historical context;
- will show you that social science goes beyond 'common sense' ideas, that it springs from a long history of philosophical and social enquiry and produces specialized knowledge needed by modern societies;
- that university study involves learning to develop your own ideas using the course material and the advice on study skills.

But we all learn best by *doing*, and Block I involves you straight away in doing social science. The first three units are a demonstration of social science in action. They analyse a variety of important social issues about *food* (see Section 1.1, below), showing you the need to see these issues in a wider context and using them to introduce the main *themes* of the course (Section 1.2). The next two units then review the methods which have been used in analysing the *food* issues and some of the problems involved in social analysis. They introduce influential *traditions of social thought* which you will be studying throughout the course and they outline some of the roles which social science plays in today's society (Section 1.3). The units have advice on how to cope with studying (Section 1.4), and the 'Block I Study Guide' (Section 2, below) shows you how to plan your work over the first five weeks using the units and the other components of the course — television, radio, audio-cassette and sections of the set books (see also the *Course Guide*).

1.1 A SOCIAL ANALYSIS OF *FOOD*

Food is a fascinating topic which raises a variety of social issues and questions, some controversial, some relating directly to your own experience. Studying them will tell you a lot of things about the society and the world in which we live. Units 1, 2 and 3 discuss food production and consumption, who eats what, and who doesn't get enough and why. They deal with historical and contemporary factors influencing what we eat, with famine abroad, undernourishment at home and modern 'consumer society'. They begin to put contemporary UK society in its historical and international context, so that you can begin building up a picture of its changing place in a changing world.

Starting with a familiar topic should help you relate to the course and make for lively Block I tutorials. But you should also begin to see the ways in which D103 can add to what you already know. From personal experience you will know a great deal about some aspects of UK society, but direct experience is inevitably limited. Any one person can directly experience only so much and there are large areas of society to which you don't have direct access. You will learn a lot about these areas from the course material, and the first three units start the process of showing how social science moves beyond everyday experience.

What we eat reflects the history and geography of our society and its internal social and cultural differences. As you will see, many long-established items of the British diet are exotic products whose adoption was part of the history of the British Empire. More recent additions reflect the considerable 'internation-alization' of our diet and cuisine in recent decades and the development of a multi-cultural society which challenges some traditional assumptions about the meaning of 'being British'.

We need food to survive but most of us in the UK are fortunate and have plenty to eat. Nowadays it's not simply a matter of survival. Indeed some of us take food for granted a lot of the time. But all of us are influenced in what we choose to eat by, among other things, our family background, the social circles in which we move, by what we think we can (or can't really) afford, by the range of foods available in the local supermarket, or by our response (or lack of response) to subtle advertisements which don't just tell us about particular commodities but seem to offer the possibility of a new body-shape or life-style. We may also be influenced by moral values or political attitudes to the killing of animals, or to the destruction of the environment, or to the conditions of the workers who produce the food, the political regimes exporting it, the problems of the undernourished in this country, or the plight of the world's hungry for whom food is very much a matter of survival. Even if such concerns don't actually affect your choice of food, you may have views on what should be done about some of them. You might, for instance, have views on whether the solution to undernourishment in the UK rests mainly with public aid from the government, or private charity, or 'self-help'.

Some aspects of food are clearly very distant from our everyday experience, distant historically, geographically, and in terms of our control over them. Nowadays we're not always sure where our food comes from (I've even seen a single bunch of bananas with the stamp 'produce of several countries'), and we're not sure what chemicals may have been used in its production nor what their effects might be on our health. The days are long gone when people in this country produced most of their own food in private households or even bought it from local producers in the public market. Now our food comes from all over the globe, its production and distribution organized by multinational corporations. The goods and prices in your local supermarket depend on more than local demand. They are only possible because of complex chains of social relation-ships between employees and employers, producers and consumers, interna-tional markets and government policies in many countries.

Units 1 to 3 address a series of interesting questions about these issues. For example:

Unit 1 — How has the production of our food been transformed over the last few centuries, from largely local and sometimes self-sufficient production in pri-vate households to internationally organized production with distribution chains which span the globe? And what does this tell us about the development of modern society and the making of the world economy?

Unit 2 — What causes famines in 'Third World' societies, why does food produc-tion and distribution break down, and what does that indicate about the contemporary world? What lies behind the terrible images of famine which we see on television or in charity aid appeals? Are 'common sense' explanations which stress overpopulation and natural disasters correct? And how should 'famine' be defined, because different definitions lead to different policies for dealing with it?

Unit 3 — Who is undernourished in our relatively rich 'consumer society' and how does food consumption vary for different social groups? How have the consumption patterns of the majority been changing in recent decades? What effects do glossy advertising images have on people's self-image, desires and spending habits?

1.2   COURSE THEMES

In discussing these issues the three units use the course themes of *Public and Private*, *Local and Global*, and *Representation and Reality*. Each *pair* of concepts or 'labels' is used to organize evidence and raise questions about the food issues. As you will see, we can attach each pair of 'labels' to various aspects of society in order to study relationships and tensions between them; and you will find the themes useful in organizing your written assignments. The pairing of 'labels' points us towards all sorts of interesting questions about these tensions and relationships; and it is important to grasp that each *theme* is flexible and that we can choose to apply the same 'labels' to a variety of different things. It is of course possible to *mis*-apply them, but the three themes between them cover most of the main concerns of the course and if one theme isn't appropriate another may be. Their usefulness and how to use them will only become fully apparent when you see them 'in action' and begin using them for yourself. I'm briefly outlining them here so that you'll know what to look out for.

PUBLIC AND PRIVATE

We have in fact already used this theme and it probably didn't present you with any difficulties because the labels *public* and *private* are part of our everyday language. In mentioning the historical transformation of food production (Section 1.1) I distinguished between the *private* household and the *public* market. Further, in raising the question of a solution to undernourishment I distinguished between *public* aid from the government and *private* charity from the rest of us. And in discussing the economy there is the common distinction between the *public* sector and the *private* sector — between, for example, nationalized industries and the National Health Service on the one hand and private enterprise or privately-owned firms on the other.

These different uses of the words 'public' and 'private' illustrate how the same labels can be applied to different things; and the theme shows clearly how the pairing of labels points us towards interesting questions about relationships and tensions. For instance, is 'private medicine' parasitic on the publicly-funded National Health Service, or does it take pressure off a badly strained public service? Should famine relief be a public responsibility or left to private charity? What should be the balance between the *public* and *private* sectors of the economy? To what extent should the *public* realm — in the shape for instance of newspaper publicity or state regulations — intrude on *private* lives or effect what happens within *private* households?

LOCAL AND GLOBAL

This theme is used for dealing with relationships between things happening at different levels and it is very useful in discussing the wider context of particular aspects or areas of the UK. In the simplest case *local* literally refers to something in a small, local area (e.g. your local supermarket), while *global* refers to things at a world level (e.g. food distribution chains which span the globe). But the theme can be used in different ways depending on how we choose to define 'local' and 'global'. For example, if we are studying world patterns of hunger *global* means literally world-wide and individual countries might be considered *local*. Conversely, if we were studying relationships between the European Community and a region of the UK, we could choose to treat Europe as *global* and the region as *local*. In analysing something at a *local* level (e.g. the range of food items available in local shops) we can do so in terms of a *combination* of 'local' and 'global' factors; and, as D103 will show you, the relative importance given to each set of factors is often the main thing which separates different explanations in social science.

REPRESENTATION AND REALITY

The term 'representation' is used to cover various portrayals or interpretations of social reality which are common or widespread in society. It can be applied for example to common sense interpretations of famine as due simply to 'over-population', or it can be applied to the glossy images of advertisers, or to 'stereotypes' of women as bad drivers. You might object that glossy advertising images are representations of *un*reality, or that women drivers have fewer accidents than men, but 'representations' which have a wide currency can have important social consequences whether or not they are accurate. Advertisements, for instance, often propagate 'ideals' which few of us can attain (e.g., they depict men who are rich, tall and handsome, and women who are young, slim and beautiful) and these 'ideals' can affect our attitude to others and indeed to ourselves (even if they don't persuade us to buy the goods being advertised).

Common sense interpretations, and popular stereotypes and images are an important part of the social reality which social science studies. To understand social events and processes it is often necessary to understand the attitudes, beliefs or motives of the people involved. We have to understand how *other* people see or interpret reality even if we disagree with their interpretations. Our subject matter after all is living, thinking, feeling human beings and they attach particular and often totally different meanings and values to the same social issues (e.g. the advertiser and the health campaigner will differ on some issues of food consumption).

In having to understand other people and their social interrelationships, social science is like the study of history or literature. Many of its scientific procedures may be similar to those of natural science, but whatever the complexities facing the physicist, chemist or biologist, they don't face atoms, molecules and cells which can 'think for themselves'! In contrast, when the social scientist arrives on the scene as it were, he or she finds that the people involved already have their own interpretations of reality. Their different interpretations are what the *Representation and Reality* theme is designed to investigate.

1.3   METHODS AND TRADITIONS

The first three units of D103 use the themes and cover some of the concerns of the disciplines in social science — economics, geography, political science, psychology and sociology. They begin to show you how social science goes about its business of making sense of society: how it formulates questions — and formulating appropriate questions is 'half the battle'; how it collects and classifies evidence; how it constructs and compares explanations.

Units 4 and 5 then pull together and reflect on these scientific methods and procedures. Drawing on examples from Units 1 to 3, they review and reinforce what you will have learned about social science from studying the *food* issues, in preparation for the first assessed Tutor-marked Assignment (TMA 01) in week 5. With selected examples from the rest of the course, they preview and explain its main features.

Unit 4 concentrates on the methods used in the 'social analysis of *food*'. It explores what it means to *do* social science, from the painstaking collection and classification of evidence to the following up of imaginative hunches from which new explanations are developed. Our subject matter, however, includes issues of public debate and controversy, such as some of the *food* issues already mentioned (Section 1.1, above), where our understandings are influenced by moral or political values. *Unit 5* introduces D103's treatment of these matters by looking at the relationship between social science and society, and by outlining four major *traditions of social thought* — liberalism, conservatism, marxism and social reformism. These traditions embody different conceptions of society and how to understand it, and they have long been influential in society and in social science.

Unit 5 thus begins to put social science in its historical and social context. It will give you more substantial answers about the nature of social science and how it compares with other subjects you may have studied. You will see how social science procedures enable it to go 'beyond common sense', questioning assumptions and assertions and asking for evidence. 'Common sense' ideas are sometimes misleading, and an uncritical acceptance of them can prevent the exploration and exchange of ideas which is what university study is all about.

1.4 COPING WITH STUDY

But how will you cope, you may still be wondering? Well, the important point to remember over the next five weeks or so is that this is a time for you to acclimatize yourself to studying the course at your own pace. The units and their associated study skills material provide advice and suggestions, and the first television programme provides guidance on using television for study purposes. There is also the *Course Guide*, designed to be used throughout the course. If you haven't already done so, it's advisable to look through Section 2 of the *Guide* to get a quick overview of what D103 involves, and for information on particular items such as study skills and tutorial support. Your Tutor-counsellor is a vital link in the learning chain, advising you on how to get the most out of the course material, clarifying issues, and ensuring that you have the opportunity of exploring ideas with fellow-students in your local Study Centre group.

As for the material in Block I, it's worth emphasizing that you are *not* expected to *memorize* a lot of detail. It's there to illustrate and enliven general features of society and social science, but it is the general issues and approaches to them which are most important rather than the details. This isn't a quiz show! The main points in the units are usually contained in periodic 'Summaries' and it sometimes helps to re-read these. But don't worry if you haven't as much time as you would like. And if some things aren't clear, keep going! Block I provides lots of 'food for thought' about society, social science and how to study. However, it is only the introductory block, the important points are dealt with again in the course and you're not necessarily expected to fully grasp new ideas first time around.

Besides, many of the ideas will have a familiar ring, and some you'll know from everyday experience. The periodic exercises or *Activities* in the units provide space for you to respond to the course material, and the short unassessed practice TMA (08) based on Unit 1 is an early opportunity for you to start expressing your own ideas. It will give you practise in the crucially important study skill of essay-writing and it will enable you to get advice back from your Tutor-counsellor hopefully before you write the first assessed TMA (01).

So studying D103 really is a 'dialogue' between what you already know and what is in the course. Indeed it's a 'multilateral debate' in which tutors and students all learn from each other. And here the OU has a 'head start' over other universities because of the wealth of experience in its exceptionally diverse and mature student body, as I'm sure you'll find in tutorial sessions.

2   BLOCK I STUDY GUIDE

Block I introduces you to most of the components of D103 described in the *Course Guide*. Their introduction is phased over the five weeks so that you don't meet them 'all at once'. Here the block components are listed along with advice on allocating your study time between them, and you can refer back to this Study Guide as you study the block.

2.1   BLOCK COMPONENTS

The five *units* have already been described. The other components are:

COURSE READER

When signposted in Unit 1 you should read the first chapter of the Reader which gives historical and international background for understanding the contemporary UK. Unit 2 will send you to Chapter 2 and Unit 3 to Chapter 3 for a study skills exercise. In Unit 5 you will be advised to read the section on *Conservatism* in the essay in the Reader on *Traditions of Social Thought*.

STUDY SKILLS SECTIONS

(see *Course Guide*, Section 2.7)

The *Study Skills Sections* within Units 1, 3 and 5 concentrate mainly on organizing your study routines, and on reading, note taking and essay writing in preparation for your written assignments. You will be advised when to read the relevant chapters or parts of chapters of *The Good Study Guide*. There are also study skills exercises in the units, including exercises in Unit 2 on using numerical evidence.

TELEVISION

(see *Course Guide,* Section 3.1 and the *D103 Media Booklet*)

TV 01, the first television programme, comes in week 2 and is about the use of television in D103. TV 02 comes in week 4 and begins 'The UK in Context' series. Transmission times for broadcasts (of radio as well as television, and of the repeat transmissions of television) are given in the *Broadcast and Assignment Calendar.*

Before each viewing you should read the background material in the *Media Booklet* and do the exercises on the programmes afterwards. The programmes illustrate and reinforce what you study in the units and will be helpful for answering TMAs.

RADIO

(see *Course Guide,* Section 3.1)

Radio is first used in week 3, for a programme about the wider context of the contemporary UK. The second programme comes in week 5 and has topical comment and advice on answering TMA 01.

AUDIO-CASSETTE

(see *Course Guide*, Section 3.1)

The cassette for Block I will be mainly used in association with the *Study Skills Sections* particularly to discuss Unit 1 and essay writing.

ENDNOTES

You should always check if there are any footnotes, corrections or updating to block material in the block *Endnotes*.

ASSIGNMENTS

(see *Course Guide*, Section 2.8 and 3.7)

TMA 08 at the end of week 1 is a short practice essay based on material in Unit 1 and you're advised not to spend more than about two hours answering the question. In contrast, TMA 01, the first assessed TMA, can take up about half your study time in week 5.

The *Assignments Booklet* gives advice on how to answer the questions. The *Broadcast and Assignment Calendar* gives the cut-off dates by which your Tutor-counsellor should have received your assignments. It is important to send off your Unit 1 practice assignment (TMA 08) in good time in order that you get personal advice on essay writing before doing TMA 01.

USING THE *GLOSSARY INDEX*

(see *Course Guide*, Section 3.2)

You can begin referring to its definitions of technical terms right away, but it will be most useful later in the course when you are revising or wish to refer back to earlier material.

RESOURCE FILE

(see *Course Guide*, Section 3.3)

Compiling a resource file of newspaper and other cuttings on block topics is encouraged but not obligatory as you are informed in the *Course Guide*. It will help to relate course material to current affairs, provided you don't stray away from block topics or spend too much time on it. If you need advice or simply wonder whether you will have the time to compile a file as well as studying the course material, consult your Tutor-counsellor. For Block I we suggest that you confine yourself to just *two* of the following topics from Units 1 to 3:

food production and trade in the UK;

food production and famine in the 'Third World';

famine relief and aid from the UK;

poverty in the UK;

food-related health problems;

food buying and diet patterns.

2.2 STUDY TIME ALLOCATIONS

These time allocations will enable you to plan roughly what *proportion* of your available time to devote to each component.

Block components	Approximate study time (hours)
Block introduction and Study Guide	1
Unit 1: The world of food production	$5\frac{1}{2}$
Study Skills Section: Getting started (and Tape 1)	2
Reader: Chapter 1	$1\frac{1}{2}$
Practice TMA (08)	2
Total	12
Unit 2: The production of hunger	$6\frac{1}{2}$
Reader: Chapter 2	1
The Good Study Guide: Chapter 2	2
TV 01: Using television (and D103 Media Booklet)	2
Total	$11\frac{1}{2}$
Unit 3: The consumption of food	$6\frac{1}{2}$
Study Skills Section : Note taking Reader: Chapter 3	3
Radio 01	$\frac{1}{2}$
Total	10
Unit 4: Making sense of society	5
The Good Study Guide: Chapter 5, Sections 1 and 2	2
TV 02 Lifestyles, work and the family	2
Total	9
Unit 5: Social science in society	3
Study Skills Section: Writing TMA 01 (and Tape 1)	1
Reader: Chapter 22, Section 2.4 (Conservatism)	1
Radio 02 (Assignment 103)	$\frac{1}{2}$
TMA 01	6
Total	$11\frac{1}{2}$

UNIT 1   THE WORLD OF FOOD PRODUCTION

Prepared for the Course Team by Doreen Massey

CONTENTS

I   THERE'S NOTHING SO ENGLISH AS A CUP OF TEA?

Figure I   Afternoon Tea

What words and images does the picture bring to mind? — a cup of tea in the afternoon. 'Afternoon tea' is a ritual that is as English as oak trees or cricket. Set, in the picture here, in a garden, quite possibly in 'England's countryside ... a vital part of our national identity' (Shoard, 1980, p.9) ... a 'patchwork quilt of fields, downs and woods, separated by thick hedgerows, mossy banks, sunken lanes and sparkling streams' ... an image (a *representation*) which 'has knitted itself into our idea of ourselves as a nation'. Words such as 'quintessentially' come to mind. There is nothing so English as a cup of tea — in an English country garden.

Some of you may already be objecting. It is not an image of England which resonates with the windswept moors of Dartmoor or Northumberland, or with the high-density life of inner cities. What does it mean to people of Asian roots, or Afro-Caribbean? And the term 'Englishness' anyway, so often unthinkingly equated with 'Britishness', leaves out of account completely the other nations of the United Kingdom. One of the lines of enquiry of this course will be to investigate this internal variety and the ways in which it is held together.

In this first unit I want to use this same image to look outwards. What has it taken, thinking broadly both historically and geographically, to get quiet, sunlit afternoon teas on to the table in country gardens?

Well, it has taken the East India Company, and tea plantations in India, Sri Lanka and Africa; it has taken dairy farming somewhere in Europe, the Milk Marketing Board, pasteurization, and the Common Agricultural Policy; it has taken the trade in slaves from Africa to the sugar plantations of the Caribbean, and the development of huge refineries in Liverpool and London (if it is cane sugar) or sugar-beet farms stretching to the horizon in East Anglia or continental Europe (if it's beet). The bread will be made of wheat whose history involved 'opening up' the pampas of Argentina and the prairies of Canada and the USA (with all that that implied, from battles with indigenous North Americans to the building of thousands of miles of railway). Getting afternoon tea onto the table has taken the transformation of butter production from the domestic scale, where it was done mainly for home consumption, through a period of trade within Europe, to an industry which today spans the world. Let's say the butter is from New Zealand. And, to complete the classic imagery, if there are cucumber sandwiches, then:

> Even the humble cucumber has a history which started in south east Asia, where it was first cultivated three thousand years ago. It arrived in Europe as an expensive delicacy. It was cultivated in monastic gardens and served on medieval tables, before being mass-cultivated for pickling factories all over the world.
>
> (Rowling, 1987, p.8)

Perhaps you can think of more examples yourself. What about the water, for instance? And finally, of course, someone in the house had to make the tea.

ACTIVITY 1

Look back at that last paragraph. What types of change does it mention? What types of change has it taken, over the years, to get afternoon tea on to the table? Before you rush into an answer, stop a moment.

What does 'types' of change mean? What is the question trying to get at? Read through the paragraph again with this question in mind. What this question is asking for is not just a list of the particular changes mentioned in the paragraph. It is asking you to classify them into types. Thus a shift in the butter trade from local to European level to the world scale is an example of a *particular* change; as a *type* of change, where it could be classified with others of a similar type, it might be better called:

'a change in patterns of trade'

I stopped at that point because being sure about the question you are being asked is one of the most fundamental skills of social science (indeed of any science). It is a skill which will be essential to you in answering TMAs! If you are clear about the question (and sometimes, as in the case above, it might need interpreting), then you are well on the way to a good answer.

So what other types of change can you pick out? Try to find one, or perhaps two.

Did you find any of the following?
- Changes in where crops are grown (the case of the cucumber).
- Changes in the economic activities in particular places (the US mid-west is turned over to cereals, parts of East Anglia to sugar beet, British ports become centres for processing raw materials such as sugar cane — and also wheat).
- Technological changes (the coming of the railways, the development of mass production).
- The development of different ways of organizing production (from domestic production in the home to commercial production in the case of butter, slavery (and its subsequent abolition) in the case of sugar cane, and plantation-production of tea).

TMA

- The emergence of different groups of people doing particular tasks which are linked together in the production process, but which may be geographically far apart (plantation work, factory work, housework).

That paragraph in fact mentions just a few of the social processes and transformations which have gone into the production of afternoon tea. I am sure you can think of others. But even this list brings out two important points which are fundamental to this unit and to the course more widely:

First: *that behind even the apparently simplest objects and events may lie complex social stories*. That quotation, which I began above, about the history of the cucumber, continues: 'The processes of that transformation constitute the history of the cucumber; not an earth-shattering history perhaps, but a history nonetheless. The perspective of this kind of history is necessarily global because it stresses the links between economic, political, social and cultural developments in different parts of the world' (Rowling, 1987, p8). Not everything has as exotic a history as a cucumber sandwich, of course, but many of the things we look at in social science — like the English afternoon tea — come out of particular relations, or connections, between people, relations which themselves are the result of long historical processes of change. And it is part of the purpose of social science to elucidate these things.

Second: *that in order to understand the United Kingdom today, its characteristics and how it works, it is necessary to see it in its wider context; and that means wider both geographically and historically*. Quite how we *analyse* the links between the United Kingdom and the wider international setting — the *type* of links which exist — is a subject of much debate, which we shall be exploring. But there is no doubt that the *fact* of those links is an important part of what made the United Kingdom what it is today.

Afternoon Tea
From a chromolithograph by Percy A. Craft.

SUMMARY — AND INTRODUCTION!

Block I focuses on food, and in this unit we focus on the *production* of food. So one question we shall be exploring is: what kinds of social activity are involved, and have been involved in the past, to get food on to the tables of people in the UK? We shall be examining the enormous range of social relations, and social changes, in virtually all corners of the globe, which have gone into the production of the food we eat in the UK today. But examining this question will allow us also to do two other things. *First*, it will enable us to explore how an international economy is made, and to understand this country's place within it. In this sense we shall be using the production of food as an introduction to a bigger story. It will enable us to fill out a bit our statement that in order to understand the United Kingdom today it is necessary to see it in its wider context.

Second, our investigation will allow us to develop further our ideas about social science and how to do it. In fact, we have already covered some pointers in this direction. Let's recap what they were:

- We have begun to appreciate the importance of being absolutely clear about the question we are dealing with.

- You have also had some experience of another fundamental skill of social science — that of using particular examples to draw out more general lessons. That is what you were doing in the *Activity* — using a particular story to begin to think about more general types of change.

- We have met a recurring theme-tune of social science, and one which we shall continue to explore throughout the course — that behind even the apparently simplest objects and events may lie complex social stories.

You will also begin to see how the course themes outlined in the *Block Introduction* can be used to make sense of these stories.

So, this unit is about more than the production of food. It will be using that story to draw out more general lessons. This means that the important thing about this unit is not the particular factual detail. Certainly you should *not* try to remember it — it is there to be used, not to be memorized. Indeed, one of the things you will be learning is how to pull out the important points from a complex discussion. The cassette at the end will help you to do this.

For instance, this unit will introduce you to using the themes of the course. It will raise some issues which arise in the exploration of the production of food, and which we hope will get you thinking. This unit, then, is like a taster, an introduction to a range of ideas and ways of thinking which you will develop further as you go through the course.

2   THE PRODUCTION OF FOOD

2.1   FOOD BECOMES A COMMODITY

One of the most important things which made that afternoon tea possible is the fact that, while food may be a basic human necessity, much of it is also produced, sold and bought as a *commodity*. Few if any of the things on the table are the product of that garden. This food has been bought from producers elsewhere.

Much of the food that we eat today comes in the form of commodities. This may seem a very straightforward statement. But in fact it is not. *First* of all, there is debate between social scientists about how exactly to define 'a commodity'. Definition (sometimes called conceptualization) is basic to social science. Any attempt to produce a social scientific explanation forces us to define our terms more precisely. Indeed, many of the advances of social science have been made through more perceptive definition. But definitions are also often the subject of fierce debate. They are themselves rarely 'neutral'. This is because the particular definition which any social scientist adopts will depend on their wider theoretical viewpoint. For the moment, let us adopt a fairly minimal definition on which many would agree, which is that *a commodity is something which is made to be sold.*

Second, that definition of a commodity may also seem perfectly natural and obvious to us now, but things were not always so. Although real local self-sufficiency disappeared centuries ago in Britain to give way to a money-economy and considerable trading of produce between countryside and town, and between regions, the explosive growth of commodity production is relatively recent, in the case both of food and of other products. Up until the mid-nineteenth century much butter production, for instance, was done on a domestic scale and for home consumption. If there were surpluses to the requirements of the home, these were sold at markets, first local ones and then as transport improved, especially with rail transport, to markets further afield. It was only later in the nineteenth century that production shifted decisively out of the home and into larger dairies where workers were employed specifically to produce butter for sale.

There is a more general point here about the nature of social science. And it links back to our earlier discussion. A good social scientist should always be wary of thinking of anything as 'natural'. 'Never take anything for granted' and always ask 'why?' are good maxims, and they reflect our earlier point — that behind even the most obvious and normal-seeming thing there may be an interesting social explanation.

The story of tea itself illustrates such shifts even more dramatically, and at an international level. Tea was first developed as a drink in China, where it was called ch'a (from where we derive our own word 'char'). In AD 805 a mandarin, Lu Wo, wrote *The Ch'a Ching* (The Book of Tea) and by that time tea was part of the internal Chinese tax and finance system. By 1200, it was a major item in commerce between provinces, and by 1400, Hunan farmers had begun to specialize in its production (Rowling, 1987, pp. 74-5). But it was still unknown in Europe.

Indeed it was not until the 1650s that tea was first brought to Britain. It did not immediately catch on. It was only when Charles II married the Portuguese Princess Catherine of Braganza (itself an arrangement stimulated by considerations of trade) in 1662, that things began to change:

She arrived with her dowry, which was Bombay and Tangier ... and her tea-chests. The king neglected her and she found solace in tea. As a bribe, the directors of the East India Company gave her regular presents of tea; the Court ladies imitated her, and the taste for tea spread to bourgeois housewives like Mrs Pepys and thousands like her. However, at 50 shillings a pound, tea did not spread far beyond the Court; tea drinking and brewing became a high status ceremonial which only the richest and most refined ladies, allegedly, understood.

Throughout the eighteenth century the cost of tea fell and the taste for it spread. The bourgeoisie was soon commenting on the habits of tea-drinking servants who aped their betters ...

(Rowling, 1987, p.76).

Before we go any further, pause and relate this to our opening images, and to our theme of *representation and reality*. If tea did not even arrive in Britain until the middle of the seventeenth century, then the representation of taking afternoon tea as quintessentially English is really of quite recent origin. Moreover it dates back to 'foreign' practices! Popular representations of what it is to be English (let alone the relationship of that to being British) clearly have their own histories, and change and develop over time.

But back to tea. By the end of the eighteenth century events were pushing towards an expansion of its trade. On the one hand, demand continued to increase as the taste for tea spread downwards through broader strata of the population (in other words the representation of tea as 'fashionable' in turn affected demand). On the other hand, the East India Company needed to increase its tea trade. (It had been bringing textiles from India for sale in the British market but was now prevented from doing so by the expanding British textile-manufacturers.) The problem was that the British merchants had not been involved in *producing* tea, they had only been *buying* it in Asia and *selling* it in Britain. Moreover, the only place where tea could then be bought was China. But the Chinese kept a strict and highly secretive control over the tea industry and wanted very little that Europeans could offer in return for tea. It seemed impossible to increase supply.

In fact, it *was* possible. Tea could be won from the Chinese in exchange for opium, grown under the supervision of the company in India and smuggled into China. It was an illegal trade; China had banned the import of opium in 1800, but smuggling was nevertheless carried on on some scale. The situation led to war (the 'Opium Wars' of the mid-nineteenth century). The British navy won, and the United Kingdom gained the right to trade in the five Treaty Ports of China, as well as being ceded the territory of Hong Kong. Most importantly perhaps in the longer run, free trade with China had been established.

But while these events increased the amount of tea which could be bought, they still did not give the British traders control over production itself. In 1851 a botanist working for the East India Company supervised the transfer of some tea plants, plus some Chinese advisors, to Assam in north India. Land leases were granted to aspiring planters. Since to establish a plantation they had to have capital these planters were virtually all European. Workers were employed, and tea production boomed. Plantations spread, railways were built and new workers were recruited from outside the region. By the beginning of the twentieth century, half a million plantation workers in Assam were supplying half the world's demand for tea.

In 1875 the tea plant had been taken to Ceylon (Sri Lanka) where similar events occurred, many of the workers in this case being poor Tamils from the south of India. By 1905, there were 150,000 hectares (about 370,500 acres) under tea plantations in Ceylon. There have been many changes since. For instance, the crop was transferred once again in the 1930s to East Africa, and further plantations were established. In the 1940s it was taken from Ceylon to Brazil. But it was these years of the nineteenth century which marked the crucial shift in control over production from the Far East to British interests, and when British interests themselves shifted from being merchant-traders in tea to making profits also from its production.

SUMMARY

About social science:

- Social scientists are wary of accepting things as 'natural' — they tend to demand an explanation of *why* things are as they are.

- A good definition, or conceptualization, is fundamental to providing a good explanation.

About the production of food:

- Much of the food we eat in the UK today is produced in the form of a commodity.

- A minimal definition of a commodity is that it is something which is produced to be sold.

- Food has not always been produced and distributed as a commodity. The development of commodity production has been a long historical process.

Reminder! You do not have to worry about the details of this history. The three points above are the important ones, which you should make sure you understand.

As you read the next section, write down your own notes of the main points being made about the production of food.

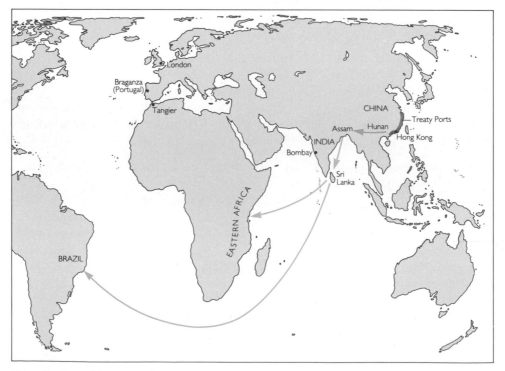

Figure 2   Part of the story of tea

2.2   A REVOLUTION IN FOOD PRODUCTION

The long historical process of turning food into a commodity has brought with it major changes in societies all over the world. The fact that food was traded meant that not everyone had to be self-sufficient. They could purchase food from others. Specialization in particular products became possible on a larger scale (one region could concentrate on one product, another on a different one). As the trading links extended geographically so the possibilities of exchange became wider, the need diminished for local communities, regions or even whole countries to be self-sufficient in food, and the possibilities expanded for a more varied local diet. Trade enabled specialization; and specialization encouraged trade.

 But the story of tea illustrated a further and possibly even more dramatic shift, when the merchants moved towards taking direct control over production itself. Making a profit from *trade* involved the relatively simple process of 'buying cheap and selling dear', although in between those two operations there may be, as we have seen, journeys half-way round the world. Making a profit from *production*, by contrast, meant employing workers to make the products in the first place, and organizing the production process in such a way that the products can be sold for more than it costs the owner to make them. This is *capitalist* commodity production. One immediate and obvious result of it is a division between those who own the places of production and who employ others to do the production, and those who work in them (waged labour).

 Such workers find their food not from what they themselves produce directly, even though they may be working in a factory where food is produced, but in exchange for the fruits of their labour — wages. Indeed, the government regularly produces calculations of how long workers earning different levels of wages per hour have to work in order to buy other commodities, including food. Table 1 gives some of the calculations for recent years. What do you make of these statistics? They reflect a number of the points we have already considered. They are based on a very particular *definition* of a household, and the definition used will affect the calculation of the numbers in the table. What is more, that definition presumably reflects what Department of Employment and Treasury officials think of as a 'normal' household. In fact the description applies to only a minority of households in the country!

Table 1   Length of time necessary to work to pay for selected services. [1]

	1971		1981		1986	
	hrs	mins	hrs	mins	hrs	mins
1 large loaf (white sliced)		9		8		7
1 lb of rump steak		54		57		45
500 gr. of butter (home produced)		20		20		16
1 pint of fresh milk		5		4		4
1 dozen eggs (medium size)		22		16		14
100 gr. of coffee (instant)		22		19		22
125 gr. of tea (medium priced)		9		7		6
1 pint of beer		13		12		12
1 bottle of whisky	4	17	2	24	2	4
20 cigarettes		22		20		22

[1] These figures are for a 'married couple with husband only working', and refer to the length of time necessary for a married man on average hourly male earnings for all industries and services, with non-earning wife and two children under 11, to work so that his net income pays for the various goods.

Source: *adapted from* Social Trends 18, *based on Department of Employment and HM Treasury statistics.*

The revolution in the production of food was thus one with many aspects and huge results. Take, as they say, the biscuit:

> … what could be more convenient or handy than the biscuit. The biscuit came to be such a British taste from naval roots. From the eighteenth century, navy bakers made biscuits suitable for long journeys. Hard ones, with low water content. And they were made in traditional, small output bakeries around the docks. Early mechanisation was also state sponsored. … Machines were borrowed from printing works to increase output and cut down on labour costs. Private capital moved in to the biscuit trade in a big way only in the nineteenth century, with the development of the fancy biscuit. Prior to this time, fancy biscuits were made domestically. The new firms … sold to the upper and middle classes. And they sold at prices which although expensive (because sugar was dear) could undercut the skilled wage rates of domestic female cooks. This process of deskilling a domestic and, therefore, usually female task is to be found repeatedly in food history …
>
> (Clutterbuck and Lang, 1982, pp. 92–3).

There is a whole host of things to note from this quotation. Here are just two:

- the reference to a national 'taste' again, though this time it is British not just English, and with a recognition that it has not existed from time immemorial but is the product of specific historical circumstances (what were they?);

- most important of all for our argument are *the kinds of changes* in the way in which the production of fancy biscuits was organized.

―――――――――――――――― ACTIVITY 2 ――――――――――――――――

What types of changes were these?

Before you rush into an answer, remember what was said earlier about considering questions carefully. What *types* of changes were they?

―――――――――――――――――――――――――――――――――――――――

I'd say there were lots of different kinds of change in the way in which fancy biscuits were produced. They include:

- the *place* of production changed, from the home to the factory;

- the *control* over the production of fancy biscuits changed, from the householder to 'private capital';

- the *reason* for the production of these biscuits changed, from consumption by the household in which they were made, to production for sale at a profit;

- in a parallel way, the *employment relations* of the people who actually made the biscuits changed, from being employed as domestic servants from whose labour no profit was expected, to being workers whose labour would contribute directly to the making of profit in production.

So, the fact that much food is produced and exchanged in this way is a relatively recent phenomenon on the scale of human history, and it has brought with it many different types of social change. It has often also been the subject of conflict and protest. Even the imposition of the laws of supply and demand (what we now often call the 'free market') met with fierce resistance. From the late eighteenth century up to the 1840s there were bread and food riots in almost every town and county in Britain. The '"laws" of supply and demand, whereby scarcity inevitably led to soaring prices, had by no means won acceptance in the popular mind' (Thompson, 1963, pp. 67-9). It is another example of something which we tend nowadays perhaps to think of as 'natural' being no such thing at all.

Afternoon tea

The bread riots resulted from the conversion of food into a freely-traded commodity. The conversion of food production (and other production) into capitalist commodity production resulted in even greater changes. It was part of a much wider transformation which we refer to now as the Industrial Revolution. In Britain agricultural methods had been transformed and many people had left the land. They found work in the new factories in the fast-growing towns and cities. The 'old moral order' of traditional deference in small communities where the old classes lived close together and everyone, supposedly, knew their place, was torn apart both socially and geographically. It was a social upheaval which also gave an enormous spur to the development of social science — as you will see when you come to read the essay on Traditions.

Britain was early into the field of capitalist commodity production and was the first industrial capitalist economy. Other European powers soon followed suit (see Figure 3). Traders and industrialists from Britain and the rest of Europe were the first to bring capitalist forms of commodity production on any scale to those countries we now count as part of the 'Third World', but which already had for long had great civilizations and complex systems of production and trade. Here too the impact was dramatic. But it was different from the impact on most western European countries. We saw earlier how vast areas of Assam and Ceylon were turned over to the production of tea for export; in such cases the local people either had to become workers on the plantations or migrate to the towns. It was a situation ripe with potential conflict, which was repeated again and again in different parts of the world. On the one hand, such commodity production might contribute to the growth of an economy based around a crop (which might itself be a food) produced for export abroad. On the other hand, local people could sometimes be worse off due to a shortage of land on which to grow food for themselves. In the case of some plantations, workers had small plots of their own on which to grow food. These workers, therefore, were not (indeed *are* not, for the practice still continues) waged labour in the sense we know it in the UK.

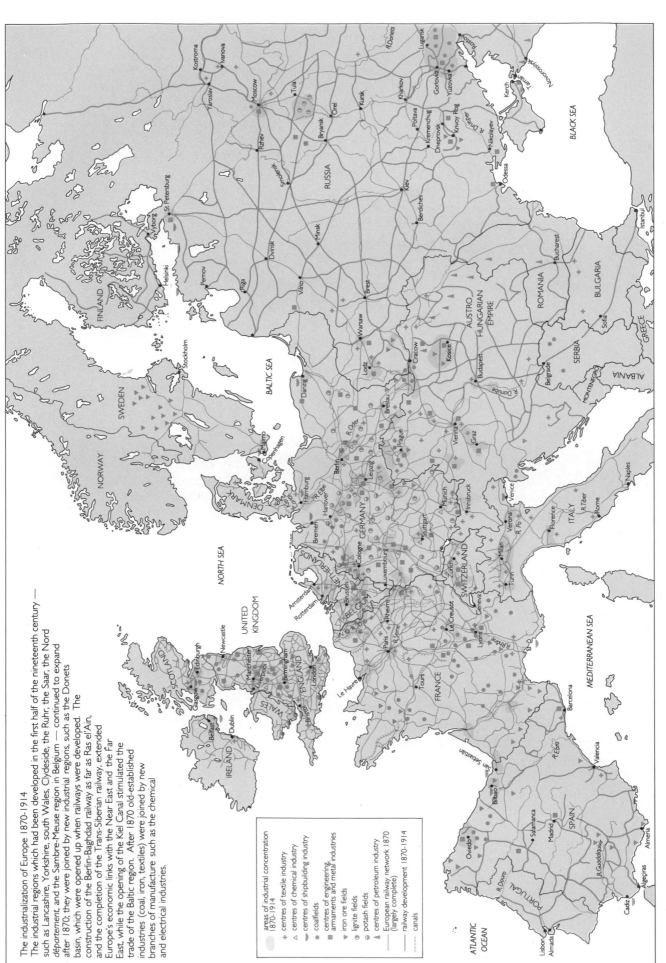

The industrialization of Europe 1870-1914

The industrial regions which had been developed in the first half of the nineteenth century —
such as Lancashire, Yorkshire, south Wales, Clydeside, the Ruhr, the Saar, the Nord
département, and the Sambre-Meuse region in Belgium — continued to expand
after 1870: they were joined by new industrial regions, such as the Donets
basin, which were opened up when railways were developed. The
construction of the Berlin-Baghdad railway as far as Ras el'Ain,
and the completion of the Trans-Siberian railway, extended
Europe's economic links with the Near East and the Far
East, while the opening of the Kiel Canal stimulated the
trade of the Baltic region. After 1870 old-established
industries (coal, iron, textiles) were joined by new
branches of manufacture such as the chemical
and electrical industries.

areas of industrial concentration 1870-1914
+ centres of textile industry
△ centres of chemical industry
○ centres of shipbuilding industry
● coalfields
■ centres of engineering, armaments and metal industries
▼ iron ore fields
◉ lignite fields
◯ potash fields
▲ centres of petroleum industry
— European railway network 1870 (largely complete)
— railway development 1870-1914
⋯ canals

Figure 3   The Industrialization of Europe 1870-1914

In the case of sugar, another commodity which went to make up our afternoon tea, the process was somewhat different. As in the case of tea, production of sugar on a large scale as a commodity entailed transplanting the crop itself half across the world. This time the main passage was from southern Europe, via Madeira and the Canary Islands in the Atlantic across the ocean to the West Indies and Brazil. Again, labour too was transplanted. The demand for labour outstripped that available from the local population and between 1601 and 1870 nearly ten million people in total were shipped from Africa, between 3 and 4 million to Brazil, over 5 million to the Spanish Americas and the Caribbean, and one-third of a million to the USA, to work on plantations of sugar and other crops. Here, the system of 'employment' was not capitalism at all in the early years, but slavery, with the worker the property of the owner of the plantation.

Once again we see the importance of precise definition. Terms such as 'work' and 'employment' can refer to a number of different ways of organizing labour.

SUMMARY

What points did you draw out about the revolution in food production? That:

- the period when European merchants made a profit from trade was succeeded by one in which profits were increasingly made by Europeans from production itself;

- commodity production, and capitalist commodity production in particular, is a historically-specific way of organizing production — that is to say it has not always existed;

- the emergence of commodity production has been the result of major historical shifts which have had huge impacts on society, both in the UK and in the wider world;

- behind any object which is a commodity, therefore, lies a particular way of organizing production and trade and a long, and eventful, history.

2.3   THE MANY FORMS OF PRODUCTION

From the way I have told 'the story so far', you could be forgiven for thinking that commodity production, and especially capitalist commodity production, had swept all before it and that all production is now done in this way. Yet, certainly as far as food is concerned, that is not the case. Not even in the First World.

ACTIVITY 3

Go back to Section 1 and the case of afternoon tea. What types of labour do you think would be involved today in producing it? What part of that production is almost certainly not done on a commodity basis?

However, it is most especially true of the Third World that not all production is commodity production. Recent calculations indicate that almost *one-third* of the world's population grow most of their own food. Such food, since it does not enter market exchange, is not a commodity. Not all 'products' are 'commodities'. (Looked at from this point of view, the way we do things in the United Kingdom is certainly not 'natural', and not even 'normal' in the sense of being similar to the way the majority of peoples and societies do them.) In some parts of the Third World, there have been attempts to move *away* from commodity production in a capitalist form. In both Guyana and Jamaica, for instance, there have been attempts to reorganize the production of sugar, in both countries a major source of export-earnings, along cooperative lines. Ownership of production was taken out of the hands of the multinationals (like Booker McConnell Ltd in Guyana, and Tate and Lyle which had been important in Jamaica) and nationalized (Latin America Bureau, 1984; Larkin and Widdowson, 1988). By this action, it was hoped that better trading terms on the world market could be established. In Jamaica, while the land taken over from the company was taken into state ownership, control over production on the plantations themselves was given over to the plantation workers. Cooperatives were established, wages were increased, some workers learned new skills in management and administration, and more services were provided. The cooperatives were started in 1976 and there came to be twenty-three of them, together producing a half of the country's total output of sugar.

Figure 4   The location of Jamaica and Guyana

The cooperatives were established by the People's National Party (PNP) under Michael Manley. But they were not to last. Some of the problems they faced were the result of simple misfortune — a disease on the plants, for one. Others came from external political antipathy towards the cooperatives on the part of the USA and the International Monetary Fund (IMF). Yet others arose from the structural difficulties of Third World countries such as Jamaica — that is, their position in the world economy, which makes them dependent on selling primary products on the international market. This can be especially difficult for countries with only a few major exports. Jamaica was in this situation, and had to face the world market for its primary products, and world market prices. Just between 1976 and 1977 the price of sugar in the European Community fell by 28 per cent. In 1980, with the economy in great difficulty, the PNP lost the elections. The cooperatives were closed down and Tate and Lyle was invited back to manage the industry.

The point of this illustration is not to suggest that such experiments are impossible — in a sense, it is precisely the opposite. Some Third World countries which have decided to follow such policies *have* managed, through taking control of production and shielding themselves from world market forces, to insulate themselves partially and to pursue alternative paths. Cuba, and

China at certain periods, are probably the clearest examples. But the illustration does demonstrate the power of the world market.

It is however in 'the Second World' (the Soviet Union and Eastern Europe, for instance) that capitalist commodity production in its pure form has been perhaps of least importance. I say 'in its pure form' because such countries do participate to some extent in world markets. Moreover, the degree to which they do so is increasing. Workers do still work for wages, and as I write this unit major economic changes are taking place which may, it has yet to be seen, lead some of them to introduce more characteristics of capitalist production and a market economy. Nonetheless, for much of the twentieth century these economies have been organized on substantially different principles. Most production has been owned and run by the state — it has not been 'private'. These have been centrally-planned economies. Individual plants have not been under such compulsion to turn in a profit, and prices and wages have been subject to controls.

Afternoon tea — the product of much domestic labour

But even in the capitalist market economies of the First World, not all parts of production take the commodity form. What was your answer to Activity 3? (Don't just read on! Go back and check.) What part of the production of afternoon tea is probably not done even on a commodity basis, let alone a capitalist one? Well, of course, the tea itself has to be brewed, the bread buttered, the cucumbers sliced, and the sandwiches cut. In the example of fancy biscuits in the last section 'the upper and middle classes' were assumed to have a cook as a domestic servant. This was not, as we have seen, capitalist production, but it was a major sector of employment in the economy throughout the nineteenth century. By today, the end of the twentieth century, such labour has been divided two ways. Domestic servants have dwindled in number; domestic labour in almost all strata of the population is now provided free. Cooking is certainly part of 'the production of food', but if it is done in the home without a wage it does not find its way into the employment statistics. Indeed, it is very often not even counted as production. Many writers describe 'the home' as a place of consumption, as though no production took place there at all! Once again we are faced with issues of definition, and of the need to be clear about our interpretations. Our theme of *public and private* can be helpful here. In part, what these statistics reflect is a distinction between the 'private' world within the household, where work is done without payment of wages, and where statistics on production and exchange are not collected, and the 'public' world of the formal economy and paid employment, which is fully recognized and carefully documented in the data. This latter (the public domain) is what is normally thought of as 'real' production. But is it? This question does not only apply, in relation to food production, to cooking. It also applies, for instance, to growing food on private allotments. All the 'digging for victory' which people were urged to do during the Second World War, to contribute to national food supplies, never entered the national statistics on production.

─────────────────────────── ACTIVITY 4 ───────────────────────────

What do you think? — *ought* the official statistics to include production and exchange within the household?

You might want to argue *NO* — it is a private matter, between individuals and their families.

On the other hand, as a true individualist, you might want to reply — *YES*. It is individuals which matter, not households. Perhaps we ought to know who are the producers, and how much is produced, even here.

But (you might retort) — *NO* — really, accepting all those things, *this* data is about the real economy, which means paid jobs and monetary exchanges. What goes on inside the household may be worthy of study in its own right, but it's not related to statistics on the real economy.

Oh but — *YES* — (you could reply) because they *are* related. If everyone decided to cook their own fish and make their own chips from scratch (i.e. from potatoes!) there would be:

> no fish-finger industry
> no frozen-chip industry
> no fish and chip shops.

It would certainly affect the 'real economy'.

───

But some of the food production which was done within the domestic economy in the nineteenth century has been taken out of it. It has been turned into commodity production. Fish fingers, canned fruit, commercially-produced jams, pre-prepared vegetables, ready-mix sauces, frozen pastry, TV dinners and 'take-away' meals, all represent in different ways and different degrees the commodification of parts of the process of food production which used to occur within the household.

But, as you are probably already objecting in response to that last paragraph, the movement is not all in one direction. As I write this, a move away from pre-prepared food is happening. Parts of food production may be being taken back into the home as some people prefer to cook and bake for themselves rather than buy food ready-made. (Though that in turn might mean more kitchen gadgets can be sold!) Household production, just like commodity production, has its own history, though it is much less often told. And the boundary between commodity production and other forms of production is always under negotiation. The popularity of allotments, for instance, has waxed and waned dramatically. In the Second World a major restructuring of the form of economic organization began in the late 1980s; in the Third World experiments continue with alternative forms of production. The forms of production which are dominant in the United Kingdom today are historically-specific, geographically-specific, and always — at least potentially — open to change.

Nonetheless, it *has* been commodity production organized on capitalist lines, and the impetus to trade and technological change which it engendered, which has been the major force in constructing the modern world economy. And that is the second part of our story in this unit.

SUMMARY

- There are many different forms of production, in each of the First, Second and Third Worlds.
- Moreover, the boundary between different forms of production (for instance between commodity production and household production) is continually shifting as a result of social changes.
- Once again, conceptualization is vital. There are debates even over what should be counted as 'production'.

=== READER ===

This is a suitable place to read Chapter I of the Reader, which will give you a wider picture of this history. (If you have already read this chapter, have a quick read through it again.)

---

3   THE MAKING OF A WORLD ECONOMY

3.1   FROM THE 'VOYAGES OF DISCOVERY' TO THE EIGHTEENTH CENTURY

There had, of course, been major international trading routes well before the Europeans set out to 'discover' the world at the end of the fifteenth century. There was trade in salt from the Mediterranean northwards up the rivers of Europe, there was trade in grain from North Africa to Rome — indeed there was a very complex trade centred on the Mediterranean — there was a major trade in agricultural products centred on Malacca on the west coast of what is now Malaysia, and one in spices which extended from the east coast of Africa across the Indian Ocean and on to Japan. A succession of empires rose and fell. The most extended trading empire in the world in AD 1500 was that of the

Arabs. From Europe, Portugal and then Spain developed trading empires encompassing their colonies in the 'new world'. They in turn were succeeded by the Dutch: by AD 1600 Amsterdam had achieved pre-eminence in trade. Nonetheless, before the eighteenth century, the only really long-distance trade controlled from Europe was in silver and gold plundered from the Spanish Americas, and in spices from the Dutch East Indies. But the eighteenth century saw the rise to dominance of European merchants making their profits from trade across the world. And by the eighteenth century, after a struggle with Holland, London in turn had won supremacy. This trade was still tiny in comparison with that of today, and because of its difficulties and costs it was primarily in luxury goods (in sixteenth century Europe, pepper was worth almost as much as gold; and sugar was the fourth most valuable commodity in Europe after gold, silver and pepper).

Lloyds coffee house: a caricature of 1808

But small though it was, the trade had major impacts on all the societies it touched. In other words, and to put the same point in more general terms, changes at global level had local effects. Here, then, we can pick up another course theme: the *local and the global*. Let us look at just two of the *local impacts* on Britain of these global changes.

First, the trade led to a major expansion of port activity in Britain, and a shift in the regional geography of the country. The southern half and the eastern parts of England had for long been the most densely-populated and the main

Lloyds of London: the "86 Building'

centre of economic activity, with many small ports engaging in trade with Europe and serving quite restricted hinterlands. With the development of the new trade, that was to change. While London retained its importance, it was the ports on the west of the country (Glasgow, Liverpool, Bristol) which grew fastest around the new sea-going commerce (Jackson, 1986, pp.94 and 96).

Figure 5 shows some of the commodities being imported into Britain at the turn of the eighteenth century. It was to be just the beginning.

Second, although much of the trade brought into Britain was for consumption here, not all of it was. A considerable amount was re-exported. From such beginnings, London, and particularly 'the City', was to become a major international centre for trade in commodities. Today, the London Commodity Exchange in the City is the umbrella organization for a massive trade in what are called 'soft' commodities, things such as cocoa, coffee, sugar, tea, potatoes, grain, soya bean meal, feed, oils, seeds, fats, jute, timber, wool and rubber (Clarke, 1986, p.8). It is one among many institutions of the City which date from this period. The Baltic Mercantile and Shipping Exchange, which covers wheat, barley and other commodities, and deals with chartering and brokerage of shipping, Lloyd's the international insurance market, and the Stock Exchange itself, all have their origins 'in the coffee houses of the seventeenth century, where the ships' captains and merchants met to arrange cargoes' (Clarke, 1986, p.113). These years of the dominance of British merchants established London as a world centre of international commerce. And that in turn influenced the geography and society of Britain. Merchants and bankers became a powerful and wealthy part of the population, and their concentration in London further increased the pre-eminence of the capital city within the economy and society as a whole.

Thus, changes happening at international level had a significant impact on the regional geography of Britain (the global affected the local). Moreover, the results of those changes are still with us. Liverpool and the other western ports have declined dramatically as the pattern established in these years has shifted again more recently. And the significance of the City in British geography and society is still with us today.

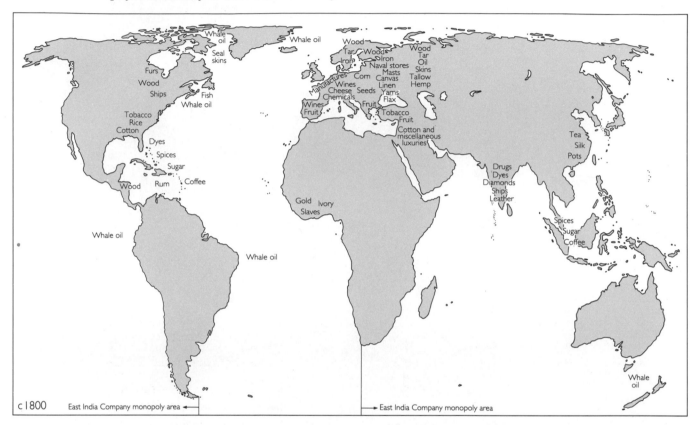

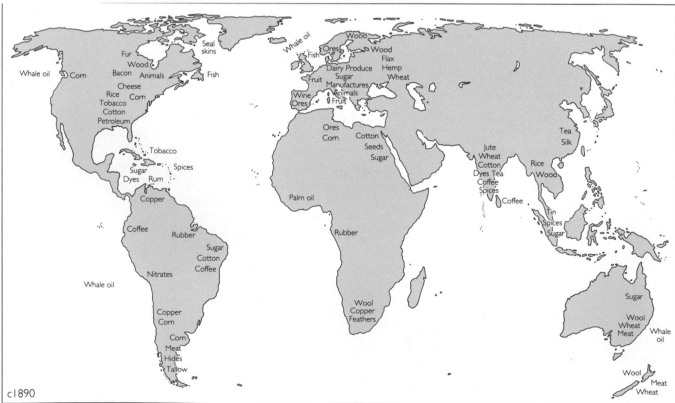

Figure 5   Commodity imports 1800 and 1890

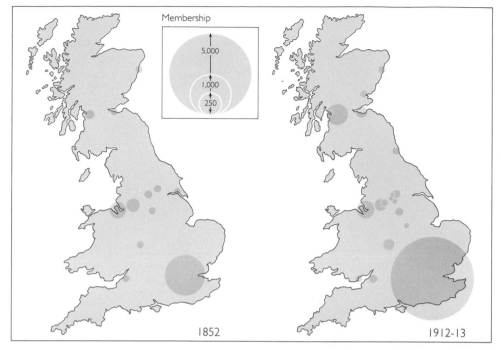

Figure 6   Stock exchange membership 1852 and 1912–13. The green circles indicate the number of members in a particular area. In both time-periods London had by far the biggest number of members. (Note that as in many cases data on Northern Ireland is not given. In this case it is because of political changes between those dates and today.)

3.2   FROM THE INDUSTRIAL REVOLUTION TO THE EUROPEAN COMMUNITY

The information contained in Figure 7 is concerned with the second half of the nineteenth century and the beginning of the twentieth. The Industrial Revolution was well established in Britain, factory employment was increasing by leaps and bounds, and was growing too in other European countries. What the maps and diagrams represent are some of the main changes going on in each of the countries selected.

─────────────── ACTIVITY 5 ───────────────

Picking up the message from the last section, about the links between changes taking place in widely-separated parts of the world, the question now is: *how* are these changes, taking place so far away from each other, linked together? In other words, how did these global changes have local effects in different continents? We shall be exploring these issues in this section. But have a go at thinking about some of them for yourself first. The questions below are meant to give you a start. I'd be very surprised if you could answer all of them right now. Some of the information you can get from Figure 7, but for the rest just give yourself a moment to speculate before reading on:

1   How did the growth of the industrial cities in Britain affect the demand for goods from parts of Africa?

2   Industrialization in Britain went along with large-scale emigration. Where (from the countries shown) did people go? What effects did that have in the countries they went to?

3   How did the building of railways in Argentina, the USA and Canada affect the countryside of Britain?

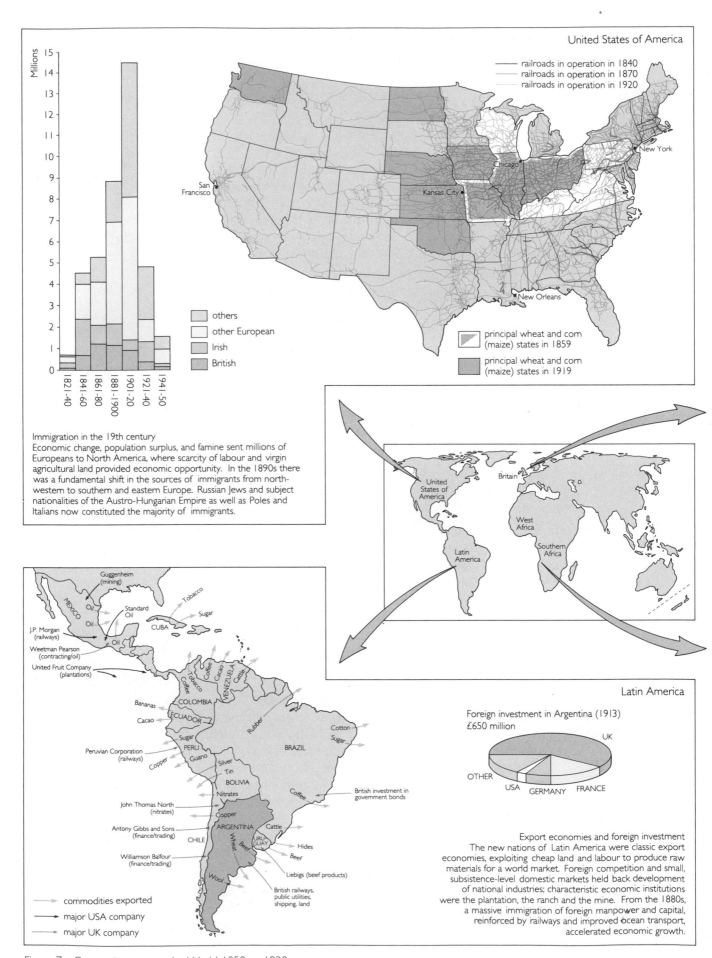

United States of America

railroads in operation in 1840
railroads in operation in 1870
railroads in operation in 1920

principal wheat and corn (maize) states in 1859

principal wheat and corn (maize) states in 1919

Immigration in the 19th century
Economic change, population surplus, and famine sent millions of Europeans to North America, where scarcity of labour and virgin agricultural land provided economic opportunity. In the 1890s there was a fundamental shift in the sources of immigrants from north-western to southern and eastern Europe. Russian Jews and subject nationalities of the Austro-Hungarian Empire as well as Poles and Italians now constituted the majority of immigrants.

others
other European
Irish
British

Latin America

Foreign investment in Argentina (1913)
£650 million

UK
OTHER
USA   GERMANY   FRANCE

Export economies and foreign investment
The new nations of Latin America were classic export economies, exploiting cheap land and labour to produce raw materials for a world market. Foreign competition and small, subsistence-level domestic markets held back development of national industries; characteristic economic institutions were the plantation, the ranch and the mine. From the 1880s, a massive immigration of foreign manpower and capital, reinforced by railways and improved ocean transport, accelerated economic growth.

commodities exported
major USA company
major UK company

Figure 7   Connections across the World 1850s – 1920s

Britain (Comparable data for N. Ireland not available)

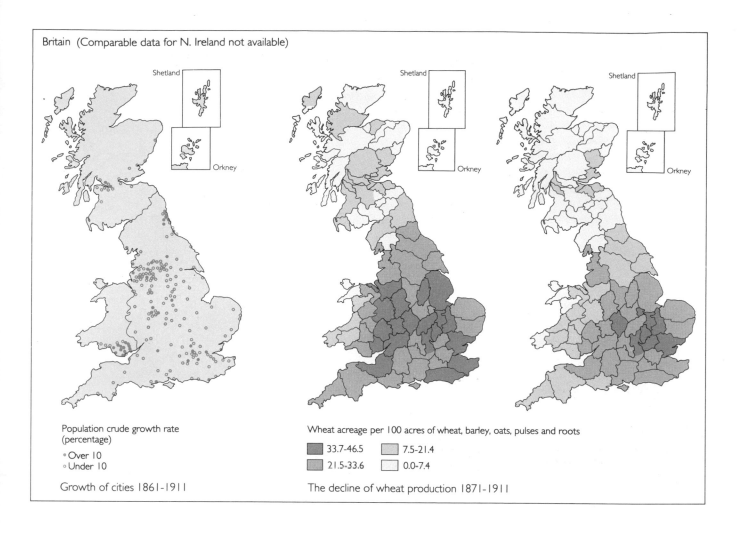

Shetland

Orkney

Shetland

Orkney

Shetland

Orkney

Population crude growth rate
(percentage)

• Over 10
◦ Under 10

Growth of cities 1861–1911

Wheat acreage per 100 acres of wheat, barley, oats, pulses and roots

■ 33.7–46.5	▨ 7.5–21.4
▨ 21.5–33.6	☐ 0.0–7.4

The decline of wheat production 1871–1911

West Africa

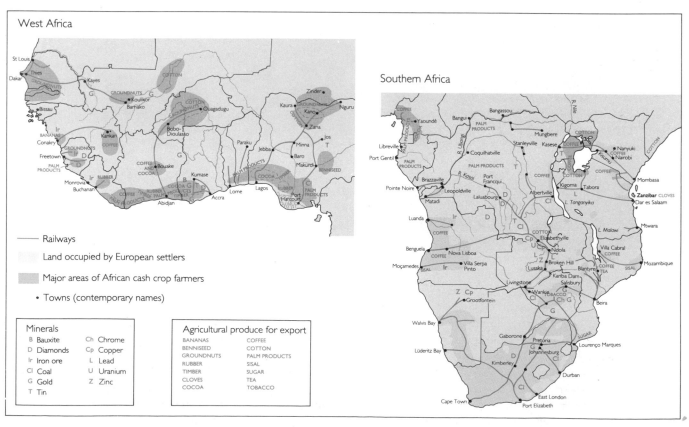

Southern Africa

— Railways

▨ Land occupied by European settlers

▨ Major areas of African cash crop farmers

• Towns (contemporary names)

Minerals

B	Bauxite	Ch	Chrome
D	Diamonds	Cp	Copper
Ir	Iron ore	L	Lead
Cl	Coal	U	Uranium
G	Gold	Z	Zinc
T	Tin		

Agricultural produce for export

BANANAS	COFFEE
BENNISEED	COTTON
GROUNDNUTS	PALM PRODUCTS
RUBBER	SISAL
TIMBER	SUGAR
CLOVES	TEA
COCOA	TOBACCO

As we saw in Section 2.2, and in Chapter 1 of the Reader, the rise of industrial capitalism in Britain was accompanied by the growth of a working class, and by rapid urbanization. More and more people therefore had to buy food out of their wages. Moreover, in general they had more money with which to buy a greater variety of food. The result was a massive increase in demand. For a while, this increased demand was provided for within the country. Even as late as 1850 the (fast-growing) population of the UK was still largely fed by home production (Overton, 1987). Developments in other continents were to change that, however. British entrepreneurs had meanwhile been investing abroad. In particular, they had been investing in railways. The inland plains of the USA and Canada, and the great open stretches of south-central Argentina were made accessible by railways often built, particularly in the latter case, with British capital. The wheat that was grown there was shipped back to the UK. Indeed, these new sources of grain proved so cheap that they totally undercut the price of home-grown wheat. After the period of 'high farming' from 1850 to 1870, when British farmers had grown rich on the profits from their expanding urban and industrial markets, they were suddenly faced with 'the great agricultural depression' of the 1870s to the 1890s. Many wheat farmers could no longer compete with foreign produce and turned their wheatfields over to the production of vegetables, milk and dairy products which were less vulnerable to competition from abroad (see Figure 7, and Activity 5, Question 3). During this period, the whole look of the countryside (so often represented as unchanging) changed completely over large parts of Britain. (How then can a particular image of this countryside be 'a vital part of our national identity' (Section 1)?!)

Family teatime

It was not just food which had to be imported. So did many of the raw materials needed for the expanding manufacturing industries. Africa provided both (see Figure 7, and Activity 5, Question 1). Colonialism extended from Asia, where the Dutch had already taken over much of what is now Indonesia and the British had taken India, Pakistan and Burma. The period from 1880 to the First World War saw the European powers competing with each other in what became known as 'the scramble for Africa'. Whole areas were handed over to European companies for their mines and plantations. The forerunners of companies such as Unilever obtained concessions in what was then called by Europeans the 'Belgian Congo' to find vegetable oils for soap (manufactured at Port Sunlight near Liverpool) and that newly-invented wonder product

margarine, a cheap substitute for butter for the working class of the First World. White settlers and African farmers produced cash crops. Thousands of local people became workers in the new export-oriented commodity production. Railways and ports, built by Europeans and designed solely to serve their export trade, transformed the transport system and the geography of the areas. Settlers went to Australia and New Zealand (and Canada and South Africa) too, where they produced wheat, meat, butter, cheese, wool, hides and many other things to feed the growing European populations and furnish their factories with raw materials.

This history both confirms some of the things we have learned so far and takes them further:

- International trade was accompanied by an increasing specialization of economies at the international level. A 'division of labour' was established at international level. While the UK (and other European countries) specialized in manufacturing (and finance in the case of the UK) many countries in the rest of the world, especially those which were to become part of the Third World, were more important for the export of food and raw materials. The raw materials which they produced were processed (manufactured) elsewhere.

- There can be little doubt that this transformation of the world economy had a major impact on all the societies it touched. *However*, and this is a development of that point, the nature of the impact varied between societies (Activity 5, Question 2). Take the example of the enormous international migration of those years. In the case of the United Kingdom it was emigration, and in many ways this eased the process of industrialization through reducing the population pressure which went with it. In Australia, New Zealand, the USA, East Africa and West Africa, for example, it was immigration. But there were still variations in the impact it had. In the first four of these areas, there was major immigration and settlement. In the first three, the populations and societies of the indigenous peoples were decimated. In parts of West Africa white immigrants arrived only as commercial operators and colonial administrators.

In other words, while in general it is true that global changes had effects locally, the nature of that effect varied quite dramatically between different parts of the world. The establishment of an international system of production and trade located different countries in contrasting places within it.

Many of the patterns established at that time are still important elements of the geography of the world economy. But there have been many changes since, some of which we shall be looking at in the course. One of the most important, as far as food is concerned, is that there has been a significant change in balance between the First World and the Third. One aspect of this has been a concern in parts of the First World about vulnerability. Specialization is all very well, but what if your food supplies are cut off? Two World Wars brought home the acuteness of the problem in Britain, and it led to major changes in policy: not only urging people to dig for victory during the war, but a major reorganization and encouragement of agricultural food production in general. And the trend has continued in more recent years through the European Community (EC) — though here there are other reasons too for the encouragement of farming. There is today a lesser degree of reliance by the First World on the Third for food. Indeed, in some commodities the First World is now a major exporter. For instance, the EC is now one of the largest exporters of *white sugar* in the world! We shall look at how that happened in a later section. But remember the Jamaican cooperatives? Here we have yet another case in which political concerns and economic changes in one part of the world (in this case Europe) have had major implications for the opportunities available to people thousands of miles away.

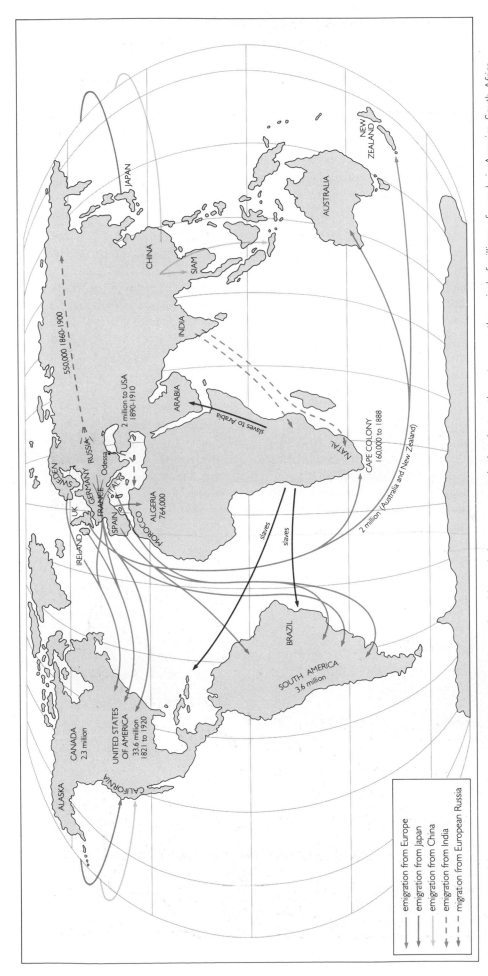

Figure 8   World population movements. The most important aspect of world population movements in the nineteenth century was the arrival of millions of people in America, South Africa, Australia and New Zealand. At first they came mainly from the United Kingdom and Germany; later also from the Mediterranean region and Eastern Europe. There were also population movements overland from east to west across North America to the Pacific and in the opposite direction from European Russia to Siberia. Figures shown are from 1821 to 1910, unless otherwise stated.

But if we accept that what happens in the world economy, or in one part of the world, can have effects in other parts of the world, the next questions are: what is the nature of those links, and how can they be explained?

We shall take up these issues in the next unit, but we can begin to raise the questions now. I have done my best to tell the story of these years in a 'neutral' or 'objective' way. But in fact it is impossible to do that completely. I had to choose which facts to put in and which to leave out. I had to decide on a particular type of terminology. Should I, for instance, say that Britain and other European countries *developed* other parts of the world, or should I say that they *exploited* them? (I tried to avoid both terms.) The implication of one's choice of terminology is not only in the flavour which it lends to the account. It is also that those two different terms imply different explanations — deriving from different theories — of what was going on. Moreover, it is not possible to resolve this kind of theoretical debate simply by recourse to 'the facts'. Even in

Cotton production — one end of the process.

39

Cotton production — the other end of the process. A mill near Preston, Lancashire in 1835. (Note how close together the farming and the factories still were.)

the very brief account I have given here you could probably find evidence to support either position. The subsequent histories of Canada, Australia, Argentina and the USA might incline one to an argument that the crucial processes were modernization and development (although there would still be questions to be answered about the fate of indigenous peoples). On the other hand, what of events in central and West Africa? At the very least, a consideration of that history would force us to examine more clearly what we mean by 'development'. In other words, once again, conceptualization would be a central part of building an understanding and an explanation.

Moreover, this is not the only theoretical debate lying behind the account in these sections. How, for instance, should the term 'division of labour' be interpreted? Was the division of labour between national economies which was established in these years an equal one, implying mutual interdependence, each country specializing in the kind of economic activity it was best at, and exchanging its products with other countries specializing in other kinds of production? The Third World was certainly dependent on the First for manufactured goods and for demand for its primary products, but then the First World also later realized its dependence on external supplies of food. Or was it clearly a case of dominance and subordination, with control remaining in the First World, the Third World being subordinate to developments emanating from there?

I am discussing these issues, though, as though it were *countries* which were the main actors. And there are theories which would stress this. 'It was Britain which exploited/developed Africa' they would assert. Certainly the British state had a very important role to play in this whole history. But can one talk of whole *countries* doing things? Other theories would begin their analyses through examining the interests and actions of important *social groups*. The financial sector of the City would undoubtedly be important here, and so too might be British manufacturers, working class and landowners, each with distinct interests, and white settlers and dominant local groups in other countries.

These various debates are linked together. There is no simply neutral way of 'telling a story'. Indeed the whole point of social science is anyway to do more than that: it is to *understand* and to *explain*. But as soon as one enters this territory the debate begins. The questions I have just raised are tough ones and it is not possible to answer them from the arguments we have developed so far. But one of the things we shall be doing throughout this course is examining the terms of such debates and how we, as social scientists, take up positions within them.

SUMMARY

- At *global* level, the last five centuries have seen major shifts in the pattern of world trade, and the rise and fall of empires, with London's period of dominance beginning during the eighteenth century.
- At *local* level, these developments had impacts on the geography and society of individual countries.
- The impacts on individual countries varied, as their economies took up different roles within the international system.
- There can be no simple description of this process. Explanation, and even defining the process in the first place, is a matter of theoretical debate.

3.3   ECONOMIC POWER AND POLITICAL INFLUENCE

And it is not just in social science that these developments have provoked debate. The changes themselves were also the subject of often bitter social conflict at the time. Let us explore just one example, and one that will allow us to follow a bit further our theme of *the public and the private*.

We have seen that global changes affected different parts of the UK in contrasting ways (Section 3.1). In fact, this produced fierce debate about what should be the UK's economic role in the world. The second half of the nineteenth century was the hey-day of Free Trade. But, as we have seen, 'the laws of supply and demand' are not natural. They are a particular way of organizing exchange which was evolved in a particular historical period, eventually to gain (for how long we do not know) a kind of dominance. And it was not just the price of bread in the English countryside that provoked resistance to these new-fangled ways. So did international Free Trade.

In the mid-nineteenth century the United Kingdom adopted a policy of international Free Trade. In 1846, import duties were abolished on all but a few items. It was, of course, as has often been pointed out, to the advantage of the United Kingdom that trade should be free. In the middle of the nineteenth century its manufacturing base and financial power were both the strongest in the world. They would benefit from lack of controls on trade, and cheap food would benefit workers and manufacturers alike (through better diets and less pressure on wages through the cost of living).

But the policy was not established without dissension, even within the United Kingdom. Indeed, it led to conflict both between different social groups and between different parts of the country. Most of all it was the abolition of import duties on corn which provoked opposition. The opposition came from the farmers and landowners, and in many ways it was a battle between the new industrial towns and the countryside. It was the industrial areas, and London, which wanted Free Trade, for it would benefit their manufacturing and financial interests; the headquarters of this strand of opinion were in Manchester. This was a political conflict, in other words, which reflected the geography of the country. Global changes here produced local conflicts. For the international trade policy adopted would affect different parts of the country in different ways. Political positions here had economic bases, and these in turn had particular geographies. (Can you think of any parallels today?)

It was the rising manufacturing classes of the cities which won. In fact, in spite of the fears, the abolition of the Corn Laws did not lead to immediate disaster for farmers. Continued growth in demand and the lack of competition for two decades resulted in the period of 'high farming' which we mentioned in Section 3.2. But when foreign competition did become intense after 1870 there were no longer any protective import duties, and British farming entered a long depression from which it was only to emerge in a completely changed form.

So the adoption of Free Trade was in part the result of a social struggle between the old established landowners and farmers, and the rising manufacturers. But Free Trade was also seen as something more than that. Free Trade became a principle, almost an ethical stance. It *must* be true — so the argument went — that for things to be free (unconstrained) is better. This was an argument which was part and parcel of a wider (liberal) view of the world which was rising to dominance along with the new industrial and commercial class.

Pause for a moment and consider this argument. Go behind its apparent obviousness, and pick out what it is really saying.

One important thing it is saying is that 'freedom' means freedom from constraint. The argument is also implying that the state is the potential threatening constrainer. This is a *particular* view of freedom, and a particular view of the state. It is also a particular view of what should be the relation between 'private' and 'public' spheres in the economy. The argument is that private individuals (and in this case specifically entrepreneurs and traders) should be allowed to go about their lives as much as possible unconstrained by interference from public authority.

Whatever the arguments, in the middle of the nineteenth century, and on the basis of such principles, the UK adopted a policy of Free Trade. As we have seen, it led — as would be expected — to greater specialization between national economies. While the UK forged ahead in manufacturing production and financial services, its agriculture, relatively, declined. Other national economies took over the role of providing food (and raw materials) while this country specialized in the export of manufactures (and finance). And indeed the idea of the UK as 'the workshop of the world' — that is as a major manufacturing exporter — dates precisely from these times. And its implication was that the manufacturing towns and London grew while parts of the countryside were forced to cope with increasing competition. (It is another example of the relation between global and local changes.)

But already by this time, the end of the nineteenth century, other European countries and the USA were beginning to compete with the UK in selling manufactured goods to the rest of the world. Doubt began to creep in about the principle of Free Trade. Indeed, some of the competition came from countries which had established their new industries with state protection, or state assistance, or both. (In other words, they had a different relation between public and private.) An important group — the Tariff Reformers — grew up in the UK, who saw dangers ahead from this growing competition and who argued for a degree of protection for British production.

Once again, the debate had a particular local geography. If the argument about Free Trade in the mid-nineteenth century had been essentially between town and country, this time the division was more between the manufacturing towns and the financial City of London. The City wanted Free Trade, but the Tariff Reformers had their most important base in the heartland of the workshop of the world — Birmingham.

Birmingham in 1886

Once again too, the Free Traders won. But this time it was not to be for long. Gradually, the pressures of competition from other countries built up, and measures were adopted to protect 'key industries'. The 'principle' was being watered down; the Free Trade argument was seen to be open to exceptions. If industries were vital to the national economy then maybe 'freedom', in the sense defined above, was not such a good thing after all. Maybe there could legitimately be a different relationship between public and private. This position is called 'social reformist' and it argued that maybe government action could sometimes be interpreted as protection, rather than interference. Maybe freedom was not just freedom from constraint but the freedom of being enabled positively to do things. By the thirties, with the economy beset by severe crisis, the principle of Free Trade was abandoned altogether, and general protective tariffs were introduced.

The discussion of these issues has continued since then, along with further changes in policy. As I write this it is the policy of the European Community which is the focus of discussion. It is a debate which brings together social science arguments about how economies work, with major political decisions which could have important implications for different parts of the country, and indeed for other parts of the world.

Moreover, the debate itself raises some important issues:

• on some occasions the state is seen, not as interfering or constraining, but as protecting (for instance in the case of key industries);

• on other occasions it is seen as enabling — making things possible — (for instance in enabling new industries to grow, through state assistance).

We have here, then, a debate about how to interpret the relationship between *public* and *private*. Here the debate is about what should be the relationship between them. Both sides seem to agree on what is public (the state) and what is private (private industry). You might have noticed, however, that this is a rather different kind of distinction between what is 'public' and what is 'private' from the one we examined in Section 2.3. There (in the case of employment statistics) the distinction was between the private world of the household and the public world of paid employment. Here, when we bring the state into the picture, it is government and the state which are defined as the public authority, while the world of employment, so long as it is not owned by the state (nationalized), is private.

One of the tasks of social science is to go behind terms such as these, which we often use so casually, and examine their complex and often contradictory meanings.

SUMMARY

- Behind all that we have discussed so far in the unit, are questions of political power and economic interest.
- Local-global relations were reflected here too, with local economic interests taking up distinct political positions about what should be the national policy towards the international economy.
- The different political arguments were based on contrasting views of the world with, for instance, their own interpretations of the most appropriate relation between the state and the rest of the economy.
- Even the distinction between 'public' and 'private' can have different meanings in different contexts. So far we have discussed two such meanings (in this section and in 2.3).

─────────────────────── ACTIVITY 6 ───────────────────────

Let us look again at the example of sugar, about which you now know quite a bit. Here is a series of quotes from books and articles about some more recent events in that story. As you read them, take note each time a relationship is mentioned in which the terms 'public' and 'private' can be applied. Do *not* worry about the detail — it's there just to give you an idea of the incredible complexity of it all!

1 We saw earlier that in the seventies the Jamaican government intervened in the sugar industry of that economy in an attempt to strengthen its position in the world market and to improve working conditions. One of the problems, among many, that it faced was competition from cheap EC sugar.

2 In 1925 the British government had created the sugar beet industry through the British Sugar Subsidy Act. The initial reasons for setting up the industry were economic, to save on imports; by the end of the thirties these reasons were reinforced by strategic considerations (Pollard, 1969, p.141). Because 'of the large surplus capacity of the cane sugar plantations in the colonies and of the subsidized and experienced beet sugar industry in Europe' (ibid., p. 136) the subsidy was supposed to last only ten years. In fact it was renewed.

> The Sugar Industry Inquiry Committee reported in 1935 that such heavy expenditure could be justified only if the producers were forced to reorganize. Accordingly, under the Sugar Industry (Reorganization) Act of 1936, the Government amalgamated the existing 18 factories into the British Sugar Corporation Ltd (ibid., p.137).

The Corporation had Government nominees on the Board, and limited profits. There was also a Sugar Commission appointed, to supervise research, education and other matters.

3 An attempt after the war to take public control of the *cane* sugar industry was fought off by the British refiners, Tate and Lyle, in a campaign in which they used their popular cartoon figure 'Mr. Cube'.

Top, the south-west prospect of Liverpool in the County Palatine of Lancaster. An early eighteenth century view of the city's riverscape. Below, Liverpool today: the Pierhead with the Liver Building and the Mersey pilot.

4   Then in 1973 came EC entry:

> Before Britain went into the EEC the official European sweetener was
> sugar beet. But with the UK entry, special arrangements were negotiated
> to allow Britain to import sugar cane from its old colonies. The British
> Ministry of Agriculture together with the British Sugar Corporation
> (representing UK sugar beet) and Tate and Lyle (representing the ex-
> colonial cane) slugged it out with Brussels to keep CAP's beet-sugar derived
> surpluses out of Britain [CAP means Common Agricultural Policy].
>
> (Clutterbuck and Lang, 1982, p.75)

Concessions were won, Tate and Lyle was protected from the full impact of EC
surpluses, though its cane sugar import quota was somewhat reduced.

5   With the future of the cane industry clearly more restricted, Tate and Lyle
closed its refinery in Liverpool in 1981. Over 1,000 workers lost their jobs, and
demand from Jamaica was reduced (note that this represented the end of a link
— Jamaica-Liverpool — which was established right at the beginning of our
story of food production on a world scale).

6   EC production of beet sugar continued to soar:

> Buoyed up by high internal support prices, maintained via variable
> levies on imports, the Community has moved over the last 10 to 15
> years from a position of net importer to become one of the largest
> exporters of white sugar in the world. The surpluses generated with the
> help of Brussels' protective shield have been a major factor in driving
> down world prices and clearly damage returns to suppliers which do
> not provide comparable levels of domestic support.
>
> (*Financial Times*, 1 December 1988)

7   Countries in the Caribbean, recognizing the world-market problems for cane
sugar, decided to do something else with all their output. They decided to use the
sugar to produce ethanol (a form of alcohol) and export it to the US. For a while
this went well. Then in 1988, the US government decided to protect its own
ethanol industry:

> The Caribbean ethanol industry, once regarded as an alternative outlet
> for the region's troubled cane sugar producers, is on the verge of
> collapse. Amid claims of increasing protectionism in the US, the main
> market for the region's ethanol, producers are shutting up shop.
>
> (*Financial Times*, 30 June 1988).

8   But another sugar then came on to the world market, neither cane nor beet.
Maize sugar (or isoglucose). It was even cheaper. Why?

> The Reagan administration spent $6 billion subsidizing the export of $2
> billion worth of corn [maize] in 1986. The price of corn was driven so
> low that high fructose corn syrup (HFCS) has replaced cane and beet
> sugar as the sweetener of choice for the US beverage and food-
> processing industries. To protect US sugar producers, the government
> reduced the import quotas on foreign sugar. This struck a devastating
> blow against countries like the Philippines, which saw its US market
> share quota cut by 60 per cent. 'There are now nearly a quarter million
> people slowly starving to death on the Philippines sugar island of
> Negros, thrown out of work because of the loss of the US sweetener
> market to heavily subsidized corn' (Ritchie, 1987). If the price of corn is
> pushed down further, the United States would become a major exporter
> of HFCS, which could ruin the sugar producers of the Third World.
>
> (Danaher, 1989, p.37).

Teatime

Such a cheap sweetener was also a threat to the EC, which already had more sugar than it knew what to do with. But the EC (the 'public sector' at a more global level) decided to keep isoglucose out.

9   In 1980 the National Health Service (another part of the national public sector) in the UK spent £271 million on the treatment of tooth decay. One of the main causes of tooth decay may be sugar in the diet. Yet another 'public' body, the Health Education Council, therefore urged us to *eat less sugar*!

Health Education Council's view

There are two main problems with eating too much sugar. Firstly, sugar promotes tooth decay, especially when you have sugary snacks and drinks frequently throughout the day. Secondly, sugar promotes obesity. Adding sugar to foods makes it easier for us to eat too much — partly because our taste buds have been trained to crave for sugary foods. And sweet foods are usually low in fibre so they don't fill you up very much. Cutting back on sugar is the easiest way to cut calories without losing any nutrients.

Guide to Healthy Eating, Health Education Council (cited in Larkin and Widdowson, 1988)

Others, however, would dispute this view and point out that sugar is a valuable source of energy.

These are just some of the complexities — I could have gone on for much longer. There is also an International Sugar Agreement, for instance. But that is quite enough for now.

Have a look at the questions which follow. But first, a further health warning: there are no simple 'correct' answers to them — they are issues for debate.

1   Can you find cases of:
    • the state *protecting* parts of society? (which parts?)
    • the state *enabling* things to happen?
    • the state *interfering*?
2   If sugar may be so harmful why does the government not *prevent* us from eating so much? (Should a *public* authority interfere in something as *private* as what we eat?)
3   Who won in the end, out of the sugar story?
4   Is the sugar industry in Europe private sector, or public?

You might also use the exercise to reflect back on the debate in Section 3.2, and the equality or otherwise of these local-global relations. What relations are reflected here between First World and Third? Are they relations of mutual, equal, interdependence, or relations of dominance and subordination?

3.4   COMING UP TO DATE ... AND ON TO UNIT 2

The rest of the course will be looking in more detail at developments which have taken place in recent decades. But one of the things which became evident in the last sections is that the pattern of the world economy has changed quite a lot from that which was dominant in the nineteenth century. The pattern of some countries producing and exporting agricultural goods and raw materials while others produce and export manufactured goods, is not so clear. The First World has become a much more important producer of food. Indeed, in the EC and the USA there are numerous government policies to try to *restrict* produc- tion. In the 1980s, just over a century since the arrival of wheat from the 'new world' devastated English farming, the UK became a net *exporter* of wheat. In manufacturing, the First World economies have been joined by Japan, and a few Third World countries (the newly industrializing countries) are fast developing their manufacturing sectors. Oil, its production concentrated in a few countries, has further changed the pattern of world production and trade.

But important aspects of the old world economy remain. The exports which First World countries most clearly dominate are chemicals, machinery, and other manufactured goods; Third World countries outside the Organization of Petroleum Exporting Countries (OPEC) are more important for food exports than for any other kind of export; and perhaps most significantly there are many Third World countries still heavily dependent on the export of a single primary commodity, in many cases a foodstuff. You can check this out for yourself from Figure 9.

So there are both similarities to and differences from the trading patterns of a century ago. Figure 10 is an attempt to put together information on production and trade specifically for food. It is based very much on estimates and was extremely difficult to construct. For the truth is that production statistics, especially for food in the Third World, are very hard to get hold of. Trade statistics are easily available. Can you think why this might be so?

We have the elements of the answer from earlier in the unit. International trade statistics are quite easy to collect because they deal with the 'public world' of commercial exchanges (remember the debate in Section 2.3 about household production?). Production data, however, are far more difficult to collect, especially in the Third World. Remember we found that almost one-third of the world's population grows most of their own food. Very little of this production ever enters the official statistics because it takes place in the 'private world' of the household. So production data, for countries where this is important, are often incomplete or unreliable.

Nonetheless, Figure 10 is the result of one such attempt. It puts together production and trade. And its results are, in some ways, alarming. First, there are large numbers of countries which have insufficient food (this does not refer to the occasional famine, but to a *normal* state of insufficiency). Second, there are countries with insufficient food which are actually *exporting* food. So one question we have to ask is: how can such things be? Is it because of some innate disadvantages of the places concerned (the climate? or even the culture?). Is it just that such countries have not yet started out on the path of development which Britain set out on two centuries ago? Is it that they are now locked into a world system in which they are dominated (by the First World, perhaps, or

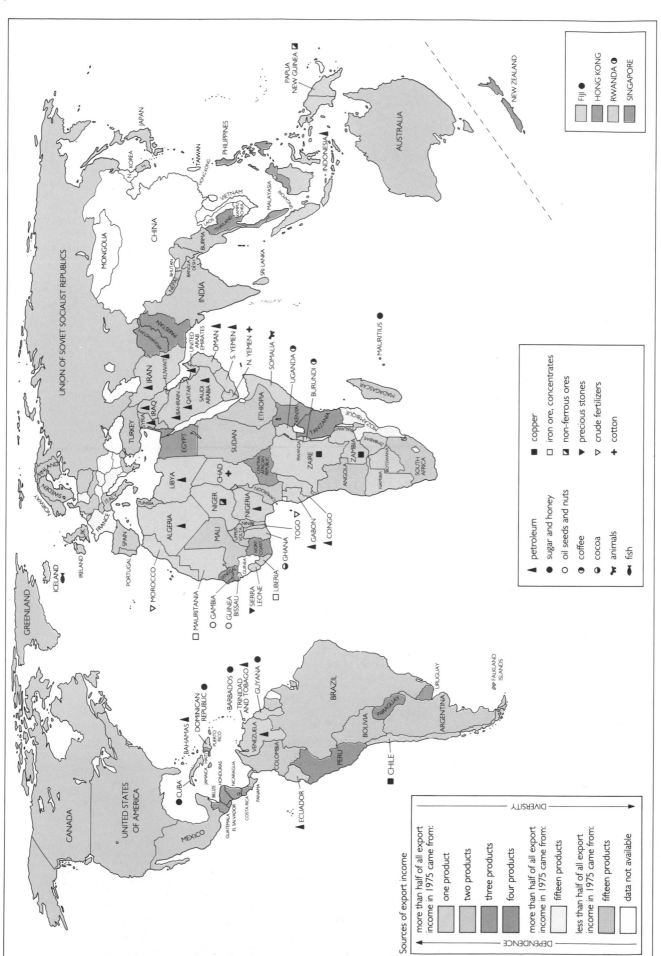

Figure 9 Dependence and diversity

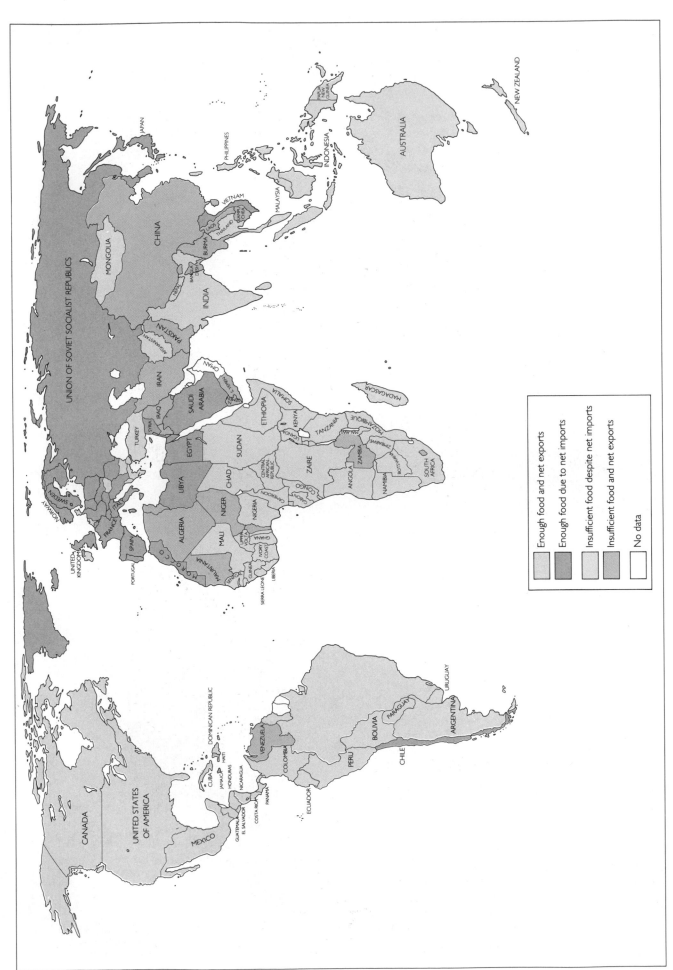

Figure 10   Food imports/exports against overall food requirements

multinationals) and from which there is no escape? Even to begin answering such questions requires us to get to grips with the debates raised in Section 3.2. It requires us to address the issue of the *kinds* of relations which exist, and why, between the local and the global. The next unit will take up these questions in relation to the specific issue of famine.

All the changes in production and trade which we have examined in this unit happened unevenly. The concentration of early capitalist industrialization in Britain and continental Europe influenced the development of other countries, on the other side of the world. A particular form of world economic system

A traditional English setting.

The timeless quality and craftsmanship of Royal Albert fine bone china has set the scene for perfect summer days since the 1800's.

Gracing the tables of royalty and gentlefolk alike, Royal Albert's distinctive gilt edged fluted curves and rich floral patterns embody everything that is English. This example of

Moonlight Rose is only one of the many traditional patterns that have made the name Royal Albert synonymous with high teas, garden parties and polite society.

You couldn't find a better assurance that when you cherish Royal Albert you hold a little piece of England.

ROYAL ALBERT

For a free Royal Albert brochure showing our full range of china visit your local department store or china shop. For a full list of stockists write to
Royal Doulton, Dept. WHF, London Road, Stoke-on-Trent ST4 7QD.

evolved, and it affected in highly-contrasting ways the different societies caught up in it. Their social structures, their economies, even their geographies, have been moulded by this history. They are not wholly determined by this wider context, of course, and the world economy has changed again since. But it would be difficult to approach an understanding of the United Kingdom today without an appreciation of its relation to this wider world.

So how English *is* a cup of tea? What do you think now about this particular popular representation? Is tea English (or even British) at all, given the many links it has with other countries and other cultures? Or should our definition of 'Britishness' somehow contain a recognition of all this history, and more?

SUMMARY

- While some of the workings of the world economy have not changed since the nineteenth century, others have changed quite significantly.
- But major inequalities remain, and the next question must be how to explain them.
- We can only understand the United Kingdom if we place it in a world context.
- Representations of what 'British' means raise all the questions of a long international history.

Well, here you are at the end of the first unit. (If you haven't read Chapter 1 in the Reader yet, read it now.) Let me also remind you once again that you do not have to worry at all about remembering the details of the history discussed in this unit. The important thing is to make sure you have grasped the main messages. One good, and reasonably quick, way to do this is to read the Section Summaries again. But to give you further help there is also a section at the beginning of the Cassette Tape which talks about some of the major issues raised by this unit. You could go on to that now; it in fact comprises the first element of your next major piece of work — Study Skills.

REFERENCES

Clarke, W.M., 1986, *How the City of London works: an introduction to its financial markets*, Oxford, Waterlow Publishers.

Clutterbuck, C. and Lang, T., 1982, *More than we can chew : the crazy world of food and farming*, London, Pluto Press.

Cottrell, P.L., 1986, 'Banking and finance' in J. Langton and R.J. Morris (eds.) *Atlas of Industrialising Britain 1780-1914*, London, Methuen.

Danaher, K., 1989, 'US food power in the 1990s', *Race and Class*, 30, no.3, pp. 31–46.

Jackson, G., 1986, 'Sea trade', in J. Langton and R.J. Morris (eds.) *Atlas of Industrialising Britain 1780-1914*, London, Methuen.

Larkin, N. and Widdowson, J., 1988, *Sweet or Sour?*, London, Association for Curriculum Development.

Latin America Bureau, 1984, *Guyana: fraudulent revolution*, London.

Overton, M., (1986) 'Agriculture' in J. Langton and R. J. Morris (eds) *Atlas of Industrialising Britain 1780–1914*, London, Methuen.

Pollard, S., 1969, *The Development of the British Economy 1914-1967*, London, Edward Arnold.

Ritchie, M., 1987, 'Alternatives to agricultural trade war', CAP Briefing, Catholic Institute for International Relations, no. 4/5, pp. 6–7.

Rowling, N., 1987, *Commodities: How the world was taken to market*, London, Free Association Books.

Shoard, M., 1980, *The theft of the countryside*, London, Temple Smith.

Thompson, E.P., 1963, *The making of the English working class*, Harmondsworth, Penguin.

ACKNOWLEDGEMENTS

Grateful acknowledgement is made to the following sources for permission to reproduce material in this unit:

Figures
Figure 1: Mary Evans Picture Library; *Figure 3*: Reproduced from *The Times Atlas of World History* by permission of Times Books Ltd; *Figure 5*: G. Jackson (1986) 'Sea trade', in J. Langton and R. J. Morris (eds) (1986) *Atlas of Industrialising Britain 1780–1914*, Methuen & Co; *Figure 6*: P. L. Cottrell (1986) 'Banking and Finance', in J. Langton and R. J. Morris (eds) *Atlas of Industrialising Britain 1780–1914*, Methuen & Co; Figures 7 and 8; Reproduced from *The Times Atlas of World History* by permission of Times Books Ltd; Figure 9: M. Kidron, *The State of the World Atlas*, Swanston Publishing Ltd.

Tables
Table 1: Adapted from *Social Trends 18*, reproduced with the permission of the Controller of HMSO;

Illustrations
p.16: Courtesy of the Board of Trustees of the V & A; *pp.23 and 40*: Mary Evans Picture Library; *p.27*: The Anthony Blake Photo Library; *pp.30 and 31*: Lloyds of London; *p.36*: William Frith *Many Happy Returns of the Day* (1850) Harrogate Museum and Art Gallery/Bridgeman Art Library; *p.35 (top)*: J. Langton and R. J. Morris (eds) (1986) *Atlas of Industrialising Britain 1780–1914*, Methuen & Co; *p.35 (bottom)*: M. Kwamena-Poh, J. Tosh, R. Waller and M. Tidy African *History in Maps*, Longman Group UK Ltd; *p.39*: Barnabys/Photo: Hubertus Kanus; *p.43*: *p.25 (top)*: Liverpool Record Office; *p.25 (bottom)*: Sefton Photo Library; City of Birmingham Public Libraries; *p.47*: The Anthony Blake Photo Library; *p.51*: Courtesy of Royal Doulton (UK) Limited.

STUDY SKILLS SECTION: GETTING STARTED

Prepared for the Course Team by Elaine Storkey

HOW ARE YOU DOING?

Now that you have just finished the first unit this is probably an excellent place to stop and review how you have got on. You can do this by relating what you read in the first chapter of *The Good Study Guide* to your own progress here.

===== GOOD STUDY GUIDE =====

Read the first chapter of *The Good Study Guide* if you haven't done so already.

Well how are you doing? Was there anything there which rang bells in your own experience? I wonder if you have encountered anything similar to Michael's and Sandy's attempts at studying?

QUIZ — SOME QUESTIONS FOR YOU TO THINK ABOUT

Try answering the questions which follow to measure how you are progressing. Tick the most appropriate answers. You may find that several boxes can be ticked.

1 Where did you read Unit 1?

(a) In a specially designed and fully equipped study. ❑

(b) In a corner of the lounge/dining room/kitchen/bedroom. ❑

(c) On the bus/train. ❑

(d) At work during breaks. ❑

(e) In the bath: the only place I could be on my own. ❑

(f) Several of the above. ❑

2 How long did it take?

(a) About two hours. ❑

(b) Two to four hours. ❑

(c) Four to six hours. ❑

(d) Six to eight hours. ❑

(e) Eight to ten hours. ❑

(f) More than ten hours. ❑

3 How did you get through the reading?

(a) Read it all the way through in one sitting, beginning at page one and ploughing on till the end. ❑

(b) Set out to read for two hours at a stretch. ❑

(c) Read for three or four hours, with breaks every twenty minutes. ❑

(d) Took several days, dipping in whenever I got the urge. ❑

(e) Read as often as circumstances allowed till it was finished. ❑

(f) Have not actually had time yet to read it all the way through so skipped on to this section. ❑

(g) Other. ❑

4 Did you find it easy to keep going?

(a) Yes, I am very self-disciplined and well-organized. ❑

(b) Yes, it was an easy read. ❑

(c) No, there were too many phone calls, interesting television programmes, etc. ❑

(d) No, I kept remembering other things I should be doing. I kept wanting to get up and make coffee. ❑

(e) No, I couldn't get the hang of it, and was bored. ❑

5 Did you take notes as you read?

(a) 8-12 sheets of detailed notes. ❑

(b) 1 to 2 sheets noting headings and main points. ❑

(c) Underlined the end of section Summaries. ❑

(d) Highlighted key words in the text. ❑

(e) Wrote comments in the margin. ❑

(f) Started a card file/computer disc for key concepts. ❑

(g) Didn't have time to take notes, or stop to underline, etc. ❑

(h) I have a photographic memory so need no notes. ❑

6 With, or without your notes, how would you describe what the unit was about? Look at the following statements. Which ones do you think best identify the key lines of argument in the unit?

(a) The food we eat and the way it is produced have developed over many centuries. ❑

(b) There is a complex history to the trading and manufacturing position of the UK, and to its relationship with the Third World. ❑

(c) Political and economic interests determine the development of food production and international trading patterns. ❑

(d) When we attempt a social science analysis of such everyday things as the food we eat, we discover the complexity and interwovenness of local and global, social and historical factors. ❑

(e) There are layers of complicated meaning which wrap around the things people take for granted, e.g. 'British' eating patterns. One of the aims of social science is to unravel these. ❑

(f) Certain themes keep recurring when we look at the world of food production, for example, the *local and global, public and private*, though these can have different meanings in different contexts. ❑

7 What kinds of things did you note down as you read Unit 1? What things do you think you might need to recall, in an exam for example?

(a) We get the English word 'char' from the Chinese word *'ch'a'* which was already in use in the eighth century. ❑

(b) By 1905 there were 150,000 hectares under tea plantation in Ceylon. ❑

(c) Events in other parts of the globe such as China, Africa or America ultimately affect something as local as the geography of the English Midlands. ❑

(d) The laws of supply and demand are not natural. ❑

(e) Between 1976 and 1977 the price of sugar in the European Community fell by 28 per cent. ❑

(f) The home is a place of consumption, not production. ❑

(g) Facts do not speak for themselves. There is no neutral way of telling a story in social science. ❑

(h) The distinction between 'public' and 'private' is an important one for this course. ❑

8   Did you do the activities in the unit?

(a) Yes, worked through them in detail — found they helped me understand the unit. ❏

(b) Did the first ones, but left the rest. ❏

(c) Read what they were about, but did not work through them. ❏

(d) Ignored them and moved on to the next part of the text. ❏

(e) Did not really have time. ❏

9   How do you feel now about the year ahead with D103?

(a) Very confident. It's going to be a doddle. ❏

(b) I think it will be hard work but I will enjoy it. ❏

(c) I hope I've got the hang of it but I will need some help. ❏

(d) I am still not sure what is expected of me. ❏

(e) HELP! I don't know when I'm going to fit it all in. ❏

COMMENTS ON THE QUIZ

There aren't really any right or wrong answers, and many of you will have ticked very different boxes, and yet should still feel happy with your progress. But in one or two cases alarm bells might be ringing. For instance:

HAVE YOU FOUND ENOUGH TIME?

If you have ticked all of 1(d), 3(f), 4(e), and 5(g), you could be in trouble! It sounds as though you were not prepared for the fact that you would have to allow quite a lot of time for studying, and maybe cannot see how you can find any more time. If that is the case, you should draw up a detailed plan of your week, and look carefully to see if there is any way of gaining more study time. You may perhaps need to talk it over with the people you live with or work with, as well as discussing it with your Tutor-counsellor. Whatever you do, don't just hope things will improve as the course goes on. They probably won't, unless you make them improve!

ARE YOU ORGANIZED ENOUGH?

The Good Study Guide points out things you can do now which will help you to manage your time better, and structure your work throughout the year. Remember to keep the Course Calendar from the *Course Guide* in a prominent position to remind you of when things have to be studied. Circle dates when assignments are due, and mark in your tutorial dates. Plan ahead to watch the television programmes for D103 and listen to the radio programmes. Life will be much easier, too, if you can create some shelf space on which to keep units, books, ring binders for notes, and box files. Make your system big enough for expansion because the OU produces volumes of paper. If you have time now try to build up a supply of basic equipment: ballpoint pens, pencils, highlighter pens, notepads, ring binders, card indexes, boxes, and a dictionary!

ARE YOU GETTING STUCK?

If you ticked 2(f) (more than ten hours) you are taking rather a lot longer than we expected for this first unit. This could mean nothing more than that you are the sort of person who is not happy unless you have read something several times, and digested all of it. Or it might mean that you have found the unit very hard to read and have not been able to make much sense of it. But whatever the reason, unless you have allocated twelve hours to read each full unit, you will need advice from your Tutor-counsellor on developing strategies which will help you to speed up. It's certainly worth remembering at this stage that you don't have to memorize any of the text that you've read. You can always go back and read it again! But you do need to be able to say what the main ideas and arguments were about.

LET'S GO THROUGH YOUR ANSWERS

1 Where did you read the unit?

(a) *In a specially designed and equipped study.* Perhaps you even have filing cabinets, a computer or word processor. Terrific! You're very lucky, so enjoy it to the full and make the most of it! But don't be too disheartened if this isn't you.

(b) *An area somewhere in the house.* Our own 'study corner' is what most of us settle for. We can even cope with a part-time corner, sharing it with other functions, as long as we have some basic equipment and space to keep things. Incidentally, one very important point, often overlooked, is the need to find a comfortable place to work. Sitting still and concentrating for a long time can produce many different kinds of physical tension, especially as we get older. So check that your chair, desk height, and lighting is right for you, and doesn't make the process of study more difficult.

(c) *On the train or bus.* Long journeys are a very good opportunity for studying, particularly when you are well into the course. But unless travelling of this kind is part of your weekly routine, you may also need to plan in other periods. You'll still need somewhere to keep things.

(d) *At work, in breaks.* You'll know yourself if this is the best place for you to work. In some work situations an extra hour or so at work either before others arrive or at the end of the day might well produce the most beneficial studying time.

(e) *In the bath?* I doubt if there will ever be enough time in the bath to get through the whole of D103.

2 How long did it take you to read the first unit?

There is not really any 'right' length of time, but you might find it useful to check the time you took against the time we had in mind.

(a) *Less than two hours.* It is unlikely that you will have been able to read it this fast and thought about the text very much. You need to give yourself time to digest some of the ideas, to do the *Activities* and to jot things down or ask yourself questions. If you have really taken less than two hours and understood it fully, then perhaps you are on the wrong course!

(b) *2 to 4 hours.* Even this is faster than we were expecting. It might be worth checking that you are not missing some of the main points of the argument. But if you are not, then you might have extra time to give to assignments.

(c) *4 to 6 hours.* Fine

(d) *6 to 8 hours.* Perhaps a little longer than we had anticipated. But if it means greater thoroughness in getting the main points then it's worth it. You may find anyway that if you are coming back to study after a long time that you need the time at this early stage in the course. There are always strategies that you can develop later to speed things up.

(e) *8 to 10 hours.* Again there is no need to worry about this for a first stab at the course. But you may need to get into a faster pace quite soon, or you'll find that you are falling behind.

(f) *More than 10 hours.* I have mentioned this above. It probably means that you are getting stuck or have not grasped the point. If you talk it over with your Tutor-counsellor you might work through some ideas on how to speed up.

3 How did you read the text?

Here again there are no right or wrong ways. What is important is that you develop an approach which suits you, both in terms of the pace you want to set for yourself, your own circumstances, and the way your mind works. So unless you are already settled into a study routine which works well it might be worth trying out a few different approaches to see which adapts most easily to your requirements.

(a) *At one sitting, going through the text from page one.* This can work well, provided you have a large amount of time available at any one stretch, and are the sort of person who is rarely distracted by anyone or anything. But my concentration is not usually like that, and on new material I often find that after a while I start to forget what I have read, or stop taking it all in. That's when I do something different and go back to it later.

(b) and (c) *Two hour or four hour stretches with breaks.* Giving yourself specific 'periods' of study, with breaks is a very good idea, and you'll get to know with experience which period suits you best. But you will also need to be flexible with the time. It's very frustrating to put something down just as you have got really into it, because now your allocated time is up. On the other hand if you have started to feel really uncomfortable, and unable to concentrate it is pointless to force yourself through to the bitter end just because there is still fifteen minutes to go. You probably will be absorbing little, if anything by then.

(d) *Read whenever I got the urge.* This is certainly a relaxed way of approaching the task! The problems come when you don't ever seem to get the urge. It's best to schedule in some regularity.

(e) *Read when circumstances permitted.* It is the same here too. Sometimes circumstances might never permit, unless we claim enough study time first. Having many other commitments might well make your study time less than ideal, but try to avoid it becoming too 'bitty'. Otherwise you might find yourself struggling to get to grips with arguments, and you never get a feeling of where the whole text is going.

(f) *Haven't found time to read the unit.* Careful here. Later in the course you may have to skip some sections, but it's a bad way to start off. If you haven't had time to read this first unit, you may well find that the time will never be there unless right now you take the matter in hand. The points in the opening section apply. Give yourself a chance.

(g) *Other.* There may be other approaches which you used, but the same points apply. Time and its organization are important in studying. There's never going to be enough time to read all that we want to read, and so we each need to develop strategies which help us to get the best we can out of the time available in our own particular circumstances.

4 Did you find it easy to keep going?

(a) *Yes, I am well organized and systematic.* Wonderful!

(b) *Yes, it was an easy read.* Good, although I hope it was not too easy, offering you no challenge at all. But however easy you find it at the moment it is still worth giving the text some careful attention just in case you missed something crucial.

(c) *No, constant interruptions.* Other people don't always understand all that is involved in being on OU student — the need for concentration, being left alone, etc. You will have to get this point across early in the course or you're in for a frustrating year! Returning to study can demand a new life-style, yet all the events which filled our time before are still around. Some students find it takes some weeks to be able to adjust and to decide what must go and what can still be fitted in.

(d) *No, other demands on my time/keep stopping/coffee etc.* It sounds as if you simply find it hard to concentrate. But as you'll have noticed from *The Good Study Guide* you are not alone in this! There are some things you can do which might help. One is to clear yourself some mental space. Do those essential outstanding things which are likely to haunt you, before you get down to study. And then write any remaining jobs down for another time.

However, many distractions are not essential. So try to create a routine in studying. Break down the study tasks and set specific targets for yourself. ('I'm going to read the next two sections, highlight the headings, make notes in the margin and do the activity. Then I'll have coffee'). Even so you might not always manage it. Be patient with yourself. It will come with practice.

(e) *No, couldn't get the hang of it and got bored.* Boredom is more likely to come through not understanding what the material is driving at, than by finding it too easy. Sometimes students are looking for a different approach—they don't see the need for developing arguments which analyse such issues as tea drinking or 'Englishness'. Why make life more complicated than it is? But social science is about analysing what we might otherwise take for granted; it is about trying to explain what goes on in society at every level. So if you try to write down what it is you can't get the hang of, you might find that already you are less bored! Bring it up at the study session with the Tutor-counsellor, or talk it over with other students. You might find you've got further than you realized.

5   Did you take notes?

(a) *8-12 pages of detailed notes.* Wow! You probably spent hours and wrote almost half as much as the unit text. You won't need this amount, and a good exercise now will be to reduce those notes to just a few sheets.

(b) *1-2 pages noting headings and main points.* Fine. You'll find this a very good revision technique for much later in the course if you reduce each unit to this length, and capture the main issues and arguments.

(c) *Underlined summaries*

(d) *Highlighted key words*

(e) *Wrote in the margin*

(f) *Began index card system/disc of key concepts.*

All these — (c), (d), (e) and (f) are excellent aids. By all means use the Summaries in the text. And any way of reminding yourself of key words and concepts is very useful. Writing in the margin is also a good idea — we've left you plenty of space. These can all be quick ways of jotting things down without interrupting the flow of reading too much. And you can use them in writing your own notes at the end of each section.

(g) *No time for notes, underlining, etc.* I've already expressed my worry here. Note-taking isn't really an optional extra. It is essential in some form if you are both to understand and recall the main points of the unit. Think again over your time commitments.

(h) *A photographic memory?* I've always wanted to meet someone like you, but in many years of teaching I haven't succeeded. If you really exist, do come along to Walton Hall, and save us all hours of having to look things up!

We're going to be giving you more practice on note-taking in the second week, looking at an article in the Course Reader.

6   Which of my statements did you feel grasped the key arguments of the unit best? (I wonder if you remembered to look over the Summaries in the unit?)

(a) O.K. but the unit was more than a piece of descriptive history. The author spent a lot of time analysing, asking questions and examining concepts, and making links between the UK and other parts of the world.

(b)   This does make those links but it doesn't give any hints of the arguments that were involved. *It simply mentions that the history is complex.* It also suggests too 'grand' a design to the unit. It was in fact a very incomplete history, deliberately focusing on only a few aspects of the UK's trade and production.

(c)   Yes, these were some of the key arguments, although there is no mention here of the UK as the context for this discussion.

(d)   Again, identifies the key arguments well, focusing also on the fact that the UK has to be seen in its wider context.

(e)   Yes, going in the right direction, but not giving any clues as to what makes taken-for-granted things complicated. In the two previous statements there was mention of those interrelated global events and social economic factors.

(f)   This picks up on the notion of themes and is a useful point to be aware of at this stage. You will find as the course progresses that these themes are picked up over and over again.

7   What will be helpful to remember?

(a)   Actually the origins of 'char' did stick in my mind. But it is not something which is important to remember, nor would you need to produce it in an essay or exam!

(b)   Again, there is no need to remember the details — you can always look them up. It is more important to remember the *general* point: that tea production shifted from local control in China to British interests.

(c)   This is more important. It reminds us that there is a strong relationship between the local and the global, and gives us some framework for understanding specific details.

(d)   It is important to remember that 'supply' and 'demand' are not natural.

(e)   Interesting fact, not necessary to remember it.

(f)   The home is a place of production as well as consumption, as Unit 1 noted.

(g)   That there is no 'neutral' way of telling a story is useful to keep in mind as the course progresses; though you will want to examine the idea carefully, and to build up your own arguments for or against it.

(h)   You could note down the two different ways of looking at the distinction between 'public' and 'private' in Unit 1.

8   Did you do the activities?

Of course, the answer we wanted was (a), but we're not too disheartened if you only answered (b). The answers (c) and (d) are more of a problem, because there is no way of knowing then if the activities would have helped you. (e) is a real problem, and has been dealt with already.

It is probably worth a minute to explain why the course team is keen on activities. They are a sort of 'pause' where the author gives you a chance to make sure you have grasped an important point, or can work out its implications. Sometimes you get the chance to use ideas in social science to work through a particular example. Of course, if you have already grasped these ideas quickly and have bags of time, you could even think out some of your own activities!

9   How do you feel now about the year ahead with D103?

(a)   *A doddle.* Well, we may surprise you yet!

(b)   *Hard, enjoyable work.* I hope so. This is certainly what we are aiming for.

(c) *Hopeful, but needing help*. The Open University is made for you!

(d) *Unsure about what is expected*. These are early days. No need to worry yet. Every new enterprise takes time to adapt to. I hope some of the suggestions I have made so far in these answers might help. It's worth remembering too that the Open University plans its year very well, keeps you informed, and is tailored especially to the needs of busy students. You won't be left in the dark about what is expected.

(e) *Help, no time*. Come on, let's try to sort out the time problem. If your diary is nearby you could do the exercise on page 8 of *The Good Study Guide*. Timetable your week, outline your commitments and mark in what 'free' time is actually hidden away in little corners. Now, how can you use those gaps? Can you move some things around to get bigger chunks of time together? Can you share some of your own commitments with other people? Is there anything you would be prepared to give up if necessary? (Other than sleep.) Prune now, if you can, and avoid that early coronary!

PRACTICE TMA

You may have noticed (!) that you have been set a practice assignment already for this unit. This is not because the course team are a bunch of sadists, but because we've found from previous experience that foundation course students benefit from an early chance to try out their writing skills. We will be focusing on essay writing over the next few weeks, so here I only want to suggest that you don't allow the task to intimidate you. Just spend a few minutes thinking about the question — what is it asking? — and try to think of any arguments in the unit which touch on the question. But do look up the sections which are relevant and read them again. It is not a memory exercise. Summarize in your own words the main points that come out, plan what you want to say under a few paragraph headings and then — just have a go at writing down your answer. Basically this assignment is for you to have some early practice at a very specifically defined task. Those of you who are used to writing essays may find it a piece of cake or it might alert you to the need for a different approach from the way you have gone about writing before. Those who have not written essays for ages will find it a useful opportunity to have a go. In any case, your Tutor-counsellor will be looking carefully at what you write, and will give you plenty of feedback. He or she will be able to help you to identify and sort out potential problems, as well as encouraging you to develop your strengths before you begin the marked work.

So, I hope you feel reasonably satisfied that you can go about studying in a way that will work well for you. Be prepared to experiment with different strategies, and do make use of everything that comes your way. Many students find that tutorials in their local study centre help to sharpen their ideas and get to grips with the material in the units. As well as having help from a Tutor-counsellor it's always good, too, to bounce issues around with other students on the course — even if on some odd occasions you may find that your views are in a minority of one!

All the best, now that you've started. I hope it is a really good year!

UNIT 2   THE PRODUCTION OF HUNGER

Prepared for the Course Team by David Coates

CONTENTS

1   INTRODUCTION

As is perhaps now becoming clear, Block I has both an immediate and an underlying purpose. Our immediate concern is to introduce you to some of the social and economic processes associated with the production and consumption of food. But as we do that we also want to introduce you to both the excitement and the relevance of work in social science. We want to demonstrate how worthwhile it is to undertake a course of this kind, and to give you some preliminary sense of how social scientists in the past have — and you in the future will — construct explanations of important social phenomena. In Unit 1 we looked at the production of food, and though our focus was on food consumed in the UK, we were obliged, when pursuing these *local* concerns, to go further afield, to explore the *global* character of complex food chains that stretch across entire continents. In this unit we have an opportunity to look at that international dimension in even more detail, to examine the consumption and production of food from the other end of those chains. Of course it will not be possible, in the space available to us here, to deal with international food patterns in the degree of detail with which food in the UK has been, and will be, considered in this block: but we can at least explore one important aspect of those patterns. We can look at the conditions under which the chain of relationships between the producers and the consumers of food breaks down, or functions inadequately, for certain groups of people in the Third World.

Our focus is on hunger in the Third World. Our task is to see how social science can bring new insights to a topic with which we are now, through television, already familiar. What I want to do in this unit is to demonstrate how our understanding of the familiar can be extended by moving in turn through a set of stages that social scientists often follow in their pursuit of knowledge. These stages are:

- the clarification of the topic (in Section 2);
- the questioning of popular conceptions (in Section 3);
- the gathering of evidence (in Section 4);
- the organization of the material that we have gathered (in Section 5);
- the building of explanatory frameworks (in Section 6); and
- the testing of those frameworks against contemporary developments (in the conclusion).

So let us take each of these stages in turn, as we explore the character and causes of hunger in the Third World.

2   THE CLARIFICATION OF THE TOPIC

In recent years there have been many news reports of quite appalling famines: in Ethiopia between 1972 and 1974, and again in 1984 and 1989–90; in Bangladesh in 1974 and 1975; in Sudan in 1984; and all along the southern edge of the Sahara (in the area known as the Sahel) between 1968 and 1973 and again in 1984 and 1985. In all these places, and in many others, literally thousands of people have starved to death, unable to obtain sufficient supplies of basic proteins, carbohydrates and fats to sustain life itself. Between these famines, and as a backcloth to them, we hear periodically of a far more generalized experience of malnutrition and undernourishment in the Third World. Basing its calculations on figures supplied by the World Bank, Oxfam estimated that in 1986 at least 750 million people were suffering from malnutrition and at least 360 million people were undernourished. So malnutrition, undernourishment and occasionally famine is still the lot of vast swathes of the world's population. Indeed, if Susan George's calculations are correct, 'if it takes you six hours to read [this unit] somewhere in the world 2,500 people will have died of starvation and of hunger-related illnesses by the time you finish' (George, 1976, p.19).

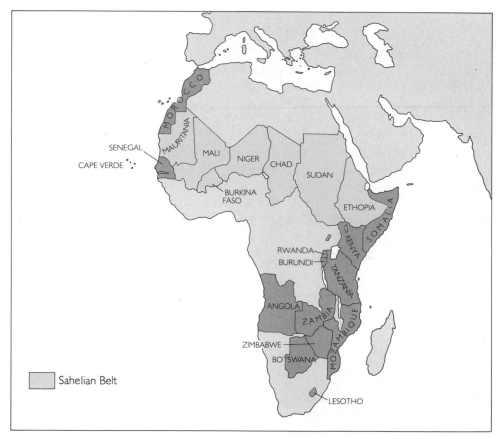

Figure 1   Twenty-one African countries affected by abnormal food shortages, December 1984

Source: UN Food and Agricultural Organization, 1985, *World Food Report*, Rome, FAO, p.12: in Bush, 1987, p.2.

2.1   DEFINITIONS

In Unit 1, it was emphasized that one of the most fundamental skills of any science is its ability to be clear and precise in the questions that it asks. It was also made clear that such precision in questioning requires an associated precision in vocabulary. If we are to ask precise questions about the causes of famine in the Third World, we will need to know what we mean by the individual words we use as we put our question together. We will need to know what we mean by 'famine' and what we mean by 'the Third World'. So the careful definition of terms is where, as social scientists, we ought to begin.

─────────────────── ACTIVITY I ───────────────────

Try this for yourself now. Jot down any definitions that come to mind for:

famine

the Third World

also, make a list of the other terms I used in the paragraphs above which need defining more precisely. What did you find? Malnutrition, undernourishment, protein … ?

Now read on, and see if your definition of each is made more precise by the paragraphs which follow.

───

FAMINE

To take famine first: terms are often best defined by bearing in mind closely related phenomena. In the case of famine, it is useful to establish distinctions between famine and the related but distinct notions of *undernourishment*, and *malnutrition*. To survive, 'people must eat both energy-producing foods (carbohydrates and fats) and a balance of other nutrients (proteins, vitamins, minerals and water)' (Dando, 1980, p.3). In that light, undernutrition or undernourishment is best understood as the consequence of inadequacies in the *quantity* of food in a diet, especially a lack of calories; while malnutrition refers to an inadequacy in the *quality* of a diet, especially its lack of essential nutrients (see Dando, 1980, p.42). The notion of *famine* is best reserved for situations *where undernourishment is replaced by food intakes too small even to sustain life*. Famine 'is a general and widespread, prolonged and persistent, extraordinary and insufferable hunger lasting for several months and affecting the majority of the … population over a more or less extensive area, resulting in total social and economic disorganization and mass deaths, by starvation' (Mariam, 1986 p.9).

It is clear however that malnutrition, undernourishment and famine are intimately related. The three taken together (famine, undernourishment and malnutrition) will be referred to in this unit as 'hunger'.

THE THIRD WORLD

The problem of defining 'famine' is nothing compared with defining so slippery a term as 'the Third World'. It's one of those terms that we all use but whose exact definition often just eludes us. Indeed, it is the elusive character of terms like 'the Third World' which makes the exercise of defining them so valuable (as well as so hard). We need to be precise with our definitions, because we are trying to analyse a world in which the terms we want to use as social scientists are also in general and looser use in popular conversation. We have to establish some distance from popular usage of these terms if our analysis is to have any chance of going beyond popular conceptions of why famines occur. So let me begin by explaining the set of distinctions we have in mind when we use the term 'the Third World' in Block I: a set of distinctions between the First World, the Second and the Third.

The First World is made up of the industrialized countries of Western Europe, North America, Australasia and Japan. D103 will have lots to say about these countries, more particularly about the United Kingdom as one of them.

The Second World consists of societies in the Soviet bloc (the USSR and other state-socialist societies, including China). D103 doesn't have much time to examine these in detail, but the course will refer to developments in the Soviet bloc as these impinge on or illuminate features of contemporary UK society.

The Third World is made up of the rest — the non-industrialized states of Asia, Africa, the Middle East, the Caribbean and South America that lie outside the Soviet bloc.

These distinctions are worth holding on to because they help us to capture important differences in the world order of which the UK is a part. But there are problems with this three-way classification system. The 'Third World' lumps together vastly different societies and sometimes it will be their differences, rather than their similarities as non-industrial and non-Soviet, that we will need to remember. For example, not all Third World countries have oil: and those without oil had a much worse time after the 1973 oil crisis than did the oil-producing Third World countries with which they are being grouped here. Some Third World countries are also industrializing rapidly while others are not. A new international division of labour is beginning to emerge, to replace the one defined by the model of three worlds. And the Second World concept is pretty leaky too. Is China Second World — because it is socialist — or Third — because it is predominantly rural? In this unit China will be treated as a Second World country, and — for lack of space — the dissimilarities between Third World countries will not be given a lot of attention.

2.2 QUANTIFICATION

Armed then with these definitions, where do we go next? We go in search of information of all kinds about food and famine: statistics, case studies, eye witness accounts, government reports and so on.

We will look at a survey of case studies on food and famine later on, but, for the moment, let us start with some numbers. Statistics about social phenomena often look more reliable, safer somehow than other kinds of information on which we have to rely; and to a degree they may be. It all depends on the accuracy and consistency of the statistics in question. As we saw in Unit 1, the statistics on food and famine in certain parts of the Third World aren't very reliable. Statistics in this area need to be treated with considerable caution, for at least three reasons.

1   It is virtually impossible to obtain accurate statistics on population, land use and crop output. Lots of Third World governments lack the bureaucracy to gather accurate and comprehensive statistics. Their farmers are often reluctant to reveal accurate figures to potential tax gatherers; and where farms are small in size — as they are in many Third World countries — it is often too costly to send government officials to each farm in turn. So quite often, when you look carefully at the notes accompanying official statistics, you find that many of them are only 'estimates', and very rounded ones at that (corrected, in other words, to the nearest 100,000 or even half million). In 1982, just to take one example, 'no less than 75 per cent of all cereal production figures for tropical African countries were based, wholly or in part, upon Food and Agriculture Organization estimates' (Raikes, 1988, p.18). The estimates may well be accurate ones (though Philip Raikes thought that there were 'few countries in sub-Saharan Africa where the level of total food production is known to plus or minus 20 per cent') — but even so the numbers they contain cannot really be treated as 'hard facts' in any genuine meaning of that term.

2   A second reason for caution about statistics on food and famine in the Third World is that — as we saw in Unit 1 — important supplies of food go uncounted

because they never enter official markets. Government figures invariably derive from estimates of marketed food stuffs — not least because this is what concerns government officials most (to feed the towns and generate tax revenue). But these figures capture neither black market supplies of marketed food (which may be large if state policies hold producer and consumer prices down) nor the vast quantities of food consumed directly by the families of the farmers who produce it. And because this is so, Philip Raikes felt that 'the statistical basis for estimating food production in Africa (at least) is extremely weak ... and is biased downwards' (ibid, p.22). In other words, the statistics understate significantly the quantity of food produced, and need to be treated with considerable caution as a result.

3   The third reason for caution is the contentious and ever changing definition of what constitutes a minimum adequate diet. The FAO (Food and Agriculture Organization of the United Nations) uses one measure, while researchers for the World Bank have used a more generous one, and that is enough to produce enormous variations in the specifications of the scale of the hunger crisis world-wide, as Table 1 shows. (The FAO had 535 million people undernourished world-wide in 1980. The World Bank study shows 1,373 million as undernourished, even with the exclusion of China — a difference of a mere 800 million!) The FAO figures measure those receiving just the very minimum number of calories necessary to maintain the human body when that body is not undertaking any heavy physical activity; and that, of course, is a very *low* calorie intake indeed. The World Bank researchers put their figures together using a higher calorie intake. However they then decided that they had overdone it in the other direction; and have since argued that 'in 1975 between 40 per cent and 50 per cent of the population of the under-developed world suffered from undernutrition, rather than 71 per cent' (Grigg, 1985, p.30). Nor should we forget, when looking at statistics on world hunger, that experts do more than just disagree with each other on minimum necessary calorie intake. They also periodically change their minds about what that minimum should be, so making comparisons between periods extremely difficult. The US National Academy of Science, for example, changed its specification four times between 1943 and 1974, first raising it and then lowering it, as public and scientific attitudes in the US towards obesity altered! (Pacey and Payne, 1985, p.23).

Table 1   Percentage of the population undernourished, 1980

	Millions	% of Population
FAO		
Africa	72	19.6
Latin America	41	11.3
Near East	19	8.9
Far East (excluding China)	303	23.1
All developing (excluding China)	436	19.3
China	99	10.0
All developing countries	535	17.0
World Bank		
Africa	243	77.0
Latin America	112	36.0
Middle East	94	51.0
Asia (excluding China)	924	82.0
All developing countries	1373	71.0

Source: Grigg, 1985, pp. 28 and 30.

Not all social statistics are as problematic as this, and even here it would be wrong to discount the statistical data on hunger in the Third World as entirely without value. All that our awareness of the problems of statistical data in this area ought to do is remind us that it is very difficult to say with any certainty *exactly* how many people are hungry in the Third World. But the statistics are sufficiently reliable to enable us to say certain things *in general* about who is vulnerable to famine, and about who, even when famine is absent, is more likely to be undernourished or to suffer from malnutrition.

2.3   HUNGER IN THE THIRD WORLD

The generalizations which the statistics do sustain include the following.

1   Famines have a long history, and until relatively recently were likely to occur anywhere in the known world. Undernourishment, too, is of long-standing and immense generality. 'Most historians would agree that before 1800 the poor of Europe — most of the population — were in a chronic state of undernourishment' (Grigg, 1985, p.31). W.A. Dando found that 'famines have decreed untimely deaths for at least 6,000 years. They were a regular but unexpected calamity dispersed throughout the inhabited world and they varied in severity, location and frequency of occurrence' (Dando, 1980, p.71). In fact he was able to locate evidence of more than 8,000 famines during the almost 6,000 years between 4000 BC and AD 1980. Such famines were 'not isolated events, but formed part of a pattern of recurrent demographic and subsistence crises which cumulatively kept mortality at a high level. In the pre-industrial world they were — along with pestilence and war — part of what has aptly been called *the biological ancien régime*' (Arnold, 1988, p.24).

2   From the vantage point of the UK, famines now seem to be things that occur elsewhere. But it was not always so. There were 187 famines in the United Kingdom between AD 10 and AD 1850, thirty-seven of which occurred after 1485 (Dando, 1980, pp.113–14). The last of these was the Great Irish Famine of 1845–1850, which claimed the lives of just over one million people and forced many more to emigrate. The last major famine in England and Wales occurred in the 1620s, in Scotland in the 1690s, in Germany, Switzerland and Scandinavia in 1732, and in France in 1795, although parts of Europe were also affected by famine in 1816–17 (and again briefly at the end of the Second World War).

3   Vulnerability to famines *within* societies seems to be heavily concentrated — paradoxically — among the producers of food themselves. Famines these days are predominantly rural phenomena. There have been urban famines in the twentieth century — particularly in the Soviet Union in the 1920s — but recently all the major famines have been experienced by rural populations, and even then, only by the poorest sections of the rural population.

4   This reminds us that societies in the Third World, like societies in the First, are characterized by distinct inequalities of wealth and power. It is the poor in the Third World who are the real 'candidates for hunger' (George, 1984, p.6). Their more privileged counterparts are not. The really vulnerable groups, 'between $\frac{1}{4}$ and $\frac{1}{5}$ of the people of the world, (constitute) a veritable village underclass of landless labourers, share-croppers, owners of dwarf holdings, and even pseudo-urban (but usually jobless and temporary) migrants' (Lipton, 1977, p.28). These groups are vulnerable to hunger because they cannot feed themselves and their dependants fully on any land they do possess, and because they find it difficult to obtain regular and well-paid work on the farms or in the factories of others.

5   The burden on women among the poor is particularly acute. In those Third World societies with strongly male-dominated cultures, women eat late, eat separately and eat less well than men. Let me give you just two examples of this. The *Diet Atlas of India* reported a Hyderabad study, showing that the average daily calorie intake of pregnant and lactating women was as low as 1,400 against the average Indian requirement of 2,200 (Sinha, 1976, p.13): and this in spite of the fact that pregnant and lactating women need a higher calorie intake than men. Again, 'a study done in Bangladesh showed that small boys got 16 per cent more food than girls: men between 15 and 45 got 29 per cent more than their wives' (Bennett, 1987, p.9) — proportions indeed that may apply in First World societies as well. What makes these figures particularly ironic in the Third World is that women there are often the main producers and certainly the main preparers of food. As Figure 2 indicates for Africa at least, it

Dürer's 'Four Horsemen of the Apocalypse'

is women who do most of the work (both in the fields and in the skilled preparation of food) — only then to find themselves disproportionately excluded from the food they produce and prepare. In fact 'the worst sufferers are invariably the young children, particularly those who are weaned at an early age, either because a malnourished mother cannot breastfeed her child adequately or because she is caught in one more sequence of pregnancy and childbirth' (Sinha, 1976, p.13).

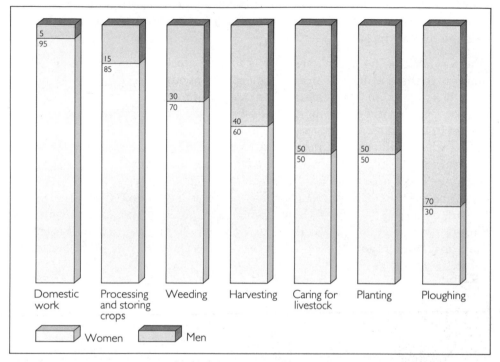

Figure 2 Percentage of types of agricultural and other work done by men and women in Africa

Source: *Women : A World Report*, 1985 (New International Book, Methuen).

SUMMARY

- A social science approach to the study of famine in the Third World must begin by establishing tight definitions of its key terms.

- Statistical data on food and famine in the Third World has to be approached with caution because of difficulties in collecting accurate data, the existence of food supplies that remain uncounted, and variations in the definition of minimum adequate diets.

- Vulnerability to hunger now seems to be largely a Third World monopoly, and falls heaviest on the food producers themselves: on the rural poor as a whole, and on women (and children) among the poor in particular.

3   THE QUESTIONING OF POPULAR CONCEPTIONS

The last point in the summary gives us our problem: how to explain the distribution of famines between societies and over time; and within societies, between different groups of the population at any given point in time. Why is it that hunger is now more common in the Third World than the First; and why do the in the Third World, and especially women and children among the poor, go hungry most?

One way of tackling these questions is to take stock of some 'common sense' answers to them which are already widespread in our society. We can bring the tight definitions and systematically-gathered information at our disposal to bear on popular understandings in the First World of why hunger is so widespread in the Third. In doing so, we will have our first opportunity to explore a theme which will occur on many occasions in D103: the relationship between the *realities* within which we live and the *representations* of those realities which we carry around in our heads. In the field of hunger, these representations are rarely entirely wrong, but invariably they simplify — often to the point of distortion — causes which are more complex than popular views allow. We can see this by looking at three commonly-held explanations of hunger in the Third World: that it is caused by *over-population*, by *food shortages*, or by *natural forces*.

3.1   POPULATION PRESSURE

'Throughout the 1950s and 1960s it came to be assumed that the major cause of hunger in the developing countries was population growth: quite simply the numbers in Africa, Asia and Latin America were growing faster than the capacity of agriculture to supply food' (Grigg, 1985, p.54). *The International Herald Tribune*, for example, published a cartoon (see Figure 3) in April 1975

Figure 3   'Chomp, Chomp, Chomp'
International Herald Tribune, 5–6 April 1975

'which gives the argument in admirably condensed form:

- The world's resources, including food, are limited.

- There are too many people in the world, and everyone knows that the poorest countries have the highest birth rates; therefore

- It is the poor who are consuming the world's resources.

QED.'

(George, 1976, p.55).

─────────────── ACTIVITY 2 ───────────────

Do you recognize this argument? Can you see any defects in it? What might it mean for policy?

The most obvious conclusion that flows from this argument is that people in the Third World should stop having babies; and that governmental policy should be directed to that end (i.e. by encouraging birth control, late marriage, sterilization etc.). But since these policies touch the personal lives of Third World peoples so intimately, and also undermine older notions of the desirability of large families — as extra producers and as insurance for old age — it is as well to check the adequacy of the original premise. What is the relationship between population growth and hunger? As ever, the evidence is mixed.

1 It is true that current population densities and growth rates are uniquely high, and that 'huge increases in population have created serious problems for some developing countries, particularly in their efforts to increase the pace of economic development' (Sinha, 1976, p.5–6). It is also true that, in Africa in the 1970s, the rate of population growth did outstrip that of recorded food production. Population growth in Africa between 1974 and 1984 rose by 3.1 per cent per annum, as recorded food output grew by only 2 per cent. The food statistics may not be entirely reliable, as we have just seen, but nonetheless this increase in population — running at twice the rate of increase of the Third World as a whole — gave African farmers by 1984 one million extra mouths to feed every three weeks! It disrupted rural labour markets and patterns of urban growth, as people migrated to find new forms of employment to pay for food for their children. It is also said to have precipitated soil erosion and deforestation in heavily-populated highland areas in places such as Ethiopia.

Population pressure can, therefore, be associated with ecological and economic changes of a traumatic kind. That is not in dispute. Nonetheless, the linkage between population growth and hunger is by no means as straightforward as is often assumed. We can see this both by looking back over time, and by making international comparisons at one point in time.

2 Many countries in Western Europe and the Soviet Union had famines in the past. But now, in spite of much larger populations, they no longer have famines. So the growth in population does not seem to guarantee famine everywhere. Visibly, factors other than population size are also at play. Perhaps the productivity of agriculture holds the key.

3 Yet there are a number of developing countries in which widespread hunger is a problem but where rates of population growth are less than the rates of increase in agricultural output: in Angola, for example, in Mozambique, Brazil, Egypt, and even Ethiopia.

4 Nor is it the case that all Third World countries have rapidly growing populations. Population growth *was* greater in developing countries than in developed ones between 1950 and 1980 (the population of Latin America, for example, increased by 124 per cent in those years, that of Europe by only 26 per cent and Australasia by 76 per cent) but not all developing countries have galloping population increases to contend with. China's population rose only by 72 per cent between 1950 and 1980, India's by only 84 per cent; while Canada's (admittedly very much smaller) population rose by 76 per cent in the same period.

5 Even sub-Saharan Africa, with its rapid population growth, is far from being an over-populated continent. The average population density of sub-Saharan Africa is only 16 per square kilometre. This compares favourably with that of Europe (78 per square kilometre): yet it is Europe, and not Africa, that has escaped widespread hunger among its population in recent times.

—————————————— ACTIVITY 3 ——————————————

So the population-famine linkage is a more complicated one than many popular conceptions would allow. You can demonstrate this to yourself by playing the 'filling-in' game in *Food for Beginners*. I hope that you, like me, find it difficult to put 'over' against all the high numbers.

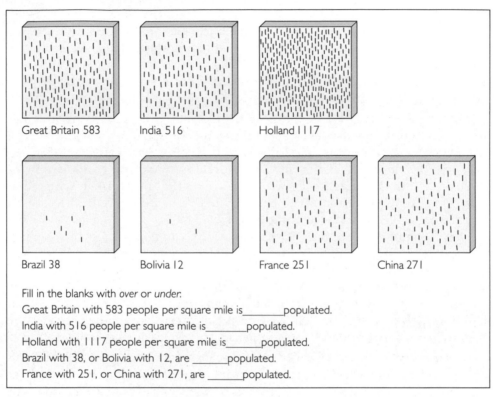

Great Britain 583   India 516   Holland 1117

Brazil 38   Bolivia 12   France 251   China 271

Fill in the blanks with *over* or *under*.

Great Britain with 583 people per square mile is_____populated.

India with 516 people per square mile is_____populated.

Holland with 1117 people per square mile is_____populated.

Brazil with 38, or Bolivia with 12, are _____populated.

France with 251, or China with 271, are _____populated.

Figure 4

Source: *Food for Beginners*, Susan George and Nigel Paige, Writers and Readers Publishing Co-op Soc. Ltd., pp. 68–9.

3.2   FOOD SHORTAGE

A second widely-held conception is that there is actually a shortage of food in the world, and that famines occur when food is not available. This explanation of famines — known in the academic literature as the *Food Availability Decline* approach (or FAD) — stresses problems of the *supply* of food as the major cause of famine; and it is clear that there have been famines in which a collapse in local food output was very important. One of the most recent examples of this is the Chinese famine of 1959–61. It would appear however that the majority of recent famines have not been caused in this way. Indeed the whole FAD approach has been widely criticized by scholars who question its emphasis on food supply, and stress instead the importance of factors of *demand*. They point out that:

1   Overall, there is no shortage of food in the world. Rather world food output 'has at least *doubled* since 1950, and only in Africa has there been any serious fall in the rate of increase in output' (Grigg, 1985, p.81). In the same period world population grew by only 76 per cent: so 'there is thus no question, at the global scale, of population having outrun food production since 1950' (ibid).

2   There are surpluses of food stuffs in the developed world, as we know. The figures for the European Community surplus build-up of cereals in the 1980s are given in the table below.

Table 2   European Community surplus build-up of cereals, 1980–91 (figures are in million metric tons)

	Usable Production	Internal Consumption	Imports	Exportable Surplus	Exports	End of Season Stocks (cumulative)
	(1)	(2)	(3)	(4)[a]	(5)	(6)[b]
1980–81	124.5	119.0	18.0	23.5	24.0	13.0
1981–82	122.5	115.5	15.0	22.0	24.0	11.0
1982–83	131.0	114.0	11.0	28.0	23.0	16.0
1983–84	124.0	113.5	10.0	20.5	20.5	16.0
1984–85[c]	143.0	114.0	7.5	41.5	25.0	32.5
1985–86	133.0	115.5	7.5	25.0	25.0	32.5
1986–87	137.0	115.5	7.5	29.0	25.0	36.5
1987–88	141.0	116.0	7.5	32.5	25.0	44.0
1988–89	145.5	116.5	7.5	36.5	25.0	55.5
1989–90	149.5	117.0	7.5	40.0	25.0	70.5
1990–91	153.5	117.5	7.5	43.5	25.0	89.0

Notes:
[a] Column (4) = (1) − (2) + (3).
[b] Net addition to column (6) = (4) − (5).
[c] Data after 1984–85 are estimates. Cereals include wheat, corn, sorghum, barley, oats, rye, millet, and mixed grains.
Sources: Home Grown Cereals Authority, evidence presented to the Select Committee on the European Communities, 6th Report (House of Lords, Session 1985–1986, London, 1986), Table 1. *World Resources 1987*, p.48.

―――――――――― ACTIVITY 4 ――――――――――

Take a close look at Table 2. Can you see any cause for caution in interpreting its figures? Which column is the crucial one for our purposes here? What does it purport to tell us?

Footnote 'c' is the key one here. The bulk of this table is made up of estimated figures. Column 6 is the key one for us, measuring the build-up of end of season stocks. Those rose from 13 million metric tons in 1980–1 to 16 million in 1983–4, and are *projected* to rise to 89 million by 1990–1. So the argument holds so long as the projection proves to be accurate. In fact we now know that these stockpiles are declining, because of a rise in global demand and government determination in the EC (and in the USA) to limit/reduce cereal production. From that I would deduce that the famines of the 1980s did go on amid stockpiles, but that famines in the 1990s may not face surplus output stockpiled on the same scale.

3   Moreover, famines occur even when there is an adequate supply of locally-produced food. Indeed this 'irony of grain being available on the market amid starvation is a regular feature of famines. It highlights the view that famines are seldom simply the result of food availability decline but instead are the result of people's inability to gain access to existing food' (Bush, 1988, p.18). People experience famine not when there is no food but when, for whatever reason, they cannot get hold of it with the speed and in the quantity they require. Even a shortage of locally produced food will only become a cause of famine if it coincides with the absence of food from elsewhere. Local areas need not know famine. If they do, it is because they cannot gain access to the world's food surpluses.

In the past, the difficulty of transporting food quickly over large distances was often the crucial thing; and to a degree it still is. But now, in a world of commercialized agriculture and modern communications, access to food turns much less on transport than on purchasing power, and on the social rules which govern the distribution of food between gender and age groups. Both monetary and non-monetary factors are at work here, shaping the *entitlement* of different groups to available food supplies. For example, women's *entitlement* to food tends to be less than that of men, to the degree to which the dominant culture of a particular society is patriarchal.[*] The poor's entitlement to food tends to be less than that of the rich, to the extent to which food has become a *commodity* bought and sold in markets. So exposure to famine is not a simple question of food availability. Rather it derives from the way in which a disturbance in local food supplies impacts upon those whose entitlement to food is already low. We can see this most clearly in a diagram of linkages, such as the one in Figure 5.

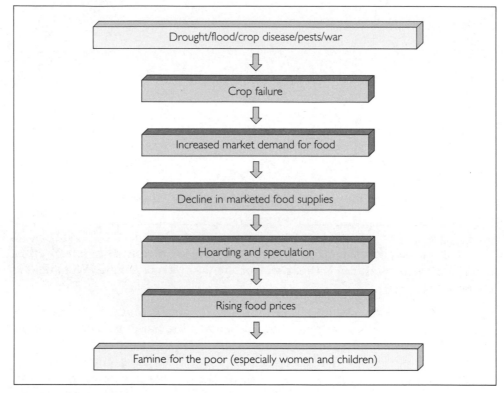

Figure 5   Diagram of linkages

Source: Amended from Devereux and Hay, 1986, p.165.

3.3   'NATURAL FORCES'

The production of food involves an intimate and regular relationship between human labour and the natural environment, and that itself helps to sustain an image of malnutrition and famine as products of natural forces. The Bible has the famine in Egypt as the product of the wrath of God. More prosaically, modern texts also exist which see 'droughts as an immediate cause in all famines' (Stewart, in Harrison, 1988, p.141). Indeed it would be strange if it were otherwise. Climate is a vital factor in all farming, and climatic changes can and do have the most serious effects. Certainly in the Horn and Sahel regions of sub-Saharan Africa, where famines attracted such publicity in the 1980s, fluctuations in patterns of rainfall have had a considerable impact on levels of food production. From the later 1960s there was an unbroken sequence of sixteen years of gradually diminishing rainfall in the West African Sahel

[*] For the meaning of this term, see the glossary.

region: and the area saw unpredictable shifts in the timing of its rainfall, with 'some areas receiving the usual volume … but at the wrong points in the growing cycle, leading to the stunting of crops' (Bush, 1987, p.3). As the Overseas Development Institute (ODI) reported in 1987:

> The human impact of the 1970s drought was so catastrophic that it became known as the 'great Sahelian drought' and it stimulated an outpouring of international assistance to the Sahelian countries. Then in 1983–85 came another widespread drought-induced crisis, this time centred eastwards in Sudan and Ethiopia. Despite all efforts during the intervening decade, again many people died, perhaps as many as half a million. And drought has continued to plague the economies of Botswana, Mozambique and now Somalia.
>
> (ODI, 1987, p.1)

But this is not to say that we can easily treat famine in the Third World as something caused simply by natural forces. Instead, the notion of the 'natural' here can and must be questioned in at least two ways, as follows:

1   Even if we can treat variations in climate and soil as natural phenomena, their consequences for agricultural production are necessarily filtered through social, rather than natural, structures. So if famines are caused by 'natural factors' (and I will come to that in a minute), such natural factors need to coincide with social ones if they are to have an impact, for good or ill. Climatic conditions can remain relatively constant in a region, but their capacity to generate famines will vary as the social organization of agricultural production

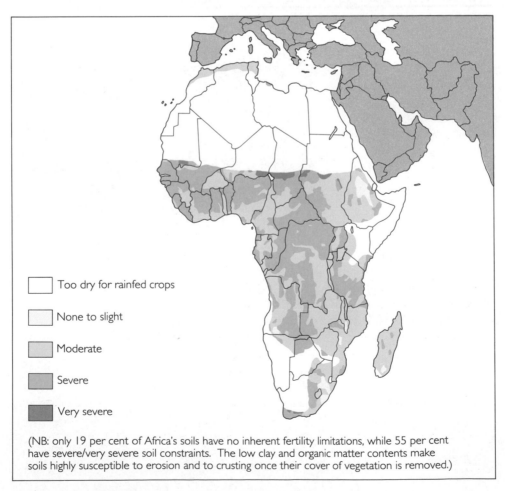

Figure 6   Soil constraints

Source: *World Resources,* **1987**, p. 223.

changes over time. We used to have famines in England — quite often in fact. Now we do not. There have been climatic changes in the UK over the years, of course, but these have not been of a kind and a magnitude sufficient alone to explain the transformation of agrarian conditions. Or again, 'the drought which is a frequent occurrence in the South Western United States is not at all the same thing as drought in the Sahel' (George, 1976, p.69) because the agricultural systems of the two regions are so different. Water is piped into the South West of the USA from Oregon, but there is no equivalent infrastructure on which the Sahel can draw. Climatic changes produce hunger only in certain *social* circumstances, and any 'natural' explanation of famines has to come to terms with this fact.

2   Nor can we, these days, talk so easily of a 'natural world' at all, if by that we mean a set of forces unaffected by (and beyond the control of) human action. We have to recognize that the social activity of men and women changes the natural world; and is increasingly doing so in ways which can disturb basic ecological systems. There are lots of examples of this. Let me remind you of three:

(a)   The rain forests of the world's equatorial regions are being destroyed at a quite alarming pace. According to Reuters, 'an area bigger than Belgium was burnt by settlers and cattle ranchers in the Amazon jungles of Brazil' in 1988 alone (*The Independent*, 3 January 1989, p.1). This has severe ecological and social consequences for the local habitat and people; and it is now occurring on such a scale as possibly to affect adversely climatic patterns a continent away. However indirect and complex, there is now the suggestion of a connection between the clearing of forests in Brazil and the steady expansion of the edge of the Sahara southwards.

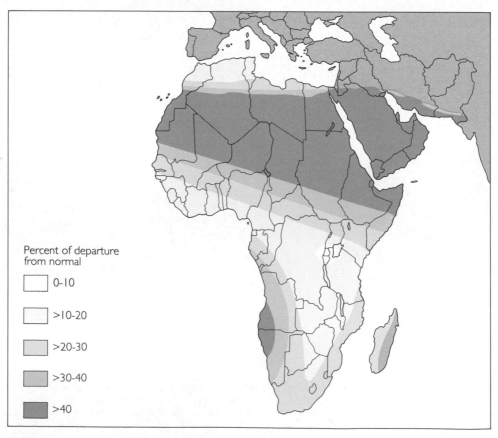

Figure 7   Interannual variability of rainfall
Source: *World Resources*, 1987, p. 224.

(b)   This steady southward expansion of the Sahara — a process referred to as *desertification* — is also partly a product of human actions. Deserts do look as though they are mainly products of nature — areas of land baked dry by the sun — as indeed they are. It is impossible to ignore the importance of climatic changes in the creation or expansion of deserts. 'In West Africa the rains *are* moving south towards the forests, ... causing the desert fringe regions to dry up' (Franke and Chasin, 1980, p.122). But human action is also playing a role. People are certainly cutting down trees in parts of Africa at quite a rate.

> In 1980 Africa's forests were being cleared at a rate of 3.7m hectares per year — 0.6 per cent of the continent's total undisturbed forests. Annual rates of deforestation reached 4 per cent in Nigeria and almost 6 per cent in the Côte d'Ivoire during the early 1980s. Throughout sub-Saharan Africa, deforestation outpaced new tree planting by 29:1.
>
> (*World Resources Institute, 1987, p.3*)

This deforestation is just one example of the social processes cited by the World Commission in 1987 as causes of the Sahara's expansion. The Commission also mentioned 'the rapid growth of both human and animal populations, detrimental land use practices (especially over-grazing), cash crops on unsuitable rangelands ... (poor international prices) for primary products and increasing cash crop production at any cost'. Once more it seems to be the interplay of natural and social forces that is eroding an area's capacity to sustain agriculture and livestock herding.

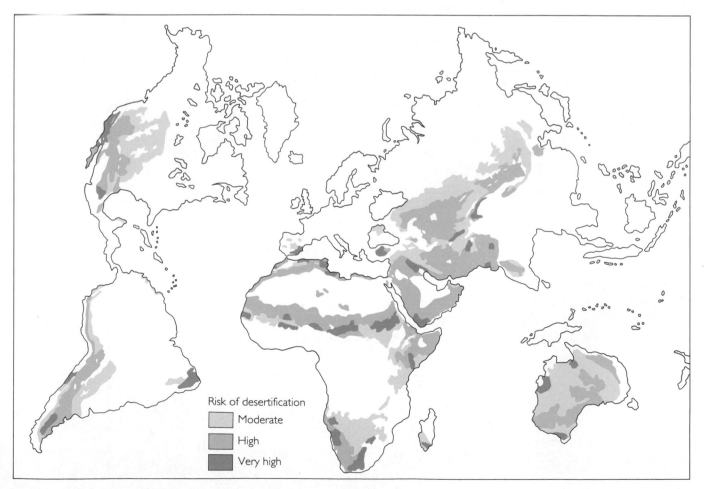

Figure 8   Areas at risk of desertification

Source: *World Resources, 1987*, p.71.

(c)   Acid rain from coal-fired power stations (many of them here in the UK) is killing the lakes and rivers of Scandinavia. Scientists now tell us that 'the release of carbon into the atmosphere as a result of deforestation, changing land use and the burning, or combustion, of fossil fuel is disturbing the natural carbon cycle' (Friends of the Earth, 1988, p.6) and producing a discernible 'greenhouse effect' on temperature levels world-wide. That, in its turn, is affecting regional climates, fish stocks, soil quality and average sea levels on exposed coastal plains. It could also affect our health. Figure 9 shows the pathways by which changes in the amount of carbon dioxide in the atmosphere may affect health.

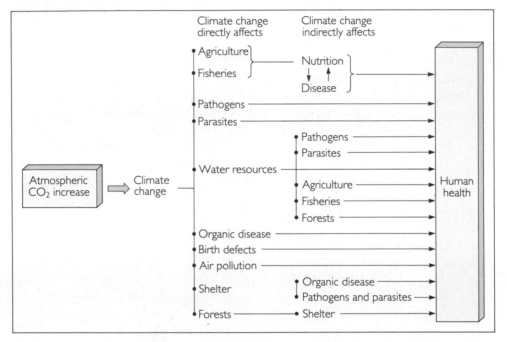

Figure 9   Pathways by which changes in level of carbon dioxide in the atmosphere may affect health
Source: Friends of the Earth, *The Heat Trap*, 1988.

Overall we are now seeing the growing impact of human action on the natural world — the creation of an increasingly *socially-constructed* natural environment. Our food still comes from that environment, so 'nature' must play an important part in any explanation of famine. But it plays that part only through the social systems created by people as they work in their natural environment; and because this is so, it is to *social* as well as to *natural* forces that we now need to look in our search for an understanding of hunger in the Third World.

─────────────── ACTIVITY 5 ───────────────

This is a good time to pause, and consolidate what we have established so far. Ask yourself, is world hunger caused by population pressure, food shortage or natural forces?

	What is the argument?	What is the evidence in support of the argument?	What are the problems with the argument?
Population pressure	1	2	3
Food shortage	4	5	6
Natural causes	7	8	9

There are nine boxes to fill in here. Here are some suggestions for the contents of each:

1   Resources are scarce, there are too many people in the world, it is the poor who consume the world's resources.

2   The world's population is growing rapidly, and in Africa at least population growth is outstripping the growth in recorded food production.

3   Many countries have increased their population while reducing their vulnerability to famine. Some countries experience famine even when their populations are growing less quickly than is their food production. Some famines occur in countries with low population densities.

4   Famines are caused by shortages of food, by a decline in food availability.

5   Some famines are caused by food shortages. China's famine between 1959 and 1961 is one example.

6   There is no world-wide food shortage. World food output has risen faster than the growth in population since 1950. Food surpluses exist in the First World while people starve in the Third. Famines occur alongside local food supplies. It is not food availability, but food entitlement, that is missing in these cases.

7   Famines are caused by natural forces: climatic changes, soil erosion, pests, etc.

8   Climate plays a part in famines — as happened recently in Ethiopia for example.

9   Natural forces only operate through social ones — societies can reduce their vulnerability to natural disasters by the way they organize themselves. The natural world is in any case increasingly a socially-constructed one.

4   THE GATHERING OF EVIDENCE

The systematic pursuit of social science permits us to go beyond popular conceptions of this kind, to probe the social processes that leave whole populations vulnerable to famine in bad years, and to undernourishment and malnutrition even in good ones. When we do this, we find a far-reaching debate going on between scholars about the relative weight of a whole series of factors which together seem to create the conditions within which famines can and do occur. Some of these factors are best thought of as *triggering factors*, as immediate causes of particular famines. Others are best thought of as *underlying causes*, creating the conditions in which the arrival of one or more 'triggers' can create widespread hunger.

4.1   THE TRIGGERING OF FAMINE

We have already mentioned the impact of *drought* as a triggering factor in certain recent African famines, in our earlier discussion of 'natural' causes of hunger in the Third World. The other trigger to famine often mentioned is more distinctly 'social' in character: namely *wars and political turmoil*. War can create famine in a multiplicity of ways:

1   It can disrupt lines of communication and food distribution — indeed in many wars the food supply channels of the rival population tend to become major targets.

2   'In war there is always a transfer of food from the civilian population to the fighting forces' (Kula, 1988, p.113).

3 Wars create an inflationary pressure in the affected countries, which erodes the purchasing power especially of the poorest sections of the population.

4 'In war situations hunger can also be used as a political weapon by one group to weaken the civilian population which may affiliate itself with a rival faction' (ibid, p.114). That use of food as a weapon may even extend to superpower relationships with regimes whose politics or social system they find unacceptable.

5 War just disrupts agricultural production. Crops are either not planted or not harvested, or are simply destroyed.

There are plenty of examples of these processes at work in the African famines of the 1970s and 1980s. Internal strife in Ethiopia, South African incursions into Angola and Mozambique, civil war in the Sudan — all played a crucial role in disturbing local food production and distribution, and exposing thousands of people to death from starvation. So it is hardly surprising that 'within the literature there is almost unanimous recognition of the role of the civil wars in Ethiopia, Chad, Mozambique and Sudan in propelling what were food crises resulting from drought, environmental and economic problems into full-blown famines' (Borton and Clay, 1986, p.265). War can create hunger in the First World too, as is clear from the near-famine conditions which existed in parts of Europe at the end of the Second World War.

Moreover, even when war is absent, there can be a definite political dimension to the incidence and distribution of famines — a political dimension whose centrality as a cause varies between famines. There are even examples of famines which were *predominantly* caused by political factors. The great Soviet famine of 1933–34, associated with Stalin's forced collectivization of the Russian peasantry, in which 10 million people died, is one major example. Arguably the great Bengal famine of 1943–44 is another, as the colonial powers confiscated grain over a wide area to prevent it falling into the hands of the Japanese. There are also examples of famines with causes rooted elsewhere, which were then *accentuated* by political errors and inactivity. Governments can make famines worse both by what they do and also by what they fail to do. Famines as far apart in time as the Great Irish famine of the 1840s and the Bangladesh famine of 1974 have often been said to have been caused in this way. In the case of the Irish famine, the British Government refused to become involved in extensive provision of food in Ireland in the 1840s; and more than a century later the US government was reluctant to release food aid to Bangladesh because of political disagreements with the Bangladesh government.

So war and politics can trigger famine just as drought can. But not all wars produce famine. Nor do all droughts. As we will now go on to see, both are most likely to have this consequence when they impact on agricultural systems that already have a particular character — one fixed over a longer period of time. In other words, famines result from the interplay of trigger factors and underlying causes. As I have already suggested, there is considerable agreement in the scholarly literature on what triggers famine. But as we will now see, there is less agreement on their underlying causes — and particularly on whether those causes are best seen as *local* or *global* in origin.

—————————————— ACTIVITY 6 ——————————————

It is always useful to clarify your own ideas *before* immersing yourself in the ideas of others. So jot down here what you think may be the underlying causes of famine.

Then come back to your list later to see if you want to amend it in the light of the reading you are now about to do.

4.2   LOW LEVELS OF AGRICULTURAL PRODUCTIVITY AS AN UNDERLYING CAUSE OF HUNGER IN THE THIRD WORLD

Vulnerability to famine down the years has been associated with low levels of agricultural productivity, itself a feature of particular ways of organizing economic activity on the land. In the long sweep of human history, men and women have lived off the land in different ways: as hunter-gatherers, as pastoralists, as settled farmers. Such agricultural activity had as its initial impulse the need to produce sufficient food to sustain the immediate producers, but over time both pastoralists and farmers raised their productivity to the point at which they were able to generate surpluses of foodstuffs which they could then exchange. Indeed the general tendency over time, in the First World at least, has been for more and more people to live in settled conditions rather than nomadic ones, and for surplus production to replace subsistence agriculture. In the process the techniques used to husband the natural world have themselves become more sophisticated, culminating since 1945 in the industrially-based agricultural systems of the contemporary First World. But legacies of earlier forms of land use remain widespread; and 'by far the largest proportion of the population of Third World countries (still) make their living as peasants ... small-scale agriculturalists who use family labour to produce food to meet their own needs' (Crow, 1985, p.6). These farmers are largely *self-provisioning*, that is they are producing food not primarily for sale but for the immediate consumption of themselves and their families. The majority of them will, in fact, produce food partly for their own consumption and partly for sale, using the income raised by selling crops to purchase essential goods (including foodstuffs) which they cannot produce themselves.

In this type of farming, productivity is often low, and when it is, vulnerability to hunger can be high. For characteristically such farmers, though capable of sustaining a low but adequate level of diet for their own needs in good times, tend to lack both the physical and financial resources to cope easily with sudden crop failures. As R.H. Tawney said of China's peasants in the 1920s, 'the position of many rural populations can be likened to that of a man standing permanently up to his neck in water, so that even a ripple is sufficient to drown him' (cited in Arnold, 1988, p.61). So no matter whether the crop failure is a product of climatic changes, or of political upheaval, the result in such societies is likely to be the same: that they will have to go through a 'famine cycle' before previously established, and always low, per capita levels of food production and consumption can be built up again. W.A. Dando has drawn the 'famine cycle' in the way shown in Figure 10.

There is broad agreement among scholars working in this field that the low productivity of agriculture in parts of the Third World is an important reason for continued hunger there. But there is no equivalent consensus on why that low productivity persists. Some scholars, as we will see in a moment, emphasize the importance of the way in which Third World economies were locked — in the eighteenth and nineteenth centuries — into the emerging *global* system of production and trade which we discussed in Unit 1. Other scholars discount that as a factor, preferring instead to emphasize the *local* character of peasant societies. On this argument, peasant societies are vulnerable to famine because they lack highly productive agricultural systems *and* the motivational structures necessary to ensure surplus food production. Their peasants neither generate a surplus to tide the society over lean years, nor are they able to export foodstuffs in sufficient quantities to buy in food from abroad when necessary. They are in some sense too 'traditional' in their technologies and in their attitudes to work and leisure — and because they are, their societies are particularly vulnerable to the famine cycle. Later in the unit we will return to look in more detail at the broad explanatory framework within which this

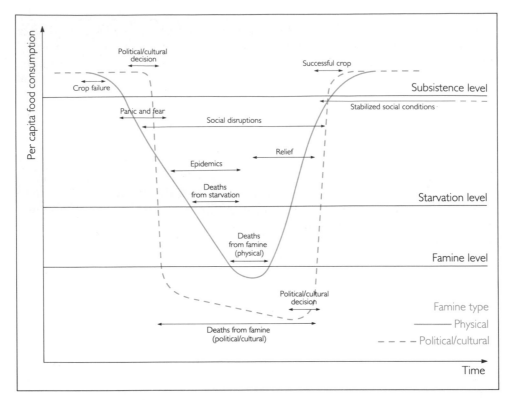

Figure 10   The famine cycle

Source: Developed by D.B. Baker, University of North Dakota.

emphasis on 'traditionalism' as a source of famine is embedded. But for the moment just notice how it is often associated with a particular set of attitudes to colonialism and to the full commercialization of agriculture. Notice in other words that this form of explanation of famine, like every other, comes with a set of associated policy consequences. We will meet this feature of social science explanation many times — this intimate connection between analysis and policy. It is a connection that helps to make social science so relevant and so controversial.

─────────────────── ACTIVITY 7 ───────────────────

If some Third World societies are prone to famine because they are too traditional in their attitudes and technologies, and too removed from contact with modern methods, do you think that the arrival of European powers — first as traders, then as colonizers — was a good or a bad thing for the local peasantry? (To help you understand what is at stake in this question, look back to Section 3.2 of Unit 1. Do you think we are looking at a process of 'development' or of 'exploitation'?)

Is the logic of the argument clear? Far from seeing the incorporation of these Third World economies into a First World dominated trading system as a barrier to their internal development as food producers, from this viewpoint famines occur because integration has not gone far enough. Instead of seeing colonialism as a burden, the argument runs the other way: that 'colonies were often established not to execute a major objective of national policy, nor even to exclude a rival economic power, but to fill a vacuum: that is, to organize a traditional society incapable of self-organization (or unwilling to organize itself) for modern import and export activity, including production for export' (Rostow, 1960, p.109). Very few scholars would want to deny the undesirable aspects of colonial rule: but some at least insist as well on colonialism's *positive* impact in the Third World. They would remind us that pre-colonial political and social systems in the Third World were often authoritarian in character, that there were famines in the Third World before colonialism, that patriarchy and poverty existed there long before the colonial period, and that colonialism helped to universalize Western liberal ideas on law and culture.

When that general view of colonialism is carried to its extreme, it becomes possible for some scholars to argue that, for example, Ireland is *now* free of famine in part because of English colonialism in the *past*, because the nineteenth century colonial power was strong enough to 'enforce a revolutionary restructuring of land tenure: the peasant was left with no choice but to adopt commercial social values' (Seavoy, 1986, p.390). India, on the same argument, remained famine-prone much longer because 'neither the colonial government nor the independent government of India had sufficient power to destroy the social restraints on food production that were enforced by the Hindu caste system' (ibid, p.390). What holds good for Ireland and India can be, and is then, more generally applied:

> [that] In order to extract more labour from the peasantry, central government must put control of land use into the hands of commercially motivated persons or organizations ... if the governments of peasant nations are to break the cycle of recurrent peacetime famine, they must use all of their political power to commercialize land tenure and *force the peasantry to adopt commercial social values*. Only after this is done can peasant nations undertake sustained programmes of industrialization and be free from the political instability that results from hunger or famine.
> (ibid, pp.31–2 and 398 my emphasis)

It is worth recognizing however that this kind of argument is not without its critics. As one of them has recently observed,

> 'The argument is certainly not devoid of all value. It gives due emphasis to an inherent frailty in peasant economies. It illustrates how historically the dissolution of peasant society through a process of capitalist transformation has been one of the routes by which famine has been evaded/overcome. But as an argument for explaining peasant vulnerability to famine it is short-sighted, superficial and almost abusive in its failure to comprehend peasant dilemmas and constraints [and runs close to] adopting the terminology of the elites, indigenous and foreign, landlords, colonial officials and the like, for whom indolence was the mark of the peasant beast'.
> (Arnold, 1988, p.58)

In contrast to Seavoy's approach, Arnold is keen to stress that 'peasant vulnerability to famine was not a self-induced nightmare but a spectre present in the very structure of the agrarian order within which they were confined' (ibid, p.59). For down the centuries a free peasantry has been a very rare thing. More normally peasants were 'subordinated to landlords and to the state, and often to the church as well, and each of these demanded and extracted some kind of payment — whether in the form of goods produced, cash or labour — from the peasant household.' (ibid, p.59). Such payments provided the base on which the sophisticated elite cultures of pre-industrial societies have flourished, but at the cost of keeping the peasantry itself on the edge of destitution. In other words, where some scholars have seen the vulnerability of peasant societies to famine as rooted in rural idleness and sloth, others have seen it as being due to the local exploitation to which peasants have been habitually subject.

4.3   THE INTERNATIONAL DIVISION OF LABOUR AS A LONG-TERM CAUSE OF HUNGER IN THE THIRD WORLD

Other scholars have found this emphasis on local features of agrarian life inadequate as an explanation of famine; and have dismissed Seavoy's solution — of a greater emphasis on the production of cash crops for export — as particularly misplaced. As was indicated in Unit 1, these academics emphasize instead the adverse effect of a new international division of labour on what had previously been self-sufficient food systems in Africa and Asia. As we saw in Unit 1, the rise of capitalism redrew the economic map of the world. Prior to its emergence, highly developed and largely self-contained economic systems were at times to be found in China, in India, in parts of Africa and South America, where productive agrarian systems and highly-developed manufacturing technologies sustained sophisticated cultures and complex political systems. These did not survive their contact with European and North American explorers, traders, missionaries, industrialists, and soldiers. Instead by 1900 a particular international division of labour was in place. It was one in which manufacturing activity went on only in the core industrial regions (basically inside a rectangle whose corners were at Chicago, St Petersburg, Milan and Baltimore), and in which Third World economies were increasingly locked into a subordinate and servicing role to that core — supplying raw materials, basic food stuffs and, where needed, cheap labour. Only Japan outside the central rectangle managed successfully to escape that Third World fate.

Elsewhere in the non-industrial world, economies were restructured to sustain this new international division of labour. This restructuring was particularly evident in those parts of the Third World which came under the direct political control of European colonial powers. Many commentators on food and famine emphasize the way in which European colonizers dismantled traditional mechanisms for coping with drought and other causes of famine, and thus prepared the way for worse famines to come. Famine was not the aim of colonial government so much as the unanticipated consequence of the way in which local economies were restructured to meet the needs of the colonial powers. In many colonies that restructuring took a number of forms.

1   Local artisan-based manufacturing was either banned outright, or destroyed by being exposed — without protective tariffs — to the full force of industrial competition. This was the fate both of the Indian and African textile industries and much of the embryonic industrial development of the southern part of Ireland after 1800.

2   Local land rights were reorganized, to give the best land to European settlers, to exclude indigenous people from participation in profitable export production, or (less frequently) to encourage local elites to consolidate land holdings for commercial purposes. Even in Ireland, parts of the Catholic peasantry were displaced by Protestant settlers in the seventeenth century, and both Catholic and Protestant tenant farmers suffered from heavy rents imposed on them by absentee landlords in the eighteenth and nineteenth centuries. In Ireland, as in other colonies, both land and labour were turned into commodities, and local food production was subordinated to the production of crops for export. This often involved the introduction of the plantation system — into the Caribbean, into Brazil, into India and Sri Lanka — from which to supply sugar, cotton, tobacco and tea to the core industrial centres. It also involved the development of extractive industries, again in the control of European and settler interests. In the process, the colonial powers commonly allied themselves with existing local elites (in the British case often using local power structures as a means of indirect rule) so freezing social relationships on the land into existing unequal forms.

3 The amount of land left available for the production of local food needs was correspondingly reduced. Local peasantries were forced out into marginal lands, whose quality was then further eroded by the over-cultivation made necessary by the arrival of so many people. India again is a classic case. The destruction of Indian manufacturing forced more and more people back onto the land. 'From 1891 to 1931 alone the population dependent on agriculture (in India) rose from 61 per cent to 75 per cent. As the artisans were driven back to the land the size of rural holdings fell, pressures on the soil increased, and hunger took possession of the whole country' (Buchanan, 1982, p.30).

—————————————— ACTIVITY 8 ——————————————

We now have two views of the role of colonialism as a long-term cause of hunger in the Third World. Check your understanding of the two positions by looking back over the last two sub-sections of the unit. Then answer these questions:

1   What were the advantages claimed for colonialism in Section 4.2?

2   What were the disadvantages claimed for colonialism in Section 4.3?

Does your list include advantages such as the 'modernization' of attitudes, the commercialization of agriculture, the filling of a local power vacuum; and the disadvantages — a disruption of established ways of avoiding famine, a redistribution of land away from the indigenous population, and a reduction of land given over to local food production? (If you are still in doubt about the nature and importance of this dispute, go back to Section 3.2 of Unit 1 again, to see how disagreements of this kind are treated.)

4.4   LOCAL AND GLOBAL FACTORS IN THE PRODUCTION OF FAMINE

I hope that it is now clear that the underlying causes of famine are in *dispute*. Social scientists disagree with each other about which features of Third World existence to emphasize, and about the ranking in importance of the features chosen. There seems a common acceptance that local and global factors play a part; but no agreement at all about where prime responsibility lies — with local features of Third World life, or with the global links of the First World to the Third. You may already be able to see that 'the local' and 'the global' here are not entirely distinct, the one from the other. What is really in dispute is the degree to which local vulnerability to famine is shaped by global forces. Is the productivity of local agriculture in the Third World low partly because of a *lack of global connections* (as those who would modernize it might suggest) or partly because of a *particular and exploitative kind of global connection* (as the critics of colonialism would argue).

The formal structures of colonialism have now largely gone away; but the debate about it, and about the causes of famine, has not. Many scholars continue to emphasize the importance of colonial legacies as the key to famine-vulnerability; others to emphasize the need to transmit the strengths of First World agriculture to Third World food producers. We can see this if we look at four suggested underlying causes of hunger in the Third World: *the export of food, agribusiness, the flow of scientific knowledge* and *foreign aid*. Take a look at each of these in turn and try to relate them to this local-global distinction.

THE EXPORT OF FOOD

Some analysts of hunger in the Third World attach particular importance to the way in which many former colonial societies were often left, upon independence, with economies disproportionately dependent for foreign earnings on single-crop exports. (This was mentioned in Unit 1, so look again at Figure 9 in that unit.) This dependence had often been deliberately fostered by the colonial power; and it left post-colonial states with very little choice — in the immediate post-independence period — but to go on exporting primary produce, usually at the price of not developing their own self-sufficiency in foodstuffs. To quote Grigg:

> Many developing countries are vulnerable because of their dependence upon one or two products. Thus tropical beverages, which are largely luxury items, make up 25 per cent of all developing countries' agricultural exports. Of 87 developing countries in 1980, half depended upon cocoa, coffee and tea for at least 30 per cent of their agricultural earnings. But concentration is not confined to these crops. Burma and North Korea derive over 70 per cent of their agricultural exports from rice alone, Bangladesh from jute, and Senegal and Gambia from groundnuts: over 90 per cent of Cuba's exports still come from sugar ... The concentration upon relatively few exports is repeated when the major regions are considered. Some 60 per cent of Africa's exports are coffee and cocoa, 70 per cent of Latin America's are sugar, coffee and soya beans, 60 per cent of the Near East's are fruit, vegetables and cotton, and 60 per cent of the Far East's exports consist of rubber, rice and vegetable oils.

(Grigg, 1985, pp.259, 261 and 262)

Not surprisingly in Third World societies dependent on foreign currency for economic development, cash crops occupy 'enormous areas of many countries' best land; and often hog most of the scarce inputs that go into successful farming' in the modern world, taking priority for 'irrigation, fertilizers, pesticides or machinery' (George, 1976, p.39). 'A total of 25 per cent of all cultivatable land in the Third World is now turned over to cash crops for the markets of the industrialized world' (Bush, 1987, p.5). This in its turn brings a new kind of dependency on the First World. For the price of these cash crops are predominantly determined in the industrial economies and not by the suppliers themselves. Third World societies can be — and often are — thrown into turmoil by a sudden drop in the prices they receive for their exported crops, by the resulting reduction in their stocks of foreign currency, and thus in their ability to import foodstuffs and manufactured products from abroad.

This is relevant to a discussion of hunger in the Third World because one consequence of this increasing concentration on production for export (including the export of food) can be a diminished capacity of such food exporters to feed their own people, as the production of staple food crops is pushed into smaller areas of more marginal land. This intensified use of the land for staple food production can in its turn increase local vulnerability to famine, as people literally 'destroy their own productive resources while attempting to survive' (ODI, 1987, p.4). Trees are cut down. Land is over-grazed. Soil is under-fertilized; and energy is directed away from essential food production into the cultivation of crops for export.

So ironically it would appear that vulnerability to hunger among the poorer sections of certain Third World societies may actually be *increased*, rather than diminished, by too great an involvement in the production of food — if that food is designed for export rather than for home consumption! Or, as Philip Raikes put it, 'there are strong reasons for doubting whether poor people's access to food is likely to be improved by increased emphasis on export-crop production' (Raikes, 1988, p.9).

Is this a 'local' or a 'global' cause of Third World hunger? On the surface it looks pretty local — not enough staple food in the local economy. But this local pattern of food production is globally driven — by the need to export cash crops to earn foreign currency. So once again it seems to be the nature of the interplay of the local and the global which is important here.

THE ROLE OF AGRIBUSINESS

There is also much discussion, in the literature on food and famine, of the way in which the production and distribution of agricultural products in both the First and the Third Worlds is now heavily influenced by a small number of very large companies (known as *agribusiness*). 'Agribusiness is an umbrella term to describe those multinational companies which control the production, processing and distribution of foodstuffs and control associated technology like tractors, fertilizers and seed' (Bush, 1987, p.4). These transnational corporations — companies such as Nestlé, Del Monte, or Cargill and Dreyfuss — are now responsible for 30 per cent of world food production, 40 per cent of total world trade, and up to 90 per cent of the world's commodity trade. These companies are truly vast. The biggest thirty of them in 1980 had combined sales that were six times the size of Britain's national income: and between them they then handled roughly four-fifths of Africa's commodity trade.

The centrality of such companies to the production and marketing of Third World cash crops has become a matter of real controversy. Their defenders emphasize the positive contribution they make to the earning capacities of Third World economies, and the role they play in the modernization of agricultural production in the Third World. Seeing no necessary tension between corporate profit-making and agrarian development in the Third World, corporate spokesmen insist that the companies merely make 'money by meeting human needs in an efficient, business-like way' (George, 1976, p.162). Here then are global institutions being presented as facilitators of greater local food production.

Their critics have found that presentation disingenuous. They have suggested instead that the companies use land that would otherwise be available for domestic food production, and that being concerned with production for profit, they seldom get involved in production of food for local consumption. Critics suggest too that agribusinesses tend to use capital intensive methods at odds with the general level of technology and availability of labour in the economy around them; and that they pay their workers badly, in spite of the profits they realize from their labour. Here then are global institutions being presented as contributors to increased local vulnerability to hunger.

It is hard to judge the relative merits of these conflicting claims — or at least to do so without undertaking extensive research that is beyond our capacities here. But it is worth noting that even moderate opinion — within the general literature on food and famine — tends to worry about the impact of these global corporations on local food systems, pointing to the increasing tendency of Third World economies to *import* basic foodstuffs, and to the *dual nature* of the agrarian systems emerging there. The incorporation of local economies into global systems of food production and distribution seems to be creating Third World agrarian sectors split 'between a large-scale and relatively capital-intensive sector producing a narrow range of export crops, and a labour-intensive peasant sector which provides the bulk of the population's food requirements' (Tabatabai, 1985, p.8). Moreover Third World nations that collectively were exporting 12 million tons of grain in the late 1930s had come to import nearly 80 million tons by the late 1970s. Imported food is, of course, more expensive than the food that a peasant could grow, and 'those who cannot afford it do not eat' (Buchanan, 1982, p.33).

THE FLOW OF SCIENTIFIC KNOWLEDGE

The advocates of agrarian modernization through agribusiness have often emphasized the advantages of 'the green revolution'. This 'revolution' began, with financial support from the Rockefeller Foundation, at a Research Institute established in Mexico in 1943; and it was extended, with help from Ford as well as Rockefeller, at a similar institute established in the Philippines in 1962. 'The Mexican institute produced new kinds of seeds for wheat, that in the Philippines for rice: varieties which would absorb more nutrients (in the shape of oil-based chemical fertilizers) and thus bear heavier kernels which would mean higher yields (hence the term high-yielding varieties or HYVs)' (Buchanan, 1982, p.50). The new HYVs were canvassed by the US government and the World Bank to wheat growers in India, Pakistan and Turkey as well as Mexico, and to rice growers in Taiwan, Sri Lanka and India as well as in the Philippines. The results achieved were dramatic. Areas with particularly favourable climates witnessed increases in yields as high as 50 per cent. As a result, the size of marketable surpluses available grew, and the capacities of these economies to sustain large urban populations was enhanced.

> Within three years, Pakistan ceased to be dependent on wheat imports from the United States. Sri Lanka, the Philippines, and a number of African and South American countries achieved record harvests. India, which had just avoided a severe famine in 1967, produced enough grain within five years to support its population. Even after the 1979 drought, grain imports were not necessary. India had become self-sufficient in wheat and rice, tripling its wheat production between 1961 and 1980.
>
> (Glaeser, 1987, p.1)

It did look as though the application of science to agriculture offered a real way out of Third World poverty and famine.

But there was an opposite side to the 'green revolution' — a side which brought new problems. Two of these problems are of particular importance here.

1 One is the greater dependency of 'green farmers' on foreign manufactured chemicals and farm machinery. The new seeds 'yielded well only if planted in conjunction with a "package" which included irrigation, massive doses of artificial fertilizers (three times those required by local varieties), pesticides, fungicides and weed killers' (Buchanan, 1982, p.50). Third World countries do not in the main produce their own chemicals and tractors. They have to buy them; and to earn the foreign currency to do so, they have to export larger and larger percentages of their agrarian output. This leaves local agrarian production heavily dependent on multinational corporations, on the relative prices of agricultural and industrial goods in world markets, and on World Bank sources of credit. Some of the 'green revolution' countries have run up massive debts. This debt was due to far more than just agrarian restructuring; but nonetheless one consequence of it has been the growing difficulties of many Third World countries to feed their own populations — rural and urban — in the face of pressures to clear foreign debts by cutting urban spending and by exporting more crops.

2 The 'green revolution' has also intensified already-existing inequalities in the Third World countryside. Only rich peasants and large landowners have been able to afford the costly inputs necessary for the new seeds; and in the pursuit of the returns needed to maintain this form of commercial agriculture, they have been obliged to hold down rural wages, put smaller competitors out of business, and intensify rural work routines. So, for example, between 1961

and 1968, as the 'green revolution' spread, the number of people below the poverty line in rural India increased from 38 to 53 per cent. The 'green revolution' has spawned a relatively wealthy landowning group, employing landless wage labourers — and it is from these landless wage labourers that the Third World recruits many of its hungry men, women and their children.

THE FLOW OF FOREIGN AID

The 'green revolution' represents one attempt to right the imbalance between agricultural output in the First and Third Worlds. The flow of aid from the First World to the Third is often seen as another means to the same end. Both public agencies and private citizens in the First World send money and/or food surpluses to the Third World in response to the visible hunger of so many people there. Their action seems — and is invariably presented — as a common-sense and humanitarian reaction to the otherwise ludicrous situation of food surpluses being destroyed in one part of the world while people starve in another. Aid goes in emergencies to provide immediate relief. It goes to assist specific development programmes; and it is given to ease balance of payments problems for hard-pressed Third World governments. Aid, like science, seems like something the First World can usefully contribute to the Third as a solution to generalized hunger there.

But can aid play this role? Does the transfer of agrarian surpluses help? How far can private altruism and state-directed aid help to reduce vulnerability to hunger in the Third World?

Aid is clearly essential in particular crises — it is all that keeps yet more people from literally starving to death. It is also clear that particular aid projects can and do increase the capacity of Third World farmers to increase their output. But aid too has its underside. The arrival of large quantities of foreign food surpluses can have a deleterious effect on the profits (and therefore future production) of local suppliers. Aid is often given for bilateral trade reasons, tying local purchasing to the supplies of the donor country. It is often given with political strings, as a way of shaping the internal social and political development of recipient economies. And even when it is not, much of it is distributed through financial agencies wedded to a particular model of development. The IMF and the World Bank have a definite development strategy. It tends to be a 'green revolution' one, and we have seen some of the drawbacks, as well as the strengths, of that. Moreover, the flow of aid out of the First World needs to be put in the context of other associated flows. The EC budget in 1987, for example, was £24.8 billion. Only 3 per cent of that went in food aid to the Third World. 64 per cent went on the Common Agricultural Policy, subsidizing European farmers. Indeed the relatively modest flow of aid out from the First World can be, and in certain years is, more than offset by the flow of debt repayments back from the Third World to the First, and by the collapse of Third World earnings on their cash crop exports. It is a sad fact that in 1985, for example, 'when an incredible £2,500 million was raised by voluntary and government agencies for famine victims in Africa ... the famine-stricken countries paid back to Northern banks, governments and financial agencies *double* that amount in debt repayments' (Bennett, 1987, p.87).

It is very difficult to resolve the pros and cons of foreign aid; but at least the advantages and disadvantages can be set side-by-side, to leave you free to decide on their relative merits. Here is how Colm Regan summarized the arguments for and against aid. How would you rank them in importance? On which side of the argument would you come down?

ARGUMENTS FOR AID	ARGUMENTS AGAINST AID
Some observers would argue that:	Some observers would argue that:
• When properly administered and used, aid can help those most in need by providing emergency assistance as well as help with long-term development. Thus aid can help save lives today and help prevent them being lost in the future.	• Aid from government to government only favours the rich of the world and has little effect on the poor. Aid has been used by authoritarian governments to consolidate their power.
• Aid can help developing country governments provide vital development infrastructure and planning, e.g. roads, water and sanitation, planning services, education. Aid can thus act as a 'pump-primer' in getting development underway. Aid can help overcome 'bottlenecks' to economic development in a country where local savings are small or where there is a lack of foreign exchange.	• Aid creates dependency by making weaker governments/countries dependent on stronger ones, thus putting them at a disadvantage in economic or political discussions.
• Aid acts as an expression of humanitarian concern, and provides people in the developed world with a channel through which to direct that concern.	• Aid is often tied; its terms dictate that recipients buy goods or services from the donor country; it is thus a hidden subsidy to industry/the professions in the developed world.
• Aid acts as a limited but effective means of redistributing global wealth.	• Aid distorts the free market which is the most important engine of growth as the experience of the developed world shows.
• Aid can help establish practical links between countries and thus foster international understanding and, hopefully, peace.	• Aid is used to divert attention from other more important areas, e.g. trade, where major structural changes would have vastly more beneficial results. We shouldn't waste time arguing about aid when trade is the issue.
• Aid is a mechanism where the experience and expertise of the better off parts of the world is made available to the poorer sections.	• Since *we* are the givers and *they* are the receivers, aid can lead to attitudes of superiority and even to those of racism. Aid re-inforces stereotypical images.
• Aid is a means through which countries and governments can pursue their own interests (both as donors and as recipients), thus giving meaning to the term 'Interdependence'.	• Aid is currently used for economic, political and strategic reasons and is thus aimed at maintaining the current character of world inequality, rather than at challenging it.

(Regan, 1986, pp.5–17)

SUMMARY

So far in Section 4 we have discussed globally-based features of contemporary agrarian life in the Third World, and seen that each has an ambiguous set of local effects — increasing certain kinds of food production at the same time as increasing the vulnerability of certain sections of Third World societies to hunger in all its forms.

- Many Third World economies emerged from the colonial period heavily dependent for foreign currency on the export of one/two primary products. This dependence has left significant sections of their societies vulnerable to hunger whenever export earnings are insufficient to cover the cost of importing basic foodstuffs.

- Much of that food export is handled by multinational corporations, whose presence has accentuated this tendency to import basic foodstuffs and to divide local agrarian systems into a capital-intensive export sector and a labour-intensive peasant one.

- The 'green revolution' has enabled certain economies to become food exporters, but at the cost of increased dependence on foreign manufactures and growing rural inequality.

- Foreign aid is often the only way to avoid immediate mass starvation, but it is often small in quantity, given with political strings, and can even disturb local production.

5 THE ORGANIZATION OF EXPLANATORY VARIABLES

If you look back over the last two sections of this unit, you will see that there are lots of explanations of hunger in the Third World, and of the incidence of famine there, available to us. There is a range of explanations that stretches from drought to agribusiness, and from over-population to inadequate supplies of overseas aid. If we are to make some sense of that range, and begin to feel our way towards an evaluation of the competing claims contained within it, we need some strategy to enable us to impose some *order* on that plethora of explanations and to find some *benchmarks* against which to assess the competing claims before us. We can do that for explanations of famine — just as for competing explanations of other social phenomena later in the course — by trying first to *list* them in some kind of order, then to *apply them as widely as possible*, and finally to *theorize* the range of explanations for the incidence of hunger in the Third World that we have gathered.

- Try the listing first. It would help if we could put all these possible explanations for the incidence of hunger in the Third World down on one sheet of paper, in some order that helps us to see the real choices involved.

─────────────── ACTIVITY 9 ───────────────

Go back through the unit and list each and every explanation in turn, in the order in which they occur.

Now take a closer look at Section 3. Can you find a big distinction, or set of preoccupations, that keeps cropping up in the discussion of a number of the explanations handled there — a distinction around which we might begin to organize the choice of explanation? Can you find a similar 'big theme' in Section 4?

These are not easy tasks to handle, and indeed they can be resolved in more than one way. It's the general strategy that is important here — one that I hope you will find useful on many occasions — of first listing explanations, and then finding some distinctions around which to compare and evaluate them.

When I did that I came out with a list of possible explanations that began with over-population, and then included food shortages, climatic and other 'natural' changes, war and politics, low levels of agricultural productivity, colonialism, the export of food, the presence of agribusiness, the absence of a 'green revolution' and inadequacies of aid. As I was writing Section 3, the argument seemed regularly to return to the natural/social distinction (are famines caused by natural forces or by human action?); and Section 4 regularly probed the role of local and global social forces. And when I realized that, I thought it might be worthwhile to re-organize the list around these two distinctions. I came up with the diagram in Figure 11 as a result.

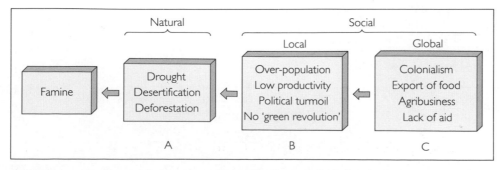

Figure 11

Now at least you have a clearer picture of what you have to decide. In which 'box' do you place your explanation of famine in the Third World? There seems to be a clear choice. It is possible to stay with 'natural' explanations (enter, that is, at box A), since at the most immediate level such factors seem to play a crucial role. Or it is possible to see these immediate factors as significant only if rooted in particular local conditions of a social kind (and so enter the explanation at box B); or it is possible to probe further still, and to ask if, or to what degree, those local conditions reflect the character and impact of past and present global forces (and so go in at box C).

So we have a diagram of choice. But the diagram alone doesn't tell us which is/ are the most important of these factors in the creation of hunger in the Third World. Nor do we know if the mix of factors is the same in each famine. To settle that (and indeed to discover other factors that we have missed) our next task must be to turn to other available sources of information — to examine detailed case studies of individual famines and surveys of case studies where these are available — asking as we do so which of these 'boxes', if any, help to explain the detail of each case in turn. In other words, we have next to *apply* our possible explanations to as many examples as possible.

=== READER ===

We only have a week. Even the quickest readers among us would be hard pressed to read every case study on famine by next Friday! So we cannot go too far down this route at the moment. But we can look at one *survey* of recent case studies on hunger in Africa by Philip Raikes. A brief extract from that survey is reproduced in the Reader, and I would ask you to read it now.

=== ACTIVITY 10 ===

When you have read the Raikes article, go back to the diagram of explanatory variables that we established a moment ago, and underline those factors which did surface in the case study you have just read. Is there evidence of drought? political turmoil? over-population? colonialism?

It does seem, from the survey, that colonialism plays an important long-term role in the creation of hunger in Africa, as does the spread of commodity production, droughts, deforestation and political factors. But Raikes also places considerable emphasis on *patriarchal cultures* (which leave women and children disproportionately vulnerable to hunger) and to the *lack of purchasing power* of the rural poor. These two need therefore to be added to box B as local

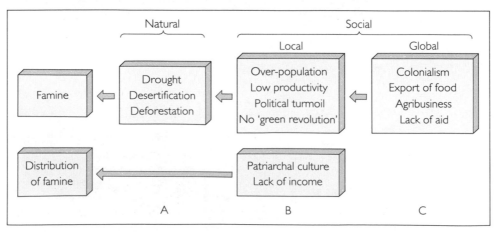

Figure 12

causes of hunger (or more accurately, as local causes of its distribution within the population). Agribusiness doesn't surface as a factor in this survey. Nor does desertification. So we will have to reserve judgement on them. Clearly if they are major causes of hunger, they are not essential prerequisites. People in Africa can clearly go hungry without their help! We can amend our diagram therefore, to absorb these new emphases (see Figure 12).

6 THE SEARCH FOR EXPLANATORY FRAMEWORKS

By looking at a review of case studies in this way we can begin to formulate at least a provisional judgement on the relative importance of all these variables, a judgement that will strengthen the more case studies we are able to examine. And that points to one important general way in which we advance our knowledge as social scientists — by the testing of different propositions against evidence wherever we can find it.

There is a related thing that we can do as well, in our search for benchmarks against which to judge the adequacy or otherwise of particular explanations of hunger in the Third World. We can relate those individual explanations to broader pictures of the way the world is organized, pictures whose general adequacy we will be able to judge only by gathering and reflecting upon all our knowledge of how the world around us is organized. These broader pictures — what I am calling here explanatory frameworks — already exist in social science, put together by major thinkers in the past; and indeed some of the explanations we have already met derive from work inspired by one framework or another. Looking at these frameworks will not instantly resolve our immediate dilemma: of what causes hunger in the Third World. But it will increase our understanding of the choices we face here as social analysts. It will enable us to see that our decision on how best to explain famine will also have consequences for our attitude towards the broad explanatory framework within which our chosen explanation normally sits: and that conversely our understanding of the causes of famine can eventually help us to choose between these broad explanatory frameworks — precisely by examining the characteristic explanations of famine which each generates.

Social science contains a number of 'big pictures' of the way the world works. From that number I will lay out briefly just three very influential ones, for you to think about — three that approach famine through a view of the world divided into:

- traditional/modern societies; or
- North–South; or
- core/periphery.

6.1 TRADITIONAL/MODERN SOCIETIES

Much development literature in the 1960s operated inside this 'picture': that all societies were engaged on the same growth path, and had to move through stages. The view was common that Third World countries were *further back* than First World ones, and had to catch up. They had to move from their status as:

traditional societies: where technology was limited, economic life was agrarian in kind and subsistence in level, social structures were dominated by loyalties of extended family, tribe and clan, the political system was decentralized and ineffectual, and thought was pre-scientific, fatalistic and dominated by religion and magic. In these societies economic output oscillated around a relatively stable point; and population growth was held back by high levels of mortality.

They had to move instead to a new status as:

modern societies: where technology was sophisticated, economic life was dominated by industry rather than agriculture, social structure was organized around divisions of class and status, the state was centralized and bureaucratized, and culture was predominantly secular and scientific in character. In such societies, economic growth was written into the fabric of the society; and population growth was held back by voluntary restrictions on birth rates made possible by new technology and new preferences for personal achievement and affluence within smaller family units.

The picture we are given is of two societies, and a common line of transition between them.

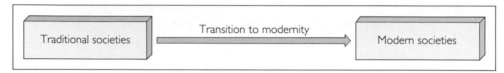

Figure 13

On this model, (as we saw in our earlier discussion of low productivity) what blocks economic development in the Third World is the persistence there of *outmoded* forms of economic activity, social life, political organization and ways of thinking. The society is just short of modern things: commercial attitudes, entrepreneurial activity, urban populations, scientific education, bureaucratic institutions, secular thought, social and private capital. These are its 'development gaps', which it needs to fill. The need therefore is to *modernize* — to chase after the First World and to catch it up. The barriers to this process are largely *local* in origin, and policy has to be directed at internal reform. If the First World can help in this 'transition', it is only by short-circuiting the process: sending 'international aid in the form of technical assistance, soft loans or grants — including flows of surplus food and fibres' (Rostow, 1960, p.142), encouraging trade, lending capital, and making available the latest and most sophisticated technology.

6.2   NORTH–SOUTH

On this 'picture', that process of change is not so easy, because the division between traditional and modern societies is overlaid by the uneven economic development of North and South. 'North' and 'South' here are conceptual rather than purely geographical categories — camps rather than regions — with the North developed and industrial, the South undeveloped and agrarian. Though both are locked into trading relationships with each other, there is nothing mutually balancing and beneficial about the interchange. On the contrary, the different production conditions in the North and the South work against any easy levelling up of their productive capacities. It is not just that the South has to catch up. It has to do so in a world in which the North is moving ahead. In the North capital investment, high rates of industrial productivity and heavy agricultural protection guarantee bountiful supplies of industrial products and farm surpluses. In the South, low investment, masses of cheap and unskilled labour, and low productivity agriculture, give it little to trade with, and few competitive advantages over Northern producers. Free trade between the two blocks will not correct the historically-created imbalance between them. On the contrary, all the evidence suggests that it will intensify it, in some cumulative process of uneven development.

So the picture we are offered is of trade between unequals pushing them
further and further apart.

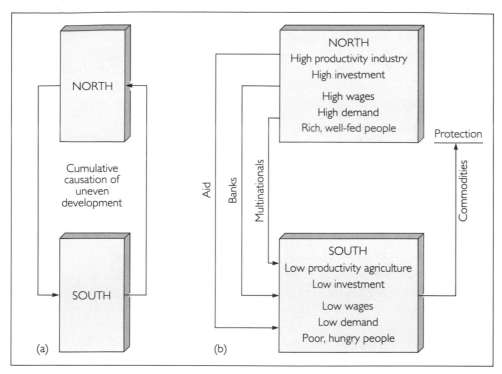

Figure 14

On this argument, if the First World is to help the Third, it has to do more than
urge it to reform its internal structures and model itself on the western economies. The First World has to give Third World producers preferential trading
terms to make up for the preferential terms it gave itself in the past. It has (in
the words of an influential report on the North–South divide produced in 1980
by a committee chaired by former West German Chancellor Willy Brandt) to
'produce structural changes with a fair balance for mutual benefit' by making
'rearrangements of international relations, the building of a new kind of order,
and a new kind of comprehensive approach to the problem of development'
(Brandt, 1980, p.18). In particular, the South needs more purchasing power, to
buy the raw materials and capital goods it requires for its internal development. It needs access to the protected markets of the North for its agrarian
produce. It needs greater control over the pricing and sale in the North of the
primary commodities produced in the South. It needs international regulation
of multinational corporations; and most of all, it needs a more generous
approach by Northern financial agencies to questions of credit and debt.

We might note too that many scholars holding this view of the world are
optimistic that this can be arranged, if the political will is there to do it. As the
Brandt Report put it:

> We are convinced that many of the world's problems can be solved in
> the mutual interest of North and South. The South wants access to the
> markets of the North for its manufacturing, which raises problems for
> specific industries in the North — but overall the North can expand
> employment by a balanced increase in its trade with the South. The
> South needs to buy from the North, and to repay its debts, but for that
> it must earn foreign currency in the North by selling its goods there.
> The South wants a code to provide more harmonious relations with
> multinational corporations — but both sides can benefit if these
> corporations can invest confidently in the South, and if the South can

97

have more confidence in the multinationals' behaviour: future mineral investment in the South depends on such arrangements. Above all, we believe that a large-scale transfer of resources to the South can make a major impact on growth in both the North and South and help to revive the flagging world economy.

(Brandt, 1980, pp.35–6).

6.3   CORE/PERIPHERY

Such a reform of the system in an incremental and mutually-beneficial way is doubted by those scholars who write of 'the development of underdevelopment'. It was not, on this view, the case that all countries were once undeveloped, and that some broke out to higher levels of economic activity. It was rather that those who broke out did so by exploiting the rest, *pushing them into underdevelopment*. The picture we are given is one of a core of industrializing nations, extracting from the agrarian societies that surround them raw materials, food and cheap labour. Fully integrated industrial societies developed in the core of the system at the cost of dividing Third World societies into two sectors: a traditional subsistence one locked into poverty and malnutrition, and an export enclave subsidized by cheap labour drawn from the subsistence sector. A system of *unequal exchange* links core and periphery. The core does not pay the full price for the resources it extracts. Labour in the periphery is underpaid, peasants are under-rewarded; and the surplus from their unpaid labour is taken away to the First World, to accumulate there as profits and as industrial and financial capital. This unequal exchange was first achieved by force of arms: in the colonial period. It is now achieved in a less political but equally effective way. In the post-colonial era, surplus is extracted from the Third World to the First through the internal pricing mechanisms of multinational corporations and through debt repayments to foreign banks. Foreign capital's hold on these economies then locks them into dependency on the First World whose wealth their people have helped, and are still helping, to create: dependency for loans, for technology, for markets, and for the arms necessary to maintain internal stability amid such hardship. Only a sharp break from these trading patterns and commercial institutions will give Third World societies any hope of achieving internal patterns of economic development free of this surplus extraction.

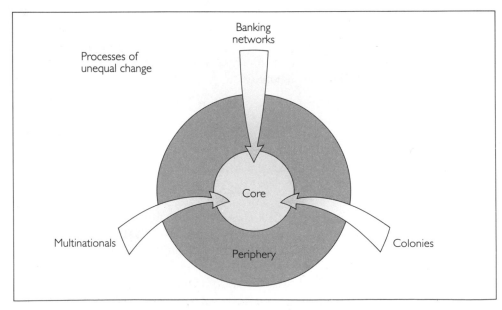

Figure 15

SUMMARY

The three views of the world order can be summarized as follows:

- The world is divided into traditional and modern societies; that low standards of living persist in the Third World because of a development gap; and that the First World can help to fill that gap by scientific and other forms of aid.

- The world is divided into an industrial 'North' and rural 'South'; that the poverty of the South is accentuated by the progressive deterioration of its position in relation to the North; and that only a fairer organization of international trade will enable the South to develop its agriculture and industry.

- The world is divided into 'core' and 'periphery'; that the core accumulates wealth, industry and power by extracting surplus from the periphery; and that only a sharp break from core-dominated trading patterns will provide the space within which Third World countries can develop their internal economies.

7   TESTING THE FRAMEWORKS

None of these three pictures, as laid out here, addresses itself directly to hunger. But each has clear implications for the exercise in which we are engaged — of trying to evaluate the different explanations of Third World hunger and famine.

--- ACTIVITY 11 ---

Complete this table of possible linkages between broad explanatory frameworks and more specific explanations of hunger in the Third World. Ask yourself: would a particular explanatory framework attach high/low importance to each of these explanations? Then ask — what would it have to say about each one to which importance was attached?

Table 3

	Traditional /Modern	North–South	Core/Periphery
1 Over population			
2 Food shortage			
3 Climatic changes			
4 War/politics			
5 Low productivity agriculture			
6 Colonialism			
7 The export of food			
8 Agribusiness			
9 No green revolution			
10 Inadequate aid			

My answers would look like this:

The *Traditional/Modern* approach would probably give a lot of weight to points 1–3 as examples of the social attitudes and agricultural inefficiency of traditional societies, and of their associated vulnerability to 'natural' forces. It would emphasize the importance of low agrarian productivity, allow a role for war and politics, and see the vulnerability to famine increased by the absence of green revolutions and of aid.

The *North–South* approach would probably give less weight to points 1–3, while recognizing the importance of population control as one way of easing immediate pressure. Its emphasis would be on low levels of agrarian productivity resulting in part from colonialism and war, and it would want to see a different role for agribusiness, better terms for food exporters, and more scientific and food aid.

The *Core/Periphery* approach would put its major emphasis on the legacies of colonialism (and of other indirect forms of Third World incorporation into the capitalist world trading system). Agribusiness would be singled out as a particular problem, as would the adverse effects on the rural poor of the green revolution. *Aid as imperialism* is actually the title of a stimulating book by Teresa Hayter written from within this broad perspective; so a core/periphery approach might be rather cautious about (and critical of) the ulterior motives and long-term consequences of the aid programmes of First World governments.

So I would mark up the table as follows:

Table 4

		Traditional /Modern	North–South	Core/Periphery
1	Over-population	√	√	
2	Food shortage	√		
3	Climatic changes	√		
4	War/politics	√	√	√
5	Low productivity agriculture	√	√	
6	Colonialism		√	√
7	The export of food		√	√
8	Agribusiness		√	√
9	No green revolution	√	√	
10	Inadequate aid	√	√	

These three 'pictures' raise questions about many things other than food and famine. They raise questions in particular about the character of First World societies, and about the nature of their international trade. These are questions which we have not yet even begun to explore — but explore them we will, at least for the UK, over the remainder of this course. So for the moment you will need to reserve final judgement on which of these 'pictures' — if any — is an adequate first approximation to the nature of the contemporary world order. But already our examination of hunger in the Third World may be beginning to predispose you towards one 'picture' rather than another, as you put the arguments of each against all the information we have now surveyed. You should keep these three pictures in your mind as you work through Blocks II–VI, so that by the last block of the course you might be in a position to decide which of them — if any — offers a useful guide to the nature of First World societies and to their relationship with other parts of the world system.

—————————————— ACTIVITY 12 ——————————————

So jot down which of the three approaches seems to you the strongest, and which the weakest: and try to say why.

Then when you revise this block in the autumn, check this again — to see if your view has changed, and if it has, to see why. For by then you will have completed the course, and will have much more information at your disposal, and a greater familiarity with the theory tucked away in each of these three pictures. At least we hope you will!

TOMORROW'S CITIZENS

the Third Horseman

THE TWENTIETH CHRISTMAS HOLIDAY LECTURES
1ST TO 4TH JANUARY 1963

'and when he had opened the third seal
I heard the third beast say, Come and see
and I beheld, and lo, a black horse
and he that sat on him
had a pair of balances in his hand
and I heard a voice in the midst of the four beasts say
A measure of wheat for a penny
and three measures of barley for a penny
and see thou hurt not the oil and the wine'
Book of Revelation

COUNCIL FOR EDUCATION IN WORLD CITIZENSHIP
an organisation of the United Nations Association
25 Charles Street, London, W1

8   CONCLUSION

This is one of the excitements of social science. Its study takes you in and out of a particular social issue, problem or area, to explore the character and causes of the social phenomena there. Each time, if it is done well, it leaves you better equipped to explain a particular issue to yourself and to others. But it also fits that *specific* study into more *general* arguments about the character of society as a whole; so that eventually you come to develop a more rounded picture of the social totality within which we all live. The journey of intellectual discovery on which you are now embarked involves this perpetual movement between the specific and the general; and at each stage it invites you to make preliminary assessments of what is going on in the world, assessments that you will no doubt later want to amend as you study more.

So for the moment just keep these three pictures of the world with you, to think about in later blocks as well; and turn your mind back to the specific questions of hunger and famine.

————————————————— ACTIVITY 13 —————————————————

As a final brief exercise list again your explanatory variables — this time in their order of importance as you now see them. And add any additional factors that have occurred to you, but which I have missed.

================ GOOD STUDY GUIDE ================

In addition, please read Chapter 2 of *The Good Study Guide* in preparation for the note-taking exercise associated with Unit 3.

REFERENCES

Arnold, D. (1988) *Famine: social crisis and historical change*, Oxford, Basil Blackwell.

Bennett, J. (1987) *The Hunger Machine*, London, Polity.

Borton, J. and Clay, E. (1986) 'The African food crisis of 1982–86', *Disasters*, vol.10(4), pp.258–72.

Brandt, W. (1980) *North–South: a programme for survival*, London, Pan.

Buchanan, A. (1982) *Food, Poverty and Power*, Nottingham, Spokesman.

Bush, R. (1987) 'Explaining Africa's famine', *Social Studies Review*, vol.2, January, pp.2–6.

Bush, R. (1988) 'Hunger in Sudan: the case of Darfur', *African Affairs*, January, pp.5–23.

Crow, B. (1985) *Famine and Plenty*, Milton Keynes, Open University.

Dando, W.A. (1980) *The Geography of Famine*, London, Edward Arnold.

Devereux, S. and Hay, R. (1986) *Origins of Famine: a review of the literature*, Food Studies Group, University of Oxford.

Franke, R.W. and Chasin, B.H. (1980) *Seeds of Famine*, New York, Universe Books.

Friends of the Earth (1988) *The Heat Trap*, London.

George, S. (1976) *How the Other Half Dies*, Harmondsworth, Penguin.

George, S. (1984) *Ill fares the land*, London, Institute for Policy Studies.

George, S. and Paige, N. (1982) *Food for Beginners*, London, Writers and Readers.

Glaeser, B. (1987) *The Green Revolution Revisited*, London, Allen and Unwin.

Grigg, D. (1985) *The World Food Problem*, Oxford, Basil Blackwell.

Harrison, G.A. (ed.) (1988) *Famine*, Oxford, Oxford University Press.

Hayter, T. (1971) *Aid as imperialism*, Harmondsworth, Penguin.

Kula, E. (1988) 'The inadequacy of the entitlement approach to explain and remedy famines', *Journal of Peasant Studies*, vol.25 (1), October 1988, pp.112–115.

Lipton, M. (1977) *Why the Poor People Stay Poor*, London, Temple Smith.

Mariam, M.W. (1986) *Rural vulnerability to famine in Ethiopia, 1958–1977*, London, Intermediate Technology Publications.

O.D.I. (1987) *Briefing Paper*, London, Overseas Development Institute.

Pacey, A. and Payne, P. (eds) (1985) *Agricultural Development and Nutrition*, London, Hutchinson.

Raikes, P. (1988) *Modernising Hunger*, London, Catholic Institute for International Relations.

Regan, C. (1986) 'International aid in perspective', *Geographical Viewpoint*, vol.15 (1986–7), pp.5–17.

Rostow, W.W. (1960) *The Stages of Economic Growth*, Cambridge, Cambridge University Press.

Seavoy, R.E. (1986) *Famine in Peasant Societies*, New York, Greenwood Press.

Sinha, R. (1976) *Food and Poverty*, London, Croom Helm.

Tabatabai, H. (1985) *Food crisis and development policies in Sub-Saharan Africa*, ILO World Employment Programme Research, Geneva, Working papers.

World Resources Institute (1987) *World Resources 1987*, New York, Basic Books.

The author is grateful for guidance on this topic from Dr R. Bush, Lecturer in Food and Famine, Politics Department, University of Leeds.

Acknowledgements

Grateful acknowledgement is made to the following sources for permission to reproduce material in this unit:

Text

C. Regan (1986) 'International aid in perspective', *Geographic Viewpoint*, vol. 15, Association of Geography Teachers.

Figures

Figure 1: R. Bush (1987) 'Explaining Africa's famine', in *Social Studies Review*, vol. 2, January, California Council for Social Studies; *Figure 2: Women: A World Report* (1985) New International Book, Methuen & Co; *Figure 3*: Copyright holder, *The Chicago Daily News*, ceased publication in 1978, current copyright holder unknown; *Figure 4*: S. George and N. Paige (1982) *Food for Beginners*, Writers and Readers Publishing Co-op Society Ltd; *Figure 5*: S. Devereux and R. Hay (1986) *Origins of Famine: A Review of the Literature*,

UNIT 3   THE CONSUMPTION OF FOOD

Prepared for the Course Team by David Coates (Part I) and Bob Bocock
(Part II)

CONTENTS

So far in Block I we have looked at some of the forces affecting the production of food, and we have examined problems of access to it in certain parts of the Third World. It is now time to complete our preliminary journey into the social world of food, by returning home. Unit 3 is written in two halves linked by a common concern with the determinants of food *consumption* in the UK. In the first, we continue the concerns of Unit 2, by looking at the relationship of hunger to poverty in the contemporary UK. In the second, our emphasis shifts, as we turn to a more general examination of the forces that shape our consumption of food. The first half of the unit is primarily concerned with the impact of income on food consumption; the second with exploring ways in which factors other than income shape patterns of food consumption. Together the two halves of the unit attempt to demonstrate the different ways in which social science can illuminate as basic a social activity as eating; and the first half offers you one possible way of building and testing an argument in the social sciences. Part I of Unit 3 will ask the question, 'Who goes hungry, and why?' Part II will ask, 'What forces shape the food choices that we make?' The two halves together will extend still further our preliminary survey of key social institutions and processes which has been set in motion in Units 1 and 2 — institutions and processes whose precise character it will be the job of later blocks to explore in more detail.

PART I: HUNGER AT HOME

1   INTRODUCTION

There is one crucial sense in which the examination of hunger at home and hunger abroad raises qualitatively different issues. In the Third World, as we have seen, people go hungry because they are poor. But they go hungry too because their societies are poor. Poverty in that second sense is a complex affair. It derives in part from the underdeveloped nature of local agriculture, from the poor quality of local farming. But it derives too from the inability of Third World societies to earn sufficient foreign currency to buy in those food-stuffs that they cannot or do not produce themselves. For these societies are also poor in terms of their purchasing power on the world market. Indeed, hunger in the Third World is a consequence of the coming together of these many poverties: the paucity of local agriculture and the lack of foreign currency at the societal level; and within the society, the lack on the part of many of its members of the money or land they need to feed themselves.

Hunger in the First World is not of that kind. First World economies are not poor as Third World economies are poor. On the contrary, their agricultural systems are bountiful, and the capacity of their agrarian, manufacturing (and even service) sectors to earn foreign currency is well established. So if people go hungry in the UK, they do so amid a general plethora of food. They do so because of the way the society is organized *internally*, and in spite of the way in which the society as a whole compares to, and interacts with, the rest of the world community. As the Brandt Report put it:

> People are poor in two kinds of circumstances: in countries which have reached relatively high average levels of income, where the income is not well distributed; and in economies which have low levels of income where there is little to distribute. Poverty in the North is entirely of the first kind.
>
> (Brandt, 1980, p.50)

It is poverty of that first kind that we want to examine here.

The question is, 'How?' One way is to do what social scientists often do — namely, formulate a proposition/hypothesis and test it. The extract from the Brandt Report suggests such a proposition: that *lack of money explains the incidence of hunger in the contemporary United Kingdom*. It's not a particularly startling proposition. On the contrary, it's the kind of statement towards which most of us might naturally gravitate. But it is worth testing anyway, for in doing so we are likely to find that things are not quite as straightforward as we now think. Testing it will therefore add to our understanding of the society in which we find ourselves. And testing so apparently straightforward a proposition will leave us the space to reflect on the testing process itself. It will thus help us to clarify some of the methods that we will need later, as social scientists, when exploring more complex aspects of contemporary life.

So let's find out if poverty is the key to hunger in the contemporary United Kingdom. To do that, we shall need to gather two sets of information: one on the distribution of poverty, and one on the incidence of hunger. If we can get both, we shall then be in a position to examine the relationship between the two. So, first, let's see who are the poor in the contemporary United Kingdom.

2 POVERTY

We shall need here, as in Unit 2, some careful definitions of terms. 'Poverty', like 'famine', is a term which is much used but little defined. Unlike 'famine', however, it is quite difficult to define and very controversial too. Intriguingly, food figures centrally in that definitional controversy, for it is possible to define poverty as an *absolute* condition, the same the world over, by defining it against a specification of minimum food intake. People are poor if they are undernourished. On that definition, our proposition is splendidly circular: people are hungry because they are poor, and we know they are poor because they are hungry! But fortunately for us, many other ways of defining poverty exist: ones which stress that poverty is something that is *relative* to the society in which it occurs. People are poor because they fall below a community-agreed definition of a poverty line; or people are poor because they experience a significantly diminished set of life chances relative to those that are normal in the society around them.

Poverty? St Anne's, Nottingham, in the 1950s

—————————————— ACTIVITY 1 ——————————————

So try your own definition of poverty here, and then check it against the following definitions and observations on poverty:

Your definition of poverty:

1 Poverty occurs when 'total earnings are insufficient to obtain the minimum necessities for the maintenance of merely physical efficiency' (Rowntree, 1901).

2 'An adaption of the Rowntree method is in use by the US government. The Social Security Administration Poverty Index is based on estimates prepared by the Department of Agriculture of the costs of food needed by families of different composition. A basic standard of nutritional adequacy has been put forward by the National Research Council, and this standard has been translated into quantities of types of food "compatible with the preference of United States families, as revealed in food consumption studies". This in turn is then translated into the minimum costs of purchases on the market. Finally, by reference to the average sums spent per capita on food as a proportion of all income (derived from consumer expenditure surveys) it is assumed that food costs represent 33 per cent of the total income needed by families of three or more persons and 29 per cent of the total income needed by households consisting of two persons' (Townsend, 1979, pp.34–5).

3 A poverty line can be defined 'to represent the level at which a person can not only meet nutritional requirements etc., but also achieve adequate participation in communal affairs ... and be free from public shame from failure to satisfy conventions' (Sen, 1981).

4 'Poverty is the lack of resources necessary to permit participation in the activities, customs and diets commonly approved by society.' It is 'the absence or inadequacy of those diets, amenities, standards, services and activities which are common or customary in society.' 'It may be hypothesized that, as resources for any individual or family are diminished, there is a point at which there occurs a sudden withdrawal from participation in the customs and activities sanctioned by the culture. The point at which withdrawal "escalates" disproportionately to falling resources could be defined as the poverty line' (Townsend, 1979, pp.88, 915 and 57).

The first two definitions cited here tend, do they not, towards the 'absolute', and away from the 'relative', notion of poverty? They emphasize physiological needs basic to human activity, regardless of culture and time; though the second is prepared to allow for specifically US standards when it talks of 'types of food compatible with the preference of United States families'. Sen's definition goes further in that direction, recognizing that poverty is an inability to participate fully in the society of the day, or to avoid exposure to ridicule for that inability. This is Townsend's view too. He in particular has stressed the difficulties of adopting too absolutist an approach, seeing in such definitions inevitably arbitrary and partial specifications of what experts think ought to be the requirements of other people's styles of life. He has argued that since 'people's needs, even for food, are conditioned by the society in which they live and to which they belong, and [since] needs differ in different societies [and] in different periods of the evolution of single societies, any conception of poverty as absolute is ... inappropriate and misleading' (Townsend, 1979, p.38). Since 'the necessities of life are not fixed, they are continuously being adapted and augmented as changes take place in the society and its products' (*ibid.*, p.915); it is better, he feels, to make a virtue of that process of social construction, by defining poverty as that condition which prevents full involvement in a socially defined and culturally specific minimum standard of life.

─────────────────── ACTIVITY 2 ───────────────────

How do those definitions compare with yours? What are the strengths and weaknesses of each? Try listing points for and against each definition in turn.

Here are some suggestions for the kinds of points you might make for and against each definition.

For

Definition 1: It is based on hard scientific data, and allows comparisons between cultures and over time.

Definition 2: It is more sensitive than 1 to variations within societies.

Definition 3: It keeps the nutritional issue to the forefront, and is sensitive to the wider social aspects of poverty.

Definition 4: It is highly sensitive to the social definition of poverty.

Against

Definition 1: It focuses on a very narrow set of concerns, and makes *value-judgements* about what is adequate.

Definition 2: It is full of arbitrary assumptions about food patterns, and will quickly be out of date as tastes change.

Definition 3: Its internal components are in tension with each other; and are not easy to reduce to a set of statistical tables.

Definition 4: It is very hard to use for making comparisons over time and cultures, and is an extremely complicated measure of poverty.

───

There are in fact very serious difficulties with all definitions of poverty. The more easily quantifiable they are, the less they capture. The more sophisticated they are, the more difficult it becomes to quantify without controversy, or to compare over time and place. There is a tension between 'rigour' and 'relevance' here — one which we shall meet in many other areas of social science too. Nor is it easy to avoid serious gender biases in the quantification of poverty. As we shall see later in Part I, this is a major problem when we seek to explore the relationship between poverty and hunger. By concentrating on money income, the measures of poverty do not easily or adequately encompass non-paid work in the home (e.g. cooking, cleaning, and looking after children). Nor do they reflect the distribution of resources between men and women inside the home itself. Nor can these measures — sweeping as they are — always capture the complexity of choice and constraint in social living. For there are diversities of life styles within societies that will not collapse easily into uniform statistical tables. What is a necessity to one house may be either a luxury or an intrusion to another. A roast joint at the weekend may be defined as essential in some homes, be of no interest in others, and — of course — be

Poverty? Bradford in the late 1970s

positively unwelcome in vegetarian households. There are still families that resist the presence of a television set in the home, not out of penury but out of principle — and so on.

All this helps to remind us of two things: that we will need to return later to consider in more detail questions of gender and of individuality; and that, even before we do, we will need to approach statistics on social phenomena, and the generalizations to which they give rise, with considerable caution. But the need for caution is not a sign that social statistics lack value, only that they have less precision than the hardness of their numbers might at first suggest. What statistics can show are broad patterns, trends and tendencies. They tap part of that complex social reality which social scientists struggle to comprehend as a whole. And what the statistics on poverty certainly demonstrate is: (1) that constraints increase, and choices diminish, as income falls; and (2) that certain sectors of the population are particularly prone to receive low incomes. We may be left, after consideration of the statistics, with much to discuss about the boundaries of poverty and its precise impact on those subject to it. We are still left with complex judgements to make about comparisons of poverty between societies and over time. But what we are not left in any doubt about is who — within this society at this time — has the highest chance of experiencing poverty at first hand. For that is obvious, even if we rely, as we shall now, on the most limited of the four definitions, and follow the Rowntree tradition by taking Supplementary Benefit as our bench mark against which to locate the poor.

3   THE POOR

The calculation of the scale of poverty in the UK, and of trends in poverty over time, is currently a matter of considerable controversy. The controversy is a relatively new one — precipitated in the late 1980s by government criticisms of the hitherto conventional practice of taking Supplementary Benefit (or Income Support as it has been known since April 1988) as the approximate poverty line. In many of the studies of poverty available in the 1970s and 1980s — including the Department of Health and Social Security's own statistics on low incomes — those living on income between 100 and 140 per cent of Supplemen-

tary Benefit levels were said to be 'on the margins of poverty'. Pressure groups
like the Child Poverty Action Group (CPAG) still insist on the validity of that
measure of poverty; and they have used government statistics to give this
picture of poverty in the first half of the 1980s. Their figures cover only Great
Britain; but even with Northern Ireland excluded, they come out as surprisingly large (see Table 1).

Table 1   Numbers of people living in or on the margins of poverty in Great Britain in 1979, 1983
and 1985

	1979		1983		1985	
	(000s)	%	(000s)	%	(000s)	%
Below SB (Supplementary Benefit level)	2,090	4	2,780	5	2,420	5
On or below SB	6,070	12	8,910	17	9,380	17
On, below and up to 140% of SB	11,570	22	16,380	31	15,420	29

Source: CPAG, 1986, 1989

According to the CPAG, 29 per cent of the population of Great Britain were
living in or on the margin of poverty in 1985, 7 per cent more than in 1979
(though 2 per cent less than in the decade's worst year, 1983). The groups most
vulnerable to poverty in the 1980s were those dependent on state pensions (the
largest single group of the contemporary poor), the unemployed, those in full-
time work but on low pay, the long-term sick and disabled, and those in single-
parent families. (In 1985, 640,000 one-parent families — 70 per cent of all one-
parent families — were living in or on the margins of poverty.) Figure 1 shows
the relative sizes of those five groups, and their 'rise and fall' as components of
the poor since 1979.

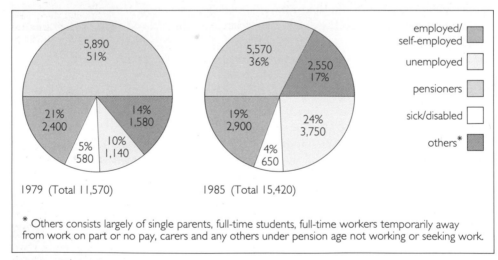

Figure 1   Numbers of people living in or on the margins of poverty in Great Britain in 1979 and
1985 by employment status (000s)
Source: CPAG, 1989

The Conservative Government of the late 1980s was no longer as content as the
CPAG to use 140 per cent of Supplementary Benefit level as its poverty line,
and Ministers criticized their own *Low Income Family Statistics* (Social Services Committee, 1987–88) for relying on this measure. They argued 'that if
Supplementary Benefit is used as a poverty line, each time Supplementary
Benefit is raised in real terms (i.e. above inflation) to improve the living
standards of the poorest, the number of people defined as poor is automatically
increased' (CPAG, 1989, p.5). Indeed, the DHSS calculated that 50 per cent of
the apparent increase in poverty in the 1980s was due to such rises in Supplementary Benefit and decided in future only to publish figures on 'households
below average income'.

For a flavour of the content and the intensity of that debate on statistics, look at the two statements in Figure 2: one a newspaper report of a speech by a senior Government minister; the other a letter in reply from Professor Townsend.

Moore says poverty levels 'exaggerated'

JOHN MOORE, Secretary of State for Social Security, yesterday accused the poverty lobby of manipulating facts to produce "arbitrary and exaggerated" estimates of the number of poor people. What was being defined as poverty, he told a conference of the Greater London Conservative Party, was only inequality. He said: "Not only are those with lower incomes not getting poorer, they are substantially better off than they have ever been before."

More and more people even in the bottom fifth of households had cars, colour televisions, and washing machines. "It is hard to believe that poverty stalks the land when even the poorest fifth of families spend nearly a tenth of their income on alcohol and tobacco," Mr Moore said.

The use by the poverty lobby of an income less than 140 per cent of benefit levels to define people as in poverty or on its margins was

By Nicholas Timmins
Social Services
Correspondent

"bizarre", Mr Moore said. It implied that one in three people in Britain was in dire need, a claim that was "false and dangerous".

On that definition, as benefit levels rose in real terms, more people would be counted in so that however rich a society became it would drag the incubus of relative poverty up with it. Using such definitions, he said, the poverty lobby would "find poverty in paradise". He dismissed attempts to assess absolute levels of what people need to live on as impracticable and arbitrary, and strongly attacked the idea of relative poverty — that those whose income is markedly below that of the community are poor. "Does it mean that in a rich community where most people have three cars, the

people with only one car are poverty-stricken?" Or that in a poor part of Africa where everyone was hungry there was no poverty?

It was the definition of poverty that had changed since Victorian times, when social reformers described the basic minimum supper as eight ounces of bread, two ounces of cheese and a pint of vegetable broth.

The Government's critics were "not concerned with the actual living standards of real people", but with pursuing the political and futile goal of equality. Claims about poverty in the UK were not motivated by compassion for the less well-off, but by attempts to discredit capitalism and the country's real economic achievements.

"Of course we will continue to give help to the individuals and families who really need it, but we cannot do this unless we can identify who they really are."

Measuring poverty in Britain

Dear Sir,
That John Moore devoted a whole speech to the issue of poverty, even if he came to a startling and quite erroneous conclusion, must be welcomed. The subject deserves a lot more prominence, investigation and discussion than the Government has been prepared to allow.

The speech is startling because it argues that there is no poverty in Britain. First, this contradicts mounting international concern about the phenomenon in rich countries. Thus, in the United States there is deep anxiety about the rise in officially measured poverty in the 1980s, especially among children.

Those younger than 18 living below the US poverty line increased 25 per cent between 1979 and 1987 (from 10.4 million to 13 million), with the sharpest rise being among children under six. The OECD has produced new material showing a more substantial extent of poverty in the UK than in West Germany, but with significant levels even in such countries as Sweden and Switzerland. The EC has recently confirmed

an increase to 44 million living in poverty within its borders in the 1980s. Ironically, I happen to be attending this week a new initiative by Unicef (United Nations International Children's Emergency Fund) to discuss "Child Poverty and Deprivation in Industrial Countries" — the first venture into the subject since its inception.

Second, the minister suggests that the estimates of poverty in the United Kingdom have been "manipulated deliberately". He does not give an accurate historical account of the development of the statistical series on low incomes by successive governments themselves. There always has been good sense in asking how many in our population live below the lowest standards of income set by governments, as well as how many benefit from its schemes or have incomes from other sources which are only approximately of the same value. The Government has now decided to shirk that responsibility to provide public information, and it is to be hoped that others will step into the

breach.

Third, he misrepresents the efforts of social scientists to establish a more scientific measure of poverty, whether in this country, Europe generally, or the third world. His attempt to suggest that these are politically motivated is rather contemptible and deserves to be ignored. What is important to call to national attention is the accumulation of evidence showing a "threshold" of multiple deprivation at levels about half as much again as current rates of Income Support.

Fourth, Mr Moore does not say what *he* means by "poverty". This, in a speech devoted to the thesis that it does not exist, is extraordinary. Should he not be challenged to define the phenomenon, so that his belief that it does not exist may be checked by others?

Yours etc
Professor PETER TOWNSEND
International Child
Development Centre
Unicef
Florence, Italy
12 May

Figure 2 The debate on the calculation of poverty

Source: *The Independent*, 12 May 1989, p.2; 13 May 1989, p.19

This controversy on statistics will no doubt continue: but its existence cannot obscure the persistence of poverty in the contemporary UK, or its uneven distribution between different social groups. Even if the DHSS is correct about the impact of rising Supplementary Benefit levels on the total numbers living close to 'the margins of poverty', it is clear that the other 50 per cent of the increase in poverty in the first half of the 1980s was not a statistical freak. It is also clear that state pensioners are still disproportionately vulnerable to poverty, that so too are the low paid and the long-term unemployed, and that they are joined in poverty by many families headed by a single parent or containing sick or disabled people.

It is worth noting too that there are definite *regional* variations in certain kinds of poverty. This regional variation is visible in the unemployment figures, but it is at its starkest in the data on dependency on social security benefits. Table 2 contains figures on both.

Table 2

	% of population registered unemployed in January 1987	% of gross household income from social security benefits 1983–4
North	16.9	20.0
North West	14.3	17.0
Yorkshire and Humberside	13.8	16.7
West Midlands	13.8	15.0
East Midlands	11.4	13.5
South West	10.4	13.2
East Anglia	9.3	15.1
South East	8.5	9.7
Northern Ireland	19.3	23.6
Scotland	15.1	17.1
Wales	14.3	19.5

Source: Winyard, 1987, pp.41 and 47

——————————— ACTIVITY 3 ———————————

It is worth pausing for a moment to look at this table in more detail, because we shall meet many similar tables in the months ahead, tables from which we shall need to extract significant information. In this table, as in others to follow, the figures are jumbled up. It is hard to see any significant patterns just by looking. If we are to see how regions relate to each other in some rank order, we will have to *impose* that order for ourselves. So do a brief exercise on this table. List the regions in order, from those with the highest unemployment to those with the lowest, and then those with the highest dependence on social security to those with the lowest. What pattern do you get? Is there a consistency in the two lists?

It does seem to be the case, doesn't it, that the heaviest unemployment and social security dependence occur in Northern Ireland, the North, Scotland and Wales, and the lowest in the South East? Things vary a little in the middle of the rankings, but the general pattern seems to be consistent.

Regional variations in the distribution of poverty are not the only variation that the detailed figures suggest. Poverty in the contemporary UK is also unevenly distributed along *ethnic* lines. *Ethnic minorities* bear a burden of poverty disproportionate to their numbers in the population as a whole. There is evidence that unemployment among ethnic minorities is far higher than among the population as a whole (see Reader, Chapter 1), and that pay levels are generally lower. Between 1984 and 1986 the unemployment rate among the

1.5 million people of working age in the UK who belonged to ethnic minority groups averaged 19 per cent; that for the population as a whole averaged only 11 per cent. In those years 'the highest unemployment rates were among the Pakistani/Bangladeshi communities, and among 16–24 year olds in each of the main ethnic minority groups: among these groups unemployment rates were frequently at least one in four, and in some cases were frequently one in three or higher' (*Employment Gazette*, December 1986, p.640). When the Runnymede Trust reported on Britain's black population in 1980, it found that 'both manual and non-manual black male workers [were] likely to earn less than white workers [because] black workers tend to be concentrated in lower status jobs and those with less responsibility' (Runnymede Trust, 1980, p.63). The Runnymede Trust found a more complex earning pattern for black women workers, who experienced, on average, lower pay rates than white women workers in the UK, but had a greater propensity to work full-time so that their earnings still tended to be higher. This extract from the CPAG report of 1987 indicates that these patterns of earnings persisted into the 1980s:

> There are no recent figures available on the pay that black people actually take home. But in 1982 there were considerable discrepancies between the median weekly earnings of white male workers and those of Afro-Caribbeans and Asians — £129.00 compared with £109.20 and £110.70 — and for Bangladeshi men the figure fell to £88.00. Bangladeshi women's average weekly take-home pay was a mere £43.80, almost half that of Afro-Caribbean women. The latter, at £81.20, actually did better than white women (£77.50). But these 'higher earnings' were achieved at a cost: Afro-Caribbean women were more likely to be doing shift work, especially at night, and they tended to have a longer working day than white women.
>
> (cited in Arnott, 1987, p.64)

Poverty in the contemporary United Kingdom is also unevenly distributed by *gender*. Women have a greater vulnerability to poverty than do men, though this is a fact which is often overlooked. Indeed, the very 'way we talk about poverty — using gender-neutral terms: the elderly, the low paid, the unemployed ... — blurs the fact that most of the poor are women' (Women's Health and Reproductive Rights Information Centre, 1988, p.2). It also blurs the fact that this has long been so: 'The simple fact is that throughout the last century women have always been much poorer than men. At the start of this century 61 per cent of adults on all forms of poor relief were women ... Today 60 per cent of adults for whom supplementary benefit is paid are women' (Lewis and Piachaud, 1987, p.28). Take a look at Table 3, on the causes of poverty among women in 1899 and 1983.

Table 3   Comparison of causes of poverty, 1899 and 1983

	Among women	
	1899	1983
Old age, sickness, disability	22%	58%
One-parent family	18%	10%
Unemployment	6%[a]	19%
Large family	14%[b]	6%[c]
Low wages	40%	6%
All causes	100%	100%

[a] Chief wage earner out of work and irregularity of work.
[b] Five children or more.
[c] Three children or more.
Source: Lewis and Piachaud, 1987, p.48

The gender face of poverty

Two sets of things stand out from the figures in Table 3 and in the previous paragraph. The first is that the causes of poverty among women have changed, as Lewis and Piachaud observe:

> Most notably there has been a growth in the extent to which poverty is associated with old age, sickness and disability. There has also been a growth in poverty associated with unemployment. On the other hand, the proportion of women's poverty associated with low wages (predominantly of husbands) has declined. Predictably, larger families are a smaller component, even using a lower definition of 'large' in 1983 than in 1899; but more surprisingly, women in one-parent families now represent a lower proportion of poor women than in 1899, primarily because of the decline in widowed women below pension age.
>
> (Lewis and Piachaud, 1987, p.49)

The second thing that stands out is that the disproportionate vulnerability of women to poverty has not changed. Women may be vulnerable to poverty now for slightly different reasons, but vulnerable to poverty they remain. Lewis and Piachaud again:

> The evidence we have examined shows clearly that the idea that poverty has only recently become 'feminised' is wrong. Women constitute a roughly similar proportion of the poor today as in 1900 and this reflects the position of women in society more generally. Paid employment is for the vast majority the main way of avoiding poverty; the nature of women's work, both paid and unpaid, and the

undervaluing of both, lead in our social and economic system to women's relatively greater income insecurity throughout the life-cycle. While there are of course exceptions, it remains true that the great majority of women are trapped in a vicious circle of domestic responsibilities and low-paid, low-status employment.

(*ibid.*, pp.49–50)

In the contemporary UK, 6 million of the 9 million elderly people are women. 90 per cent of one-parent families are headed by women, and women make up a majority of the disabled. Moreover, in paid employment women on average earn less than men: 'In 1989, for example, the average earnings for full-time non-manual female workers was 61 per cent of men's earnings' (*The Independent*, 16 October 1989, p.9), even though there has been an Equal Pay Act on the statute book since 1970. Women are more likely than men to work part-time, and unemployment amongst women workers has been rising more rapidly than it has for men during the 1980s (as indeed it did for all but two years in the 1970s). Women constitute a majority of the low paid: 'Two-thirds of the 8 million people whose wages are below the poverty line are women, with British Asian women being the hardest hit' (London Food Commission, 1988, p.33). More women than men work at home unpaid, dependent for income either on their male partners or on state benefits. And 'less directly, women bear the burden of managing poverty on a day-to-day basis. Whether they live alone or with a partner, on benefits or low earnings, it is usually women who are responsible for making ends meet and for managing the debts which result when they don't' (Glendinning, 1987, p.60).

Finally, there is the question of *age*. We have already noted the disproportionate vulnerability of the elderly to poverty. But what about children? The CPAG suggests that in 1985 there were 3.5 million children in the UK living in or on the margin of poverty — and that these 3.5 million children constituted 29 per cent of all children in the UK. Children in one-parent families were particularly vulnerable to poverty. In 1985, 65 per cent of all children in such families were living on or below Supplementary Benefit level as against 12 per cent of all children in two-parent families; and there were some 360,000 children living in families whose collective income was actually lower than Supplementary Benefit in that year. The CPAG figures on children in poverty are reproduced in Table 4.

Table 4   Numbers and proportion of children living in or on the margins of poverty in 1985 broken down by family status (figures are rounded)

	Children in: two-parent families	Children in: one-parent families
Below SB level	310,000 (3%)	50,000 (3%)
On SB level and below	1,290,000 (12%)	960,000 (65%)
140% SB level and below	2,460,000 (23%)	1,090,000 (74%)

Source: CPAG, 1989, p.8

So overall it does look as though vulnerability to poverty in this society is not randomly distributed through the population as a whole. Poverty is concentrated among certain groups — groups which include the low paid, the unemployed, those in one-parent families, and in certain ethnic communities. Poverty seems to fall more heavily on women than on men, on the very young and very old rather than on the middle aged, on the sick more than the healthy, and on certain sections of Northern Irish society more than on the people of Surrey.

SUMMARY

- Poverty can be defined in different ways: against an absolute standard of minimum social needs; or with a greater sensitivity to variations of living standards between societies and over time; or by locating that point at which lack of resources qualitatively reduces capacity to participate in the full range of normal social activities.

- Even on a modest definition of poverty based on state-defined minimum income requirements, anywhere between 17 per cent and 29 per cent of the population of the UK live in or on the margin of poverty.

- The members of contemporary UK society most vulnerable to poverty include the elderly, children, the unemployed, the low paid, single-parent families and the long-term sick and disabled. Women have a higher vulnerability to poverty than do men. Poverty is also unevenly distributed between regions and between ethnic groups.

4   THE HUNGRY

What we have to decide now is whether vulnerability to hunger is also unevenly distributed on similar lines. We have some statistics on 'who goes hungry', though not an enormous amount; and as with the statistical data in earlier units, we have to proceed with as much definitional care as we can.

By hunger in the UK we do not mean famine. There have been no large-scale deaths through starvation in the UK in this century, as far as I know. But there might be *malnutrition*, and there might be *undernourishment*.

Undernourishment, as I hope you recall (from Unit 2, Section 2.1), is best understood as the consequence of inadequacies in the quantity of food in a diet. *Malnutrition* refers to inadequacies in the quality of diet: in its composition of essential proteins, minerals, vitamins and water. We do have a lot of information on the nutritional value of particular foods. We know, for example, that food scientists currently award white bread less nutritional value than brown bread, and that a diet full of sugar and fats is less healthy than one full of fresh fruit and vegetables. We know too that overall the quality of diet in the UK has improved over time. Rationing during the Second World War was critical here: 'Pre-war studies had called attention to widespread malnutrition. Wartime studies showed a marked improvement' (Townsend, 1979, p.167). What the war also did was to reduce variations in diet between social groups, so that, by 1945, 'the diet of nearly all population groups was on average very close to or above recommended nutrient requirements' (*ibid.*, p.167).

Since then there seems to have been little further reduction in inequalities of diet between social groups. But we have to proceed with some caution here, since our data on food distribution between different sections of the population are very limited, and very unsophisticated and indiscriminating in their organizing categories. Moreover, no two people are exactly alike; so where natural scientists can generalize on the basis of their data with relative ease, social scientists have to generalize with far greater caution. But what data we do have indicate that there is a relationship between *income and diet*. It does look as though those on lower incomes spend a higher percentage of their income on food than do those on higher incomes, and that the nutritional value of typical diets goes down as income goes down. The poorer you are, the more proportionately you are obliged to spend on food, but the less well you eat.

Poor food, tired times?

There are two sets of statistics for you to look at on this. The first shows the percentage of income being spent on food in households with different levels of income (see Figure 3).

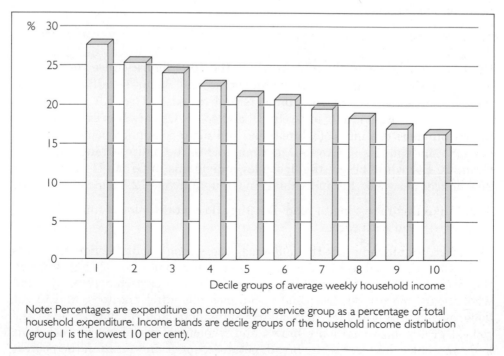

Note: Percentages are expenditure on commodity or service group as a percentage of total household expenditure. Income bands are decile groups of the household income distribution (group 1 is the lowest 10 per cent).

Figure 3   Variation of expenditure pattern on food by decile group of household income (1986)
Source: Department of Employment, *Family Expenditure Survey, 1986*, p.7, HMSO

I hope it is clear from Figure 3 that, as income falls, the percentage of that falling income spent on food rises. According to the data summarized in Figure 3, those in the bottom 10 per cent of income earners (group 1 on the horizontal axis of Figure 3) spend nearly 28 per cent of their meagre income on food. Those in the top 10 per cent (group 10 on the horizontal axis of Figure 3) spend less than 20 per cent of their much larger earnings in this way.

The second set of statistics is taken from Margaret Whitehead's article 'The health divide', published in 1988 (see Table 5). It shows food consumption by income group in Great Britain in two years — 1976 and 1984. In the table, 'Groups A to D represented households with at least one earner. Group A contains the richest 10 per cent, group D the poorest 10 per cent, and groups B and C are intermediate, each representing 40 per cent of households with one earner' (Whitehead, 1988, p.293).

Table 5   Food consumption by income group (Great Britain, 1976 and 1984) (oz./person/week)

Income group	White bread		Brown bread incl. wholemeal		Sugar		Total fats		Fruit (fresh)		Vegetables (fresh)		Potatoes	
	1976	1984	1976	1984	1976	1984	1976	1984	1976	1984	1976	1984	1976	1984
A	19.8	12.3	4.1	8.0	12.3	8.0	9.8	9.1	22.5	25.3	27.3	30.7	29.8	33.0
B	26.2	18.3	3.0	6.0	13.4	9.4	10.5	9.5	18.3	19.0	24.0	24.4	35.0	36.5
C	30.4	23.0	3.0	5.9	14.5	10.9	11.0	10.4	15.2	16.0	24.8	25.5	38.2	42.4
D	29.9	26.0	2.7	5.2	15.7	11.5	11.0	10.0	15.2	13.0	24.9	21.5	42.3	48.3

Source: Whitehead, 1988, p.293

———————————— ACTIVITY.4 ————————————

Table 5 shows a general move away from white bread and sugar across all income bands; but it shows too a differentiation of diet between income bands. Can you see that in the table? What sort of comparison between figures in the table sustains the claim that: (1) there is a general move away from white bread and sugar across all income bands; but (2) a differentiation of diet between income bands.

Claim (1) is evident in the way in which the 1984 figures were consistently lower than the 1976 figures under 'White bread' and 'Sugar' — falling from 19.8 to 12.3 ounces per week of white bread for individuals in Group A, from 26.2 to 18.3 ounces for individuals in Group B, and so on. Claim (2) is evident in the higher numbers of ounces of white bread and sugar consumed per week by, for example, individuals in Group D as compared to the figure for individuals in Group A. For white bread, the figure for individuals in Group D in 1984 was 26.0 ounces per week. For individuals in Group A it was 12.3 ounces per week.

Tables like this take time to read. But they do contain a lot of information, if read slowly and with care.

Margaret Whitehead made the following observation about the figures in this table. She reminded her readers that recent nutritional advice 'has stressed the need to eat more fibre (for instance in bread, particularly brown and wholemeal), more fresh fruit and vegetables including potatoes, and to cut down on sugar, salt and fat, particularly animal fat'; and yet in both years 'the richest group consumed more brown and wholemeal bread, more fresh fruit and vegetables, and less white bread, potatoes, sugar and fat than the poorest group' (ibid., p.283). This observation was in line with the findings of an independent research body, the London Food Commission:

... compared with the highest income groups, households with low incomes eat considerably more processed meat products, eggs, margarine, lard, sugar and jam. These are mostly foods with relatively high fat or sugar contents and are comparatively nutrient dilute. They tend to provide concentrated cheap energy sources but with fewer other useful nutrients such as protein, vitamins and minerals. At the same time households with low incomes are eating more potatoes, canned vegetables (in particular baked beans) and white bread. These are relatively cheap filling foods. They are eating considerably less cheese, carcase meat, poultry, fish, butter, cooking oils, fresh and frozen vegetables, fresh fruit, and brown and wholemeal bread.

(London Food Commission, 1988, p.44)

The statistical data we have used so far indicates a relationship between incomes and the *quality* of food consumed, suggesting a linkage between poverty and malnutrition in the contemporary UK. The statistical data does not suggest levels of malnutrition on the scale evident in certain Third World countries, but it does suggest the existence of a poorer quality diet as less income is available. Poverty in income and poverty in diet do seem to go together. But what of *undernourishment*, the other feature of Third World hunger which we looked at last week? Again, the data is far from adequate. It is limited in its coverage, being in the main available only in the form of small-scale local studies. So it can only be indicative rather than definitive. But what it does indicate is that if there is any undernourishment in contemporary UK society it is among the poor. This is what Margaret Whitehead had to say on the subject:

> ... a study of 65 families living on supplementary benefit in 1980 found that some parents went without food to provide enough for their children ... In a study of 1,000 low-income people in the North of England in 1984, approximately a quarter of respondents reported that they did not have a main meal every day. One-third of these said that this was because of cost. Four out of ten unemployed people went without a main meal because of lack of money ... An in-depth study of 107 women living with pre-school children in Milton Keynes in 1984 found that 51 per cent of single parents and 30 per cent of low-income mothers in two-parent families were cutting down on food consumption for financial reasons.

(Whitehead, 1988, p.300)

The London Food Commission offers us more systematically gathered information, but for a more geographically restricted area. They found, as we would expect, that in London people on low incomes face serious problems. Food is a flexible item in household budgets and therefore tends to be cut back when money is short: 'As one separated mother explained "you can always make the food stretch, but you can't cut down the price of clothes" ... It is thus at meal times that the meaning of poverty is most acutely felt' (Graham, 1984, p.128). As a result, a number of groups in the population are at risk of undernourishment or malnutrition:

> *Children* — children from households with low incomes may be at risk of under-nutrition, failure-to-thrive, vitamin and mineral deficiencies and poor dental health, as well as poor nutrition generally ... ; *Young adults* — many 15–25 year olds have been found to have inadequate intakes of a number of vitamins and minerals ... ; *Women* — women often bear the brunt of poverty. They are likely to cut back on their own food to prevent their children and men from going without ... ; *Women*

who are pregnant or breastfeeding — there is evidence that the
nutritional needs of pregnant women cannot be met financially by
women on low incomes ... ; *Elderly people* — ... over one-quarter of the
people with the lowest incomes are pensioners. Elderly people are more
at risk of suffering from nutritional deficiencies than most other people.
The incidence of ... malnutrition amongst the elderly has been
estimated at about 7 per cent ... ; *people from Britain's black and ethnic
communities ... people with disabilities ... homeless people.*

(London Food Commission, 1988, pp.1–3)

The London Food Commission's findings are in line with other surveys of food
and poverty in the UK that are available to us. They all show that children
from low-income homes have less adequate diets than do children from more
affluent backgrounds; and many of them suggest that, if the children are
vulnerable to hunger, so too are their parents. Hunger in the UK seems to be
linked not just to the distribution of income *between* families, but also to non-
monetary factors which affect the distribution of food *within* families. Hilary
Graham reported on a series of surveys of diet and poverty published over the
period from 1937 to 1980. Apparently in each of them 'there are generational
differences in eating patterns. Parents in the survey noted how they went
without to leave enough food for their children' (Graham, 1984, p.128). Hilary

The baby's bottle?

Graham also found evidence of gender differences. In both two-parent and one-parent families, if anyone had to go short, it was the mother who went without food first. Hers was 'the burden of sacrifice … it's like the old saying, "in a poor family, the wife gets nowt" ' (*ibid.*, pp.130 and 131).

SUMMARY

- There is no famine in the UK as in parts of the Third World. Our concern here is with other aspects of hunger — with malnutrition and with undernourishment.

- The quality of the UK diet has improved since 1939, but the earlier relationship between income and diet remains. People on low incomes spend a higher proportion of their income on food than do people on high incomes. The nutritional value of diets seems to decline as incomes decline.

- There is less evidence of undernourishment, but any that exists is concentrated amongst poor families, and particularly among women and children within those families. There is some evidence of higher than average vulnerability to malnutrition/undernourishment among the elderly, ethnic minorities, people with disabilities, and the homeless.

——————— ACTIVITY 5 ———————

How far do you think the evidence we have now accumulated confirms or refutes the hypothesis that we are testing (*that lack of money explains the incidence of hunger in the contemporary UK*)? Is it fully confirmed, partially confirmed, not confirmed at all? Is there other evidence that I could have used, and didn't? Or can we interpret our evidence in ways that don't lay such emphasis on the relationship of income to hunger?

---

5   CONCLUSION

During your Open University studies you will often find that you are asked to evaluate the adequacy of hypotheses/propositions of this kind. When you are, you might find it valuable to look back at the *structure* of this unit as a possible model for the shape of your answer. What I have tried to do here so far is to:

1   *clarify the problem/hypothesis* — in Section 1;

2   *define my terms* very carefully *en route* to my answer — at the start of Section 2 on poverty, and Section 4 on hunger; and then

3   *marshal* what *evidence* I could for and against the hypothesis.

What I now have to do — and what you will often find yourself having to do in your essays later — is to put together a *conclusion* which returns to the original hypothesis, and tries to answer/evaluate it by reviewing the evidence we have gathered.

So let me consider the evidence we have just worked through, and come to a conclusion on the importance of lack of money as a cause of hunger in the contemporary UK. I have three reflections.

1 The first is that there is other evidence to be considered too, evidence which suggests that lack of money is not the sole cause of hunger. There is evidence of

a relationship between money and certain aspects of hunger of quite a different kind. Some forms of malnutrition, for example, are associated with rising incomes, and more prosperous life styles, rather than with poverty as such. The adverse effect upon diet of the excessive consumption of alcohol would be one example. The low nutritional value of much convenience food might be another. Moreover, there are examples of hunger — indeed of starvation — in the midst of plenty which have no monetary cause at all. Contemporary outbreaks of food poisoning from bacteria such as salmonella, listeria and botulinus — which must be among the most acute forms of malnutrition imaginable — seem these days to be linked to the way food is produced, distributed and cooked, rather than to any question of income as such. And anorexia is one — very important — cause of acute starvation, particularly among young women, a cause which is no doubt just as social in origin as is poverty, but which is quite different in kind from any lack of money. So in deciding if the original proposition is correct or not, I will have to judge what percentage of hunger in the contemporary UK derives from sources other than poverty. I will not be able to assume that all hunger has the same source.

2 Moreover, even when poverty and hunger are associated, the association may mislead, by giving causal weight to poverty without concentrating on the social processes which place people among the poor. To concentrate on poverty may not be to probe deeply enough. Racial discrimination, for example, is a powerful social process which increases the vulnerability of members of certain ethnic groups to hunger, by locking them into low-paid jobs or by excluding them from employment altogether. It is their poverty that exposes them to hunger, but discrimination that exposes them to poverty. As with ethnicity, so too with gender. Indeed, the relationship of gender to hunger is more complicated still. Women are disproportionately vulnerable to poverty in part because of the way this society chooses to reward the labour of men and women. Women do not have equal pay or equal career opportunities in the paid work they do; and much of the work they do, in rearing children and tending adult members of their family, isn't paid at all. So because of the way that this society is organized, women are disproportionately dependent on the wages of others, and on state benefits if no wage is forthcoming. There is therefore a very real monetary dimension to women's experience of poverty. In general, their monetary entitlements are less than men's. But there is more. *Within* the households of the contemporary UK there is also a division of labour between men and women; and within that division of labour women are expected to require fewer resources for themselves, regardless of the total amount of money available to the household as a unit. Their entitlements to food are less in non-monetary terms as well as in monetary ones. And because this is so, the allocation of hunger through poverty will need to be argued with a developed sensitivity to the way poverty is affected by ethnicity and gender.

3 I will want to find space too, in my assessment of the importance of money, for cultural and individual variations in attitudes to food. There are regional subcultures in the UK which affect both the availability of, and demand for, food. Such subcultures may have been stronger in the past, when interconnections between regions were less developed and when food production and distribution were handled by smaller firms; but residues of regional subcultures remain to affect food patterns in different parts of the UK. So we will need to keep a regional dimension to our argument; and we will also want to leave space for individual choice and variation. For as we examine the different ways in which social processes such as poverty shape individual lives, we also have to recognize that individuals respond to common social circumstances in different ways: differential responses that reflect variations in such things as character, motivation, energy, determination and perception. As a result, any complete analysis of the social determinants of food consumption has to include

a specification and explanation of these individual variations. We need to remember that a full social analysis has two facets, not one. It has to concentrate on broad patterns *and* on individual details. So both in our analysis of the causes of hunger, and in our later work on other aspects of social life in the contemporary UK, we will need to maintain a space for the personal, and an opportunity to examine the extent to which such personal characteristics are themselves social products.

By this point, we are beginning to meet material which needs careful and full treatment in its own right — treatment that will come in later blocks of D103. The social construction of self, and the role of regional and national cultures in shaping our individual sense of identity and meaning, will be examined in Blocks V and VI. Questions of gender and ethnicity will surface again, for consideration in a systematic way, in Block II; and the economic processes generating unequal distributions of income will be one topic for consideration in Block III.

Let me end Part I of this unit by indicating the conclusion to which I am driven by the evidence on hunger as I understand it. As far as I can tell, poverty is the single most important cause of hunger in the contemporary UK. But it is a poverty whose impact is *filtered* through powerful patterns of gender inequality and racial discrimination, and it is a poverty whose impact is *mediated* by the different ways in which individuals learn to cope with the lack of money that is socially imposed upon them. Poverty *is* the key to hunger in the UK, as in the Third World: but here, as there, poverty is itself the product of other economic, social, political, cultural and geographical processes. Income is important in determining access to food; but it is not the only factor; and because it is not, we still require a more systematic consideration of some of the non-monetary factors shaping patterns of food consumption in the contemporary UK. That is what awaits us in Part II of this unit.

PART II: THE SHAPING OF CONSUMPTION

1   INTRODUCTION

The consumption of food is of course an issue that touches all of us, whether we are poor or not. What we eat, where we buy it, what we come to think of as good food or bad, how we differ in our eating patterns from other people — all these things are integral to any complete understanding of food consumption in the contemporary UK. Every day each of us makes individual choices about what to eat, where and how; and yet as we do so our choices are influenced by all kinds of social forces. The decisions we make about what to eat are shaped (as we have just seen) by the amount of money available to us, and by such things as our age, gender and ethnicity. But they are shaped too by factors which are not so obviously tied to questions of money and status. Our choice of food is shaped by the structure of retailing which we face; by the advertising to which we are subject; and by variations of culture and personality. It is with the impact of these factors on patterns of food consumption that Part II of this unit will be concerned.

———————————— ACTIVITY 6 ————————————

Before you read on, list the main factors which you think determine what you eat. Try to list at least four, and to rank them in importance. We shall return to your list at the end of Part II, to see if anything you have read has persuaded you to change your mind.

We have seen in the first half of this unit that income plays an important role in affecting who can afford to eat an adequate diet, and that gender and ethnicity also affect patterns of food consumption in significant ways. You may well have mentioned the *price* of food as one of the important factors which affects your own household's pattern of food consumption. I know that for much of the time it is the price of food which is the main thing I notice about the food I buy. I tend to shop in a local supermarket which has reasonable quality foods at a lower price than smaller food shops, such as the local butcher, greengrocer and delicatessen. However, there are times when I am both able and willing to pay a little more than usual for meat, for vegetables, or for fresh fruit, in order

Do you use a small local shop for small items? Or have you lost access to such small corner shops?

to make a meal for a special occasion, such as for a birthday, for festivities, or for a visitor. On these occasions it is not just price which affects my choice of food, but other factors: what is available in the shop when I go shopping; what I think will be enjoyable to eat; what might appear impressive to visitors; and what I think the other people coming for a meal will enjoy eating. And I am conscious that my choice of type of shop has an important impact on the food I buy. Let's look at the organization of retailing — and its impact on food choice — in more detail.

2 FOOD RETAILING: THE EPOCH OF THE SUPERMARKET

In the not too distant past most food was bought from small local shops, as anyone over forty can still presumably remember. But these days most of us buy most of our food in supermarkets; and whether we have easy access to them, or only to a local corner shop or to a travelling shop, now has an important effect on the degree of food choice that we have.

Supermarkets offer at least the appearance of abundance which smaller shops cannot do, and the foods available in them have indeed become more varied than in earlier periods. Increasingly, the large supermarkets are telling farmers and market gardeners what fruits and vegetables to grow; their size, colour and taste can be specified to order. Supermarkets increasingly place specific orders for meats and fish, fruit, vegetables and drinks. The large supermarkets can stipulate what kind of salmon, mussels, or white fish they desire and these are then produced. This reverses the previous picture of markets as places or processes in which producers brought their produce 'to market' and sold it to the highest bidder. The supermarket chain's food purchaser now says what she, or he, requires and the produce is grown to these specifications.

As was shown in Unit 1, the process of producing and selling foods and drinks from around the world has a long history, and these days those processes are coming to be influenced by the supermarkets themselves. The large supermarkets reach out not only to growers and producers of food in Britain, but to their suppliers throughout the world. You want tomatoes all the year? Right. You will have them from the Canaries, Israel, California, even Brazil. You want kiwi fruit, peaches, grapefruit or grapes all year? Fine. You can have them. You want tulips and daffodils in December, or in August? No problem.

The range of foods available in supermarkets has been expanding during the last two decades. This expansion of choice is in part the result of an increase in the variety of foods available since the UK joined the European Community in 1973. More varieties of foodstuffs became available from France, Italy, and later Spain, for instance. However, the sources of foods within Europe as a whole, and the UK in particular, have become increasingly global. The large supermarkets send their 'food technologists, quality controllers, and buyers to the furthest edges of the globe for something new to put on the shelves' (Clinch, 1988). Salmon from Alaska, almonds from Greek hillsides, pizzas from Canada, Pink Fir Apple potatoes from who knows where? Recipes from India, China, Mexico, Japan are adapted for British taste, and ready-prepared dishes manufactured to sell in supermarkets. For not only do foods now come from distant places, but an increasing number of foods are sold as ready-made meals. Marks and Spencer started doing their ready-made Chicken Kiev and Chicken Cordon Bleu in November 1981 — and the list of such ready-made meals has expanded greatly since then. In November 1981, Marks and Spencer were not sure if they should include garlic in their new Chicken Kiev, and tested it by asking a sample of people drawn from groups throughout the country, who had already been identified from earlier research as likely to buy such a ready-made dish. The results showed that the time had come — small amounts of garlic could be included in a ready-made dish for the British! (Clinch, 1988).

So supermarkets now have a powerful influence on *what* is available for us to buy. But they also have a powerful influence on *where* we shop and *when* we shop. When they first developed, supermarkets were located on local high streets. Some are still found there, which means people can reach them by using local bus services. The use of bus-passes, giving free travel, or much reduced fares, for older and disabled people, has helped these groups shop for food. The out-of-town location of other supermarkets necessitates the use of a car to reach them. By 1987, nearly two-thirds of British households had a car, as Table 6 shows, and by then groups without cars were effectively excluded from easy access to out-of-town shopping complexes. It is therefore more diffi-cult to shop in such complexes if you are old, unemployed, poor, ill, physically disabled, or bringing up young children and you are without private transport.

Table 6   Car ownership (1979–87)

57% of households had a car in 1979
64% of households had a car in 1987
20% of households had two or more cars in 1987

Source: Central Office of Information, 1989

A variety of patterns of shopping has emerged, influenced by changes in work-ing hours, the hours shops are open, new methods of transport, and the spread of home freezers. Working people have less time for shopping than retired people, so shopping patterns for these two groups tend to differ. Retired people may enjoy a trip to the shops for food every day as it gets them out of the house. Working people may find the late opening hours of many supermarkets very helpful. The development of supermarkets outside city centres has led to one-stop shopping trips once a week, or once a fortnight, which involve the whole family going in the car to do the shopping. Home freezers have made storage of some foods easier, so enabling some households to have a large shopping trip when needing to restock. The rise of supermarkets has led, conversely, to the closure of many local, small, corner shops which used to sell foods and drinks. Indeed, the rise of supermarkets, particularly those in the new shopping complexes, has effectively:

> ... restructured leisure-patterns — shopping centres, in particular, have become new sites of pleasure. ... Weekend shopping trips are now likely to fill a whole Saturday, rather than a half day, as was customary 10 or 15 years ago. According to recent surveys, the British now regard shopping as their favourite leisure activity, after holidays and television.
>
> (Gardner, 1988, p.40; see *The Good Study Guide* for a full version and discussion of this article by Gardner)

There are intriguing questions of individual freedom and corporate economic power at play in the world of the supermarket. Supermarkets have become major organizations selling over three-quarters of the foods the British popula-tion consumes. The specific items which consumers buy are chosen from an increasing range of products displayed on the shelves of the major supermar-kets. The individual shopper can therefore make some choices about which specific items to buy. These choices are constrained both by *availability* and by *price*. None the less, to walk into a large supermarket is to feel that one could be potentially among the really affluent even though one is not rich — just to see all the goods displayed is an invitation, a request, to keep at it, to keep earning, to be a part of it all. Yet behind the appearance of choice lie powerful elements of economic power (e.g. see Reader, ch. 1, Fig. 1.3). Supermarkets require a large investment to build, supply and run. If you look at Table 7, you can see that just seven supermarket chains dominated the market for food in the late 1980s.

Table 7   Supermarket pecking order (% of all purchases of food in the UK)

Tesco	14.0%
Sainsbury's	13.9%
Co-op	12.1%
Gateway	11.5%
Safeway (Argyll Group)	10.7%
Asda	7.6%
Marks & Spencer	5.0%
	74.8%

Source: Verdict Research Ltd (1988), cited in Clinch (1988)

By the late 1980s, these seven major chains sold 74.8 per cent of all purchases of food in the UK. There were other smaller supermarket groups, locally based in particular regions of the country, so if these are added to the above list we can say that between 75 per cent and 80 per cent of food was bought in supermarkets in the late 1980s. With that degree of dependence by all of us on so few outlets for our food, it is clear that our choice of food is heavily constrained by the decisions of supermarket managements. There is therefore some tension between the appearance of choice (as we take things off the supermarket shelves) and the fact that so few companies actually decide what will be on the shelves from which those choices are made.

But how constrained are we by corporate power as we shop? Let us begin to explore the forces that operate upon us as we browse among the supermarket shelves. We shall do this in the Activity which follows the Summary.

SUMMARY

- The development of the modern supermarket has transformed the ways in which most people in the UK obtain their foods.

- Modern supermarkets have increased the range of foods available by going global in their pursuit of food supplies. The seasons are overcome by searching out supplies from all over the world.

- In the late 1980s, three-quarters of food purchases were made in shops owned by the seven largest supermarket chains in Britain. This has led to many smaller shops closing down, resulting in problems for some categories of customer: the old; the unemployed; the poor; young mothers; people without a car; the homeless; the physically disabled; and the ill. It has also left all of us heavily dependent on just a few companies for much of the food we consume.

ACTIVITY 7

At this stage, I want to suggest that *going shopping* need not be seen as an interruption to the process of studying, but rather that it can be seen as an *opportunity to observe* yourself and other people doing the monthly, weekly, or daily shopping for basic household provisions. This will not involve anything difficult, such as having to gather detailed statistics about people's shopping habits, or having to interview someone you have never met before about their shopping habits and patterns. It is simply a matter of taking note of the following:

1   Note how frequently you shop for food. You may, for example, shop for something to eat every day, or nearly every day — perhaps something which you have forgotten when you did the 'big shop' for the week, or the month, at a

large supermarket. On the other hand, you may just do errands for someone else whose main responsibility is to buy the major food items in your household.

2   Notice where you do this shopping. It may be at a nearby local shop, such as the local newsagents where it is also possible to buy some sweets, chocolate, or soft drinks; or at a local grocery shop which keeps some supplies of basic food, such as bread, milk, or fruit and vegetables. It may be that you bought some food and/or milk from the milk float; or that you use the local supermarket, travelling by bus or car. Ask yourself what proportion of the food you buy comes from shops other than supermarkets.

3   If you are able to do so next time you are in a supermarket, stand and watch the kinds of foods other people are buying. Try and spot five or six items that are commonly bought, and that you buy too. Pick ones whose price doesn't vary with the seasons (so ignore things like vegetables), and just note down what the five or six items are, and what you paid for each. You can repeat that exercise when reading Unit 12, which discusses inflation, and again when revising in the autumn. That should give you some raw data on which to base your own calculations of the rate of inflation. By the end of the course you should be in a position to complete an exercise you can begin now.

Item	Price now	Price in week 12	Price in autumn
1			
2			
3			
4			
5			
6			
Total cost	A:	B:	C:

(When you revise, just take A from C, to see how the cost has changed: and then divide your answer by A, and multiply by 100, to get yourself a rate of inflation on those six items. Then check it against government figures on inflation in the autumn!)

4   Do you see going shopping as a domestic chore or as a pleasure? You will recall the quotation from Gardner above which argued that surveys have found that 'the British now regard shopping as their favourite leisure activity'. This claim includes shopping for things other than food, but it includes food shopping in the supermarkets in the new shopping centres. How often is shopping a source of pleasure for you? How often is it a domestic chore?

You might like to compare your answers to these four questions with those of other students at your local study centre.

3   THE 'HIDDEN PERSUADERS'

Many people see themselves as individual shoppers when they are doing their food buying in one of the supermarkets. They may be with their husbands, wives, children, or partners when shopping, but basically they see themselves as being able to choose freely what they want to buy, as long as it is on the shelves of the shop. In other words, much of the time people are shopping for food, or other items for that matter, they think of themselves as free agents, able to exercise individual choices about what to buy.

This picture becomes more complicated, and is even contradicted in some respects, when we take into account all the advertising of food and drink in newspapers and magazines, and on television and radio. Much of this advertising is based upon market research into who is likely to respond and buy a particular food or food product. The main aim of market research is to work out not only who in the population can afford to buy specific goods, but which *types* of people may be motivated to buy specific brands of food or drink.

The work carried out by market researchers can be used by those who devise advertisements to try to increase the sales of a particular product, whether this be a car, items of clothing, shoes, furniture, drinks, or food. These professional persuaders aim to develop as effective an advertising campaign for a specific brand of product as they can. As the American author who first used the term 'the hidden persuaders', Vance Packard, wrote:

> What the probers are looking for, of course, are the *whys* of our behaviour, so that they can more effectively manipulate our habits and choices in their favour. This has led them to probe why we are afraid of banks; why we love those big fast cars; why we really buy homes; why men smoke cigars; why the kind of car we drive reveals the brand of gasoline we will buy; ... why men are drawn into auto showrooms by convertibles but end up buying sedans; why junior loves cereal that pops, snaps, and crackles ...

> ...The professional persuaders ... see us as bundles of daydreams, misty hidden yearning guilt complexes, irrational emotional blockages. We are image lovers given to impulsive and compulsive acts. We annoy them with our seemingly senseless quirks, but we please them with our growing docility in responding to their manipulation of symbols that stir us to action. They have found the supporting evidence for this view persuasive enough to encourage them to turn to depth channels on a large scale in their efforts to influence our behavior.

> The symbol manipulators and their research advisers have developed their depth views of us by sitting at the feet of psychiatrists and social scientists (particularly psychologists and sociologists) who have been hiring themselves out as 'practical' consultants or setting up their own research firms.

> (Packard, 1981, pp.4–7)

I shall explore the theme of hidden persuasion raised in this extract later on in this section. But first, try this activity.

─────────────────────── ACTIVITY 8 ───────────────────────

Social scientists sometimes observe and analyse the contents of the various forms of mass media — television, newspapers, magazines, radio, and film, for example. All of these media include some form of advertisements — even the BBC advertises its own programmes to attract audiences, as well as its own publications, videos, and audio cassettes.

In this activity you are asked to observe either television or newspaper/magazine food advertisements (or both if you have the time and the inclination). You will not have time to carry out a detailed analysis of many advertisements, so you should concentrate on just one or two.

Record your responses to the following three questions about your chosen advertisements. Do not spend more than a quarter of an hour on this exercise.

1   What are the main elements *in the particular advertisement* to which you respond, either positively or negatively?

2   What are the main aspects of social reality the advertisement contains?

3   Towards which group of people do you think the advertisement is aimed?

You may find it useful to bear in mind the following checklist of things to watch out for in the advertisements:

Innovation — i.e. the suggestion that new products should be tried.

Whether 'British' or 'foreign' foods are portrayed as desirable.

Is the emphasis on the really 'exotic'?

Class and status (e.g. is the implication that if someone uses this product they will be more like a particular class or status group?).

Speed and ease of preparation for modern life styles.

History and tradition (of manufacturers).

'Healthiness' of the ingredients.

Gender roles (is the appeal specifically to men or women?).

There are, of course, no right or wrong answers in this kind of activity. The aim is to help you to see that some major aspects of concern and interest to social scientists are to be found in media imagery and representations, including those in printed advertisements in newspapers and magazines, and those on television.

Again, it might be valuable to compare your findings with those of fellow students at your local study centre.

Advertising campaigns for particular products, and for specific brands of these products, are devised, and targeted upon specific sections of the population. Some advertising campaigns are broader than others; that is, they are aimed at large groups of the population. Such advertisements are likely to be shown before, during, and after popular television programmes (such as *Coronation Street* during the 1980s, for instance). Other advertising is aimed at more precisely defined potential customers, who are seen as occupying a specific 'niche' by market researchers and advertising campaign designers. Ever more finely tuned categories of potential consumers are being developed by market researchers, and used by advertising agencies.

All this kind of information can induce in many of us a feeling that we are being researched, then manipulated into buying specific items and brands of food and drink through various advertising campaigns. Of course, at a *conscious* level we are unlikely to think we are being affected by the various advertising materials which appear in the media, but the addition of some notion of 'hidden persuasion' to our understanding introduces the idea that effective advertising campaigns can work at an *unconscious* level. This suggests that we are caught up in a vortex of manipulation by the advertisers, and the fact that many of us, much of the time, may think we are not being manipulated by advertising in our buying decisions suddenly appears less secure. We may be being persuaded in hidden ways, hidden that is from our conscious level of thinking, into making purchases of particular products, or brands of food and drink. It is because such advertising can sometimes be effective in raising the sales of a specific brand that so much money is spent by manufacturers on promoting particular brand images for specific foods or drinks.

Advertisements can promote a particular product by targeting niches in the market, but they also help to shape people's self-definition. Some advertisements suggest that by consuming a particular product you, the purchaser, will become what you desire to be. You may not even be very conscious of what it is you desire to become — successful yuppie; loving mum; glamorous woman; caring dad; sexy thing; or healthy and contented elderly person — but the advertisements which we notice in the media will often be those which touch us in some aspects of ourselves; touch some desire to be a specific type of person of which we are barely conscious.

Now this way of looking at advertising starts to shift our thinking yet again. There appears to be a contradiction — most people assume they are free agents when choosing foods and drinks on their shopping trips, yet manufacturers of foods and drinks spend large amounts of money on advertising and marketing to stimulate people to buy their products. But is there a contradiction here? Not necessarily, for when we look into how advertisements sometimes work, it is possible to see a link between us and them, between ourselves as consumers and the food/drink manufacturers. This link emerges when people's desires, self-definitions, images and representations of self are taken into account by market researchers. Let us look at how market research bridges the gap between consumers and producers.

Market research is not a one-way process. Market researchers don't just find out how much money particular segments of the population spend on food. Nor do they only discover how they can manipulate us into buying products which we really do not want. They do much more than this. Market research is also about finding out what images people may have of themselves, how different types of people see themselves, and how they wish to appear to other people. Food and drink advertising is then often geared towards such research findings about how various types of people think of themselves.

The foods and drinks which we all consume are increasingly part of a complex social, economic, psychological and cultural matrix. They are not simply utilitarian. The things people consume can come to represent their aspirations to be a certain kind of person; to belong to a certain group, however imprecise the imagery of that group may be; to have a certain social identity. It is not only cars, furniture, housing, clothing, or consumer durables which can be representations of social status, of social class, or of the type of person someone desires to be. The foods we eat, and the drinks we consume, are also part of a complex social process by which we represent to ourselves, and others, the kind of person we desire to become.

There is a continuing interplay between the definitions people have of themselves, or which they are in the process of creating, and market research, advertising and consumption. Market researchers try to find out how to address specific types of people by discovering their aspirations, their meanings, their way of seeing the world, the symbols to which they might respond. The advertising they may help to design then plays upon, reinforces, and helps to sustain these self-definitions by linking a specific brand of food and drink with a certain type of person.

By finding out about different groups' definitions of themselves, their aspirations, hopes and fears, market research shapes advertising campaigns towards specific groups — 'niche markets' as they have been called. People may recognize themselves as being spoken to in some advertising, but not in other advertisements. This process of making appeals to specific segments of the buying public also helps people to define themselves as the sort of person a specific advertisement is geared to addressing. Such a process makes more explicit in the respondent's own consciousness some symbols, some shapes, colours, words, looks, body-images, which advertisements associate with a particular product, thereby helping to produce a more explicit self-definition — a conception of self which was previously implicit.

These processes are difficult to capture in words because they are operating at the boundary where pictorial imagery meets words. This may help to explain why advertising campaigns are not always successful. They can and sometimes do fail. We are not, therefore, being totally manipulated by advertising into purchasing products of specific manufacturers. Nor are we socially isolated, freely-choosing, individual shoppers, whose minds are empty, uninfluenced by the surrounding culture of advertising and its symbols, signs, ciphers and representations. Advertising is not best described as 'manipulative', nor as 'hidden persuasion'. But nor is it necessarily innocent. For example, advertising could be devised which increased the numbers of people who smoke by a campaign which was built around some people's aspirations to be urbane, well-travelled, cosmopolitan, and not fuddy-duddy. Alcohol consumption could be raised by an advertising campaign designed around appeals to social status, or class, or to the masculinity concerns of young males, their desire to appear strong and macho to their male friends. Nothing in these processes is stable, however. Self-definitions change as new fashions, new products, new experiences, arise. There is an interplay between self-imagery, advertising, and food consumption. These processes now affect the foods and drinks which we consume. Advertising does not determine our individual choices, nor does it fully shape them. It is perhaps best seen as a dialogue with different segments of the population, a dialogue mediated by market research.

SUMMARY

- Shopping for food may appear to be an individual act, free from external determinants at first sight. But are we always choosing as freely as we imagine?

- Advertisements can be seen as setting out to persuade customers to buy a particular brand. Such persuasion has been seen as a form of manipulation of the buying public by manufacturers. One aim of advertising is to generate brand loyalty, to keep people buying the same product.

- Niche marketing aims to sell specific products to particular kinds of people based on research into potential consumers' own self-definitions and concerns. This can be seen less as a one-way process of communication (whereby manufacturers cajole consumers into buying products they do not want to buy) and more as a two-way communication process (in which the self-definitions of different groups of consumers are taken into account by manufacturers).

4   CULTURE AND FOOD

People's food consumption patterns can be seen as being shaped by social factors such as income, class, gender, and ethnicity, as we saw in Part I of this unit. From a wider, comparative perspective they can also be seen as having deeper, long-established roots, which do not change easily nor rapidly. People's likes and dislikes in foods and drinks form broadly recognizable and observable patterns within what can be termed their 'culture'. Let me explain this concept briefly, starting with a definition from a popular introductory text:

> Sociologists and anthropologists use 'culture' as a collective noun for the symbolic and learned, non-biological aspects of human society, including language, custom and convention, by which human behaviour can be distinguished from that of other primates.
> (Abercrombie *et al.*, 1988, p.59)

This is a tightly packed definition, but the central points in it are:

1   Culture contains symbols or signs — these can be special clothes, gestures, pictures, words, objects which are publicly shared and convey emotions as well as ideas. Items of food and drink can be symbolic too, as in many religious rituals, such as bread and wine in Holy Communion among Christians.

2   These aspects of a culture are learned; their meaning is not given by biological instinct but by *learning* from parents, teachers, and others such as friends or peer groups.

3   Language is an important component of culture. This feature of human social groups distinguishes humans from other animals who do not possess a complex language based on the exchange of symbols and signs, although they may respond to signals (as sheepdogs respond to the whistle of a shepherd).

4   Cultures also are said to contain customs and conventions; that is, patterned ways of how to act in such a way as to avoid giving offence to other group members. Both dressing and eating are activities which are usually, if not always, governed by strong rules of custom and convention (e.g. British conventions include using a knife and fork; and not slurping when one consumes soup).

The foods which people eat vary from one group to another, from one country to another, and from one historical period to another. All of us will have acquired particular likes and dislikes about what we eat, which are partly a consequence of the period in which we grew up, partly a result of the culture in which we were reared, and partly produced by our own individual tastes and responses to specific foods. The cultural aspects of food are explored in this section, and some aspects of individual responses to food are examined in the next.

ACTIVITY 9

Before you read on, note down your own favourite foods (one or two dishes will be enough) and also several things which you could *not* eat under any normal circumstances. Re-read what you have written when you reach the end of this section, and ask yourself if you would then alter any of your answers.

Culture in the sense defined above is learned as children are brought up in a particular family. A family in turn is part of a wider social network of neighbours and kinship relationships with other extended family members, many of whom will share the same cultural 'codes' surrounding food. Codes of this kind deal with what may or may not be eaten by members of a group. So, for example, among the things which may not be eaten in normal times in the UK are cats, dogs, foxes, mice, rats, ants, and most garden birds, such as robins or blue tits. Did you include any of these in your own list of things you could not eat? You probably did not think that these animals and birds needed to be mentioned.

Look back at the list just given and ask yourself what kinds of categories are involved here which might lead these creatures to be defined as inedible.

The first two, cats and dogs, are kept as pets, and such domesticated animals are not coded as being edible. They are not wild animals which are shot or hunted, such as rabbits or hares. On the other hand, some other wild animals, which are hunted by humans, are still not eaten — foxes, for example. They fall into another category — the category of 'vermin'. Vermin are those creatures which are culturally defined as polluting food if they touch it, or come into contact with it. Rats and mice are also classed as vermin in our culture. In other cultural codings, of course, they may not be defined as polluting and so may be eaten, as in parts of Asia for instance. Ants, particularly flying ants, are not defined as edible in British culture, but some peoples, such as the Bemba people in Africa, have been observed to eat them (Firth, 1958). Finally, garden birds such as robins and blue tits are not seen as being things one ought to eat in British cultural coding — they are wild but they are seen in gardens and parks, that is in human-made surroundings, and although they are not domesticated pets they are close enough to being so defined to be seen as a taboo food in the UK.

This brief look at some of the foods which may not generally be eaten reveals that there are collectively shared codes which affect our definitions of what to eat and what to avoid eating. These codes are not vegetarian. They allow us to eat certain animals. Of course, vegetarian codes exist, within the culture, which stop those of us who subscribe to them from eating meat at all. But the dominant food codes are not vegetarian ones. The principles underlying these codes are not primarily concerned with the morality of eating meat, or even with health or hygiene, but with categorizations of foods as edible or inedible depending upon whether they are wild, domesticated or farmed. None of the examples of things which may not be eaten considered above is a farmed animal — so British codes seem to contain the notion that animals specifically reared by humans to be eaten are the best ones to be defined as edible. Domestic pets are not farm animals in this sense, nor are wild animals. The first group, pets, is too close to humans to be edible; the second, wild animals, is too removed from human control, as shown by it being in competition for the same foods we want to eat or use — chickens in the case of foxes for instance. Animals reared on farms, on the other hand, are not fully domesticated (farmers do not normally have their livestock living in their own home). On the other hand, these farm animals are not totally wild, nor are they 'vermin' which pollute food which human beings may wish to eat.

One further example will help to illustrate this set of distinctions between the domestic, the wild, and the farmed. Consider the items which make up a traditional salad in the British family diet — lettuce, tomato, cucumber, and watercress. These are all cultivated in gardens or greenhouses; they are not gathered from the wild. They are typically eaten raw, however, and not cooked. But they must be washed before being eaten. Raw foods are now defined as being 'good for you'. A raw tomato is better for you than a fried one in this scheme, but it must not be too 'raw' in the sense of being wild and unwashed. Salad food should come from a market garden, or from a domestic garden or greenhouse. It is rarely 'wild' food these days.

The distinction between the 'raw' and the 'cooked', incidentally, is one which was introduced by one of the pioneers of modern social scientific analysis of food, the French anthropologist Claude Lévi-Strauss (b. 1908). Lévi-Strauss was concerned with relating these categories — the 'raw', and the 'cooked' — to two other fundamental categories — 'nature' and 'culture' (Lévi-Strauss, 1969). He suggested that raw foods belong to 'nature', but that cooked foods belong to 'culture' in that they are transformed by a *cultural* process, not a natural process, into edible food. However, the 'raw', as we have seen, is not the same thing as 'nature', for raw foods are grown and prepared specially for eating, in modern industrial societies such as the UK. Raw foods are rarely gathered from the wild in such societies. So not all foods made edible by a cultural process are included in the category of the 'cooked'. Moreover, some foods which are eaten raw in the UK are believed to be more healthy as a consequence by some people. This is a cultural belief, however, and not a fact of pure nature. It could be said, therefore, that our 'raw' foods belong to culture, rather than to nature. They are not as 'raw' as they may seem.

There are many examples of foods which are collectively defined by some groups as being edible or inedible because of wider or deeper cultural categories. Hindus regard beef as a taboo food; orthodox Jews regard pork as a taboo food. The social anthropologist Mary Douglas used the ideas of *pollution* and *taboo* to try to explain what is going on in these categorizations of foods, which are found in all human societies, whether they are predominantly industrial, or agricultural, or based on hunting and gathering food. She argued that many of the rules about what counts as edible food which operate in modern British society cannot be seen as being based on hygiene, but instead, like those of primitive tribal societies, are best seen as being based upon ritual pollution or religious taboos — in what she called 'symbolic systems'. She wrote: '... our ideas of dirt also express symbolic systems and ... the difference between pollution behaviour in one part of the world and another is only a matter of detail' (Douglas, 1966, p.147). Furthermore, she argued: 'If we can abstract pathogenicity and hygiene from our notion of dirt, we are left with the old definition of dirt as matter out of place' (*ibid.*, p.48).

Mary Douglas argues that the notion of *dirt* is a fundamental one in all human cultures and that it pre-dates the advances in medical knowledge about food hygiene which have been made in the last hundred years or more. In other words, we might say that there are two sources for our notions of food pollution: the basic idea of dirt or pollution, which exists in all human societies, and the more recent development of scientific understanding of food hygiene.

'Dirt' is defined as 'matter out of place'. In the light of this definition of dirt it may be useful at this point to reflect upon the earlier examples of foods which may not be consumed by humans. Some of the animals are coded as being dirty — mice and rats particularly. To eat them would entail becoming polluted by them, even though their flesh may be perfectly safe to eat from a food hygiene point of view. Such vermin are coded as being 'dirty' or polluting, in part because they may leave behind 'matter out of place' in the form of droppings in close proximity to food for human consumption.

These concerns with taboo and pollution pre-date the development in the late nineteenth and in the twentieth century of knowledge about the organisms in food which can cause food poisoning of varying degrees of severity — from salmonella to listeria. There is also now known to be another source of substances which may cause harm to human consumers, namely some of the chemicals used to fertilize the soils in which crops are grown, or to promote rapid growth in young animals and chickens, or to prevent crops of fruit and vegetables being spoiled by fungi and insects. These kinds of food pollution are based in biochemical processes and are distinct from the former types of pollution which are best seen as a form of ritual pollution or taboo.

Turning to the notion of taboo — one definition of 'taboo' is as follows:

> The term, which came into the English language from Captain Cook's travels in Polynesia, refers to anything (food, place, activity) which is prohibited and forbidden. For E. Durkheim, observation of a taboo has the social consequence of binding a social group together behind common rituals and sentiments. The taboo is a symbol of group membership ...
>
> (Abercrombie *et al.*, 1988, p.251)

Notice in this definition that there is a new element which has not been mentioned so far. This is the idea of Emile Durkheim (1858–1917), a French pioneer of social science, that observing taboos has the consequence of binding a social group together. This idea is a very important one, and is found frequently in social scientific analyses of social activities. It is related to the claim that ritual meals, such as wedding meals, Christmas and New Year meals and drinks, including office parties, and other ethnic groups' New Year celebrations, such as the Chinese New Year, serve to help to bind a group together, whether this is a family, a work group or a peer group of friends. Afternoon tea, which was discussed in Unit 1, may also be seen as a ritual occasion when it is served for a group, in a situation of some formality. Durkheim's claim is that this same social consequence of binding a group together can result from observing the negative ritual rule of a food taboo. All those who avoid the same foods express by so doing that they are members of the same group, just as those who eat festive meals together make a similar statement about themselves.

Although culture operates very powerfully in affecting peoples' likes and dislikes about food, it does not fully determine the foods which any particular individual eats. Individuals develop specific likes and dislikes about food, not just ones their broad cultural group shares. In the next section some of these individual motivations and patterns will be examined.

SUMMARY

- The concept of *culture* refers to the shared symbolic and non-biological aspects of human societies.
- Culture affects the types of food which are defined as being consumable and which are seen as polluting.
- Concerns about pollution, or taboo, in the area of food *preceded* recent knowledge about the organisms which cause food poisoning.
- Group membership and a sense of group identity is created, affirmed, re-created and re-affirmed in rituals which involve members collectively eating and drinking together. That group membership can also be reinforced by the group agreeing *not* to eat certain foods.

5   INDIVIDUAL MOTIVATION AND CONSUMPTION

So far we have approached the analysis of patterns of food consumption in one particular way. We have moved in on the individual food consumer from an analysis of wider social processes shaping individual choices of food. That is quite a normal route to take. Many social scientists, as you will discover in the rest of D103, are content to understand and explain people's actions by analysing the influence of factors such as class, gender and culture. But other social scientists prefer to adopt an alternative route. They concentrate on the way different individuals respond to such shared social circumstances and processes. They emphasize in their work that although there are patterned variations in the ways in which people act, these broad patterns do not exclude specific individuals acting in ways which may be quite different from other people in the same social, cultural or economic grouping. In the consumption of food, as in other aspects of social life, individual differences are an important subject of social analysis.

One way of approaching the study of differential individual responses to common social circumstances is to concentrate on the effect of variations in personality. The concept of 'personality' refers to those distinctive characteristics of an individual which mark them out from others and which persist for long periods of time. For example, some people may be more optimistic or pessimistic about the future and about their own lives than most others in the same gender, age, class, economic, and cultural group. Optimism/pessimism can be measured by using a specially designed questionnaire, in which items have been pre-tested so that a particular answer is known to discriminate one type of personality from another. Alternatively, or in addition, other methods may be used, such as interpreting a person's responses to patterns, inkblots of different shapes and colours, as in the Rorschach test. Figure 4 shows a reproduction of Card IV from the ten Rorschach inkblots. Klopfer and Davidson have described the 'stimulus characteristics' of this card as follows:

> The blot material of Card IV appears massive, compact, yet indistinct in shape. This card is black-gray all over and highly shaded. Because of its massive structure and dense shading, it appears ominous to some people. Thus monsters, giants, gorillas, or peculiar-looking people are seen sitting or approaching, or the blot looks like a dense forest with mountains and lakes. The frequency of the giant, ape, or monster type of response has prompted some clinicians to refer to this card as the 'father card.' They believe that attitudes toward paternal authority are revealed because of the combination of masculine aggression and dependent needs related to shading.

> Subjects who are prone to select details for their responses may perceive the large side areas as 'boots', or the top side areas as 'snakes' or a 'female figure diving.' Two other areas that are easily delineated are the lower center portion and the small top center area, frequently associated with sexual responses.

> The shading of the card, if not disturbing to a subject, may suggest furriness; in that case the blot is frequently seen as a fur rug.

> (Klopfer and Davidson, 1962, p.10)

To help you to see the interrelationships between individual personality variables and those of class, gender, age, ethnicity and culture, I shall briefly explore two interrelated eating disorders — anorexia nervosa (self-starvation)

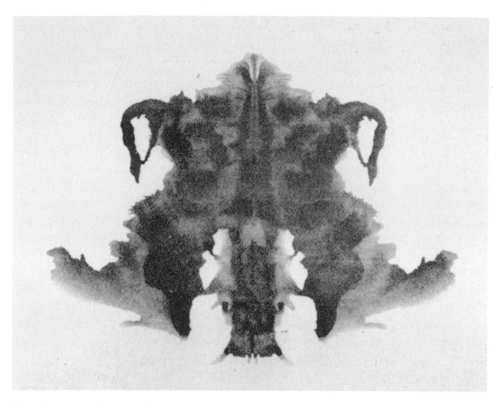

Figure 4   A reproduction of Card IV from the ten Rorschach inkblots

and bulimia nervosa (eating to excess and subsequently vomiting or defecating). These phenomena were known in earlier historical periods, but they affect an increasing number of people in the late twentieth century, especially in the United States and the UK. Moreover, these patterns of behaviour towards food are found in a particular group of people in these societies — most anorexics (95 per cent) are women, or post-pubescent girls, under the age of thirty. In 1976, one study found that one in every 200 girls under 16 in private schools in Britain and one in every 100 girls between 16 and 18 years of age had been reported as having one severe episode of anorexia nervosa (Crisp, Palmer and Kalucy, 1976). The figures for bulimia nervosa are unknown, but of young women attending a family planning clinic in Britain in 1980, nearly 21 per cent had experienced at least one bulimic episode.

Now, if we try to explain these findings, where should we start? Well we could get some help from looking at social factors first of all. Nearly all the reported cases of anorexia nervosa are of girls, or young women, from the top social classes in Britain. In the United States and in Britain, however, education, particularly higher education, seems to be an important contributory factor in the sense that most cases of anorexia nervosa have been among girls in schools aiming their pupils towards further and higher education, or among young women already attending organizations of higher education. On the other hand, bulimia nervosa is found to be more prevalent among young women not in higher education, or who did not attend college or university, or who went to schools in which they were not oriented to higher education.

There are specific cultural influences operating too on girls and young women in the UK and the United States which portray *thin* women as being desirable. In many countries where malnourishment is a problem, women usually desire to be fatter, so there is nothing universal about thin, slim women being more desirable. Indeed, in previous eras in Europe, women were seen as desirable if they were curvaceous and fleshy — as in paintings by Rubens (1577–1640). Nowadays, women are frequently portrayed in articles, and in advertisements, as needing to watch their weight, to have slim figures, and to spend time, money and energy on keeping a slim appearance.

So a person is more likely to be anorexic if:

- they are female;
- between 15 and 30 years old;
- have some higher education;
- their parents were in the top social classes;
- they belong to a culture which sees slimming as a desirable activity.

Now all women and young girls are subject to basically the same cultural influences in contemporary Britain, but not all have either of the eating disorders being discussed. Not all young women in universities develop anorexia nervosa. Among those young women not in higher education, only some develop bulimia nervosa. So although gender, age, culture, and class provide some necessary factors in the explanation of these disorders, they do not explain why a specific individual develops one or other syndrome. Other social factors seem to play a role too. Families seem to predispose some individuals to be more at risk than others. Families in which parents are overprotective, rigid and tightly-knit are more likely to predispose girls towards anorexia nervosa, for instance, but not all families which psychologists might observe to be of this kind produce daughters who develop anorexia nervosa.

The personality of individual girls plays a crucial part in explaining *which* specific girls, or young women, who are in social class, cultural and familial situations in which anorexia nervosa is found, will develop the behaviour pattern which can lead some to starve themselves to death in the midst of an affluent set of circumstances. Both those who behave in an anorexic manner, and those who behave in a bulimic way, have been found to have some personality characteristics which distinguish them from otherwise similar young females who do not show such behaviour patterns. These personality traits are: perfectionism; solitariness; submissiveness; competitiveness; high intelligence (Strober, 1981). Anorexics, in particular, lack a sense of individual autonomy from their families; they spend much of their leisure time at home but often in their own room, alone. They do not go out dancing with friends very often, nor do they go on many trips. Lack of fatness becomes a central concern for such girls in their efforts to try to make their own body-image acceptable in their own eyes.

Anorexia nervosa is, therefore, best seen as being based upon *feelings about self* rather than as a biologically based illness. It is not so much an illness as a way of being, a way of living, and as an attempt to conform to an exaggerated notion of western culture's stereotypical 'attractive female' imagery. It is a pattern of behaving which is produced by the way some girls respond to family, educational and mass media messages about being female, but is not a disease produced by any known virus, nor by any identifiable physiological abnormality. For example, one therapist, who works with women, has said:

> That food routinely plagues women is an acknowledged and discussed aspect of everyday life. An obsessive involvement with food flows out of a cultural insistence that what they eat, how much they eat, and how they cook for others is their especial domain. Food is the medium through which women are addressed, in turn, food has become the language of women's response.

> The preoccupation with food is linked with a fetishizing of the female form. Women wish to acquire that elusive, eternally youthful body beautiful. A woman's body becomes the subject of scrutiny, the recipient

of enormous amounts of attention, and the vehicle for the expression of a wide range of statements. Women find themselves obsessively engaged with both their foods and their bodies ... Women repress the knowledge of how damaging and hurtful this obsession is.

Anorexia nervosa is perhaps the most dramatic outcome of the culture's obsession with regulating body size.

(Orbach, 1986, pp.3–4)

SUMMARY

- Social scientists can approach their analysis by focusing upon individual differences in social actions, as well as the economic, social and cultural factors examined earlier in this unit.

- Personality differences in adults, such as the degree of optimism or pessimism they possess, may be one example of the influence of early experiences in infancy upon later patterns of acting.

- Certain eating disorders which affect women particularly (bulimia nervosa and anorexia nervosa) have increased in some societies in recent years. These disorders have a *social* dimension; they are *not* purely *biologically* caused illnesses.

---

6   CONCLUSION

You have seen in this unit some of the ways in which the food which people consume in the UK depends upon economic, social and cultural factors. Level of income is a fundamental element in affecting who eats or does not eat an adequate diet, even for those groups of people who are not part of the poorest 20 to 30 per cent of the UK population. Social class, gender, and ethnicity also affect patterns of food consumption among the population of the UK. So too do the kind of food shops which are readily available for a particular shopper to use. The rise of the supermarket in the last two decades has transformed the ways in which large numbers of people do their shopping for food. The advertising of foods and drinks in the press and on television has some influence on what people buy. Both necessary food items, such as bread and vegetables, and more luxury items, such as chocolate, alcoholic and non-alcoholic drinks, are advertised regularly; and those advertisements influence what people consume. The population of potential purchasers for any particular product is increasingly analysed as being a niche market by market researchers and advertising is geared to addressing such smaller groups of potential consumers. These may be differentiated by occupation, social class, gender, age or ethnicity.

At a more fundamental level, there are deeper cultural codes at work in any society which determine the broad parameters of food choice, specifying which foods may be eaten and which are regarded as disgusting, inedible, and potentially polluting. Some social scientists, following or adapting the ideas of Durkheim, have pointed out that social groups are bound together not only by eating some meals together, at which culturally acceptable foods and drinks are consumed, but also by upholding the same taboos about what *not* to eat or drink. These taboos can have an adverse effect upon perceptions of outsiders, who may be perceived as being potentially polluting persons if they consume substances which are forbidden to the insider group.

These major economic, social and cultural factors provide the primary background for understanding and explaining the social activity of food consumption. However, as you saw in considering eating disorders, the personality of the individual also has to be taken into account if we want fully to understand the food choices that we all make.

 ACTIVITY 10

Finally, you may like to look back at the list of factors determining what you eat which you wrote down at the beginning of Part II of this unit (see Activity 6). Would you still write down the same factors, or a different set? Are there ways in which you would change how you ranked factors now that you have read the unit? Are there any factors you had not thought of before you read the unit, which you now think you could have included?

Gender (and age) differences in food consumption in the UK are only now beginning to be documented systematically for the first time. A typical example of recent work is that of Charles and Kerr, reproduced in Chapter 3 of the Reader, which you will be recommended to study in the following Study Skills Section.

REFERENCES

Abercrombie, N., Hill, S. and Turner, B.S. (1988) *The Penguin Dictionary of Sociology*, Harmondsworth, Penguin Books.

Arnott, A. (1987) 'Second class citizens', in Walker, A. and Walker, C. (eds) *The Growing Divide*, London, Child Poverty Action Group.

Brandt, W. (1980) *North–South: A Programme for Survival*, London, Pan.

Central Office of Information (1989) *Britain: An Official Handbook,* London, HMSO.

Clinch, T. (1988) 'These people choose what you eat', *Daily Telegraph,* 17 December.

Child Poverty Action Group (1986) *The Rising Tide of Poverty*, London.

Child Poverty Action Group (1989) *Poverty: The Facts*, London.

Crisp, A.H., Palmer, A.L and Kalucy, R.S. (1976) 'How common is anorexia nervosa?', *British Journal of Psychiatry*, vol.128, pp.549–54.

Department of Employment (monthly) *Department of Employment Gazette*, London, HMSO.

Department of Employment (annual) *Family Expenditure Survey,* London, HMSO.

Douglas, M. (1966) *Purity and Danger,* London, Routledge and Kegan Paul.

Firth, R. (1958) *Human Types*, London, Thomas Nelson.

Gardner, C. (1988) 'Spend, spend, spend', *New Statesman and Society*, 16 December, pp.40–41.

Glendinning, C. (1987) 'Impoverishing women', in Walker, A. and Walker, C. (eds) *The Growing Divide,* London, Child Poverty Action Group.

Graham, H. (1984) *Women, Health and the Family*, Brighton, Wheatsheaf.

Klopfer, B. and Davidson, H. (1962) *The Rorschach Technique: An Introductory Manual,* New York, Harcourt, Brace, and World.

Lévi-Strauss, C. (1969) *The Raw and the Cooked*, translated by J. and D. Weightman, London, Jonathan Cape.

Lewis, J. and Piachaud, D. (1987) 'Women and poverty in the twentieth century', in Glendinning, C. and Miller, J. (eds) *Women and Poverty in Britain*, Brighton, Wheatsheaf.

London Food Commission (1988) *Tightening Belts: A Report on the Impact of Poverty on Food*, London.

Orbach, S. (1986) *Hunger Strike: The Anorexic's Struggle as a Metaphor of our Age*, London and Boston, Faber and Faber.

Packard, V. (1981) *The Hidden Persuaders*, Harmondsworth, Penguin Books.

Rowntree, S. (1901) *Poverty: A Study of Town Life,* London, Macmillan.

Runnymede Trust (1980) *Britain's Black Population*, London, Heinemann.

Sen, A. (1981) *Poverty and Famines*, Oxford, Clarendon Press.

Social Services Committee (1987–88) *Families on Low Income: Low Income Statistics,* House of Commons paper 565, London, HMSO.

Strober, M. (1981) 'The significance of bulimia in juvenile anorexia nervosa', *International Journal of Eating Disorders*, vol.1 (i), pp.28–43.

Townsend, P. (1979) *Poverty in the United Kingdom*, London, Allen Lane.

Winyard, S. (1987) 'Divided Britain', in Walker, A. and Walker, C. (eds) *The Growing Divide,* London, Child Poverty Action Group.

Whitehead, M. (1988) 'The health divide', in Townsend, P. and Davidson, N. (eds) *Inequalities in Health*, Harmondsworth, Penguin Books.

Women's Health and Reproductive Rights Information Centre (1988) *Women's Health and Poverty*, London.

STUDY SKILLS SECTION: TAKING NOTES

Prepared for the Course Team by Kay Pole

As a finale to the work of this unit, turn to the Reader, Chapter 3, entitled 'Gender and age differences in family food consumption', by Nicola Charles and Marion Kerr.

We think that this article has an intrinsic interest in that it pulls together the material on food consumption, thus integrating ideas from the two parts of the unit quite successfully. It takes some of our assertions about gender differentiation a little further, showing how differences operate even in such an apparently simple activity as catering for a family. It will also introduce you to the way research is reported, and to the skill of looking through reports for evidence in support of assertions.

At the same time, we are going to use the article as a vehicle for practising certain study skills. These will build on your previous experience in the course so far, short as that may have been, and will involve you particularly in actively taking notes. This will be familiar to you if you studied the *Preparatory Pack*, and you should have done some work on it while studying Chapter 2 of *The Good Study Guide*.

If you didn't manage to read Chapter 2 of The Good Study Guide *at the time we recommended it, at the end of the second week of study, then please do so now.* You will find that the questions we're about to ask about the article by Charles and Kerr are the same as Andy Northedge asks about the Gardner article, so we'd like to think they are not new to you. Indeed, the ideas in the Gardner article itself are still germane to the concerns of this unit, so you could also be practising the further skill of integrating information from several different sources.

In addition to polishing techniques of 'active reading' — namely questioning, note taking and recalling — you will also be studying tables in order to describe what they contain, thus building on what you did in Units 2 and 3.

———————————————— ACTIVITY 1 ————————————————

================= READER =================

Now read Chapter 3, by Charles and Kerr, in the Reader. This should take you about 45 minutes to an hour. Don't worry if it isn't all clear at this stage; we will be going over it again in the process of rehearsing the study skills.

Try to answer the following questions about the article, remembering the advice given in *The Good Study Guide* that it's always a good idea to take your own notes about what you read, since the act of putting things into your own words seems to help in their retention:

1   What was the article about? (Put down one or two sentences, without looking at it again for this purpose.)

2   Did you experience any difficulties in reading it?

3   Were there any points that you found unclear?

Here's my answer to the first question, written after my first reading of it:

> 'Different foods have different statuses in family catering and women are most likely to give high status meat or sweet things to their husbands or children, and keep themselves relatively deprived.'

Perhaps this is written in a slightly academic way (and in only one sentence), but you probably put down something about women doing the catering and fathers and children getting the best or choicest bits.

It's more difficult for me to suggest what difficulties you found or where the article wasn't altogether clear to you, though I could make a few guesses. However, if we now follow Andy Northedge's practice of highlighting words and phrases in order to make the whole thing more accessible, difficulties and lack of clarity might disperse.

—————————————— ACTIVITY 2 ——————————————

Go through the article again, using a highlighter pen or whatever suits you, to pick out important words, phrases, concepts or ideas — anything which helps you to catch the essence of what is being said.

I indicate what I highlighted below. The first thing you will have to do is to number the paragraphs. I hope, like me, you find nineteen.

(Note: what I highlighted at the time of reading is shown in quotation marks.)

PARAGRAPH 1

'food is a particularly clear indicator of social status'

PARAGRAPH 3

'social relations of food consumption'

'ideologies of food provision'

'foods were ranked hierarchically in terms of their social status'

'relative power and status of family members'

This seems a good place to pause. I don't, of course, know which phrases you marked. If, even this early in the course, you are attuned to the concerns of the social sciences, you may have picked out the same kinds of words that I did, words such as 'social status', 'social relations', 'ideologies', 'relative power', and so on. It was easier for me to do this since I've been a social scientist for a bit longer than you have, and you may not have homed in in quite the same way. But what my highlighting does for me is to signal the phrases that I should look for as the article progresses, so that I'm using the opening paragraphs in the way that they are intended; namely, to suggest what is coming and to look out for arguments and evidence to support what is being claimed so far.

Let's continue with my list of highlighted words:

PARAGRAPH 5

'women ... subordinated their own preferences'

'unequal relations of power and authority' (there we go again!)

PARAGRAPH 6

'social values' (now I'm getting rather enigmatic; social values of what, or for whom?)

'meat which endowed a meal with status'

'women were highly sensitive to gradations in the status'

PARAGRAPH 7

This paragraph is largely taken up with presentation of research results, in the form of the table, so we are now able to assess some of the evidence that the authors give for their assertions. We'll come back to this later.

PARAGRAPH 10

'"children's food" within contemporary British mainstream culture'

'important for children's health'

PARAGRAPH 11

'gender differences in food consumption'

'differential status and power within the family'

'in general men had more opportunity to enjoy a drink than women'

There may not be much of the social scientific in the last remark; I think it just fuels a prejudice of mine.

PARAGRAPH 13

'men's consumption of low status meat was higher than that of women and children' (so they just eat a lot, anyway; more prejudice!)

PARAGRAPH 14

'differentiation according to gender and age' — back to the concerns of the research and of social science in general. But I'm also getting the impression that the same point is being laboured; I'll have to read more carefully to see whether new information is being adduced.

PARAGRAPH 15

'seven occupational groups of the male partners' — a possible link here with the Registrar General's classification (which I'm already familiar with, and which will be described in Block II of the course).

PARAGRAPH 16

'necessity to limit access to scarce resources'

'inequalities ... remain a persistent and enduring feature'

(Perhaps some refinement of the data is to be made in order to strengthen the argument.)

PARAGRAPH 17

The consumption of meat for 'men in the professions ... is closer to that of women'. A detail, perhaps, but a nice one that cuts across gender, class and culture.

PARAGRAPH 18

'women and children's meat consumption is closest to that of men, in the families of unemployed men' — Ah! It's something to do with being at *work* that encourages women to give their partners higher status food. Or is it money? There is another table here that may enable us to decide this.

PARAGRAPH 19

This is the conclusion to the paper, and I have highlighted the following phrases:

'Food is not a resource to which all family members have equal access.'

'life cycle point when most women and children are financially dependent on men' — I hadn't noticed this stated in the paper before, perhaps it was one of the assumptions.

The fact that 'women did the food shopping and cooking does not necessarily lead to their wielding power in their own interests'. This is a nice conclusion that illustrates social science's concern with power relations (remember the *Preparatory Pack* again?), and how having responsibility doesn't automatically confer power.

And, finally: 'women are themselves instrumental in reproducing the social and sexual division of labour'.

There's something from nearly every paragraph here and perhaps this is fuller than you've been able to do. But it's going to give me a basis for the notes I make separately; notes that, were I a D103 student, I would keep and use later for a TMA, or, later still, for revision.

It may be the case that you are reluctant to mark the pages of a book (as opposed to those in one of the units), even when that book belongs to you. It took me a long time to overcome such a distaste — I still don't turn down the pages of a novel to mark my place, for example; but remember that the point of the exercise is to convert the article into one of your working documents, to be used along with all the other teaching materials for D103.

TAKING NOTES FROM THE ARTICLE

If you recall, and of course you will since you took notes as you read Chapter 2 of *The Good Study Guide* (didn't you?), highlighting is to some extent a preliminary activity to making notes for your own use. It is the beginning of your investment of time in studying. The investment becomes more valuable when you proceed to take notes on the piece you've been reading.

Just remember two points Andy Northedge made in his note-taking chapter:

1 Notes of the same length and complexity as the original do not do you much good. There is an old joke about lectures, that they're something that go from the notebook of the lecturer to the notebooks of the students without going through the heads of either. Voluminous notes that are made mechanistically are not going to help later.

2 While taking notes you are *writing to yourself* (see the discussion box 'What is note-taking skill?', in Section 5.2). So, since you are the audience, write in the way that suits you best.

There are various ways of organizing the notes you take, and examples are given in Andy's chapter. You may feel happy writing on index cards; at least this is a way of limiting the amount you decide to write, and normally helps in the filing and retrieving of information. Or you could simply use loose-leaf paper, that you can then keep with the units or with your TMAs for the block. This is what I happen to prefer, since it doesn't confine me to a small space, or force sets of notes from different pieces of writing into the same sized area (although you could of course use more than one index card for larger, or more complicated articles). Andy gives a very extensive worked out example of possible notes for the Gardner article in Figure 2.5 in Chapter 2.

Then, of course, you choose the *form* in which to record your notes and reminders. This could be some kind of network diagram, for example (see Figure

2.4 in *The Good Study Guide*), or something more linear. Again, I prefer the second of these. What is important is that you are clear to yourself; no one else will need to see what you take down, and certainly no tutor will come along to assess your notes. Work out what is good for you. At this early stage in the course it is still possible to experiment.

For my own note taking I would return to the highlighted phrases from the concluding paragraph of the Reader article by Charles and Kerr. I picked out four phrases about women and their relationship to the others in the family, and these statements form the focus of my notes. They will also encourage me to look more closely at the data in the tables for evidence to support them. In fact, it's often a good idea, especially when pressed for time, to look at the introduction and conclusion of reports and papers to get a 'line' on the research, so that what you're looking for has some structure.

Taking the first statement that I highlighted from the conclusion — 'food is not a resource to which all family members have equal access' — can we now find 'hard' evidence to support it?

—————————————————— ACTIVITY 3 ——————————————————

Look again at paragraphs 6 and 7 of the Reader article by Charles and Kerr, paying particular attention to Table 3.1. What do these tell you to support the assertion about unequal distribution of food within families? *Read only as far as the end of paragraph 7, since the following one gives some of the answers!*

The main conclusions I drew from the table are that men get more meat of any kind, high or low status, than either women or children; that the pattern of eating for adults seems quite different from that of children; that children don't seem to like raw vegetables or at least they don't get them very often; that men consume alcohol and crisps a great deal more frequently; and that a vast amount of tea and coffee seems to have been drunk in the two week period in which diaries were kept.

These conclusions were relatively easy to reach because of the authors' use of an index of 100 for the women's rate of consumption of the various foods. By standardizing on one set of respondents in this way, and expressing other frequencies as a proportion of that, comparisons are very quickly made. Thus, you can easily see by glancing down the columns, which items of food men were given more frequently, or less frequently, than women, and the same for the children.

You will come across the convention of using 100 as a baseline index for purposes of comparison in many contexts, such as tables, graphs, or time series. Incidentally, you can also see the number of women whose responses contribute to the data in this table by the numbers in brackets along the top, where 'N' simply stands for 'number'. Does this make you wonder what happened to 43 women, since 200 were originally interviewed?

—————————————————— ACTIVITY 4 ——————————————————

Look at Table 3.2 in the Reader article, and at paragraphs 17 and 18 where it is discussed. What variations in access to food within the family are indicated here?

I saw evidence for the statement that the authors make in paragraph 18, about changes in consumption of meat according to whether the men in the families are in paid work. Using the index again, and simply checking down the first and third columns as compared to the second, we can easily see children get much less 'high status' meat than either men or women; have a little more of the medium status meat, but still not as much as their parents; and catch up with the women, but not at all with the men, when it comes to low status meat.

You can also look at differences in consumption between occupation groups within each of the three 'status' categories. This would reveal quite a complex relationship between the 'status' and the amount of meat served, for each of the groups: men, women and children. In order to consider the relationship you might want to ask for a definition of the criteria by which meat is classified, and for that you'd need to look back at paragraph 6. There, for example, it looks as if what is classified as 'low status' meat, such as sausages or beefburgers, doesn't really count as a proper meal — so the kids can have more! Notice, of course, that in nearly all occupational class groups, the women still seem to give themselves less, even of low status meat.

CONCLUSION

This has been a limited analysis of the results of a particular piece of research. We hope that going through an article like this makes it lively and informative for you. Looking at tables is a rewarding activity in itself, and not something that should be skipped. It's a bit like scraping the mud off archeological finds to see what riches are revealed. The commentary around the tables, like the descriptions of the finds, may be insufficient — you will need to see for yourself what is contained.

In the coming months you will often be presented with more complex data than we have used here, or indeed with more elaborate hypotheses that are being tested. You will need to see for yourself whether the results are supported by the evidence, so don't be tempted to skip over the data and go straight to the discussion of results without looking at the 'facts' for yourself. In addition, you should be encouraged to cite information from tables published elsewhere, in your TMAs, or, of course, at tutorials. You may have decided to put together your own Resource File, which will no doubt include cuttings which themselves contain tables and graphs. Just don't be afraid of using them!

Acknowledgements

Grateful acknowledgement is made to the following sources for permission to reproduce material in this unit:

Figures

Figure 1: CPAG (1989) *Poverty: The Facts*, Child Poverty Action Group; *Figure 2*: N. Timmins (1989) 'Moore says poverty levels "exaggerated"', *The Independent*, 12 May, Newspaper Publishing PLC; P. Townsend (1989) 'Measuring poverty in Britain', *The Independent*, 13 May, copyright © Professor Peter Townsend; *Figure 3*: Central Statistical Office (1986) *Family Expenditure Survey Report 1986*, reproduced with the permission of the Controller of HMSO.

Tables

Table 1: CPAG (1989) *Poverty: The Facts*, Child Poverty Action Group; *Table 2*: A. Walker and C. Walker (eds) (1987) *The Growing Divide*, Child Poverty

Action Group; *Table 3*: C. Glendinning and J. Millar (eds) (1987) *Women and Poverty in Britain*, Harvester Wheatsheaf; *Table 4*: CPAG (1989) *Poverty: The Facts*, Child Poverty Action Group; *Table 5*: M. Whitehead (1988) 'The health divide', Penguin Books, copyright © Margaret Whitehead, 1988; *Table 7*: T. Clinch (1988) 'These people choose what you eat', *Daily Telegraph*, 17 December, © Verdict Research Ltd.

Photographs

p. 108: Roger Mayne; *pp. 111, 116, 119, 122*: Andrew Yeadon; *p. 126*: Wendy Latham; *p. 127*: Raissa Page/Format; *p. 131*: Collage: numbering 1–5 from the top of the page: 1, 4, 5: J. Sainsbury, plc; 2: Joanne O'Brien/Format; 3: Brenda Prince/Format; *p. 143*: C. R. S. McCully (1971) *Rorschach Theory and Symbolism*, p. 109, plate IV.

UNIT 4   MAKING SENSE OF SOCIETY

Prepared for the Course Team by James Anderson

CONTENTS

1   REVIEW AND PREVIEW

Units 1, 2 and 3 have provided lots of 'food for thought' about our social world and about the methods of analysis which social science uses to understand and explain it. Units 4 and 5 will now review this material and preview major features of the course.

Unit 4 concentrates on some of the basic social science procedures for 'making sense of society'. It does so by drawing on examples from the material about the United Kingdom and its historical and international context which you have already studied in the first three units. It deals with the following:

- the use of terms and *concepts* and how the course *themes* help us to organize our thoughts about social issues (Section 2);

- the *classifying* of factual information or evidence about society into different categories, and how putting particular aspects of society into their wider social *context* improves our understanding of them (Section 3);

- outlining how *explanations* are constructed by bringing together these methods in a series of steps or stages which combine the use of concepts and factual evidence (Section 4).

Unit 5 will then look at 'social science in society' and at how society influences the explanations and understandings which social science produces. The unit will introduce four influential *traditions of social thought* — liberalism, marxism, social reformism, and conservatism — which embody different overall conceptions of society and how it should be understood.

You will be aware, from the first three units of the course, that the subject matter of social science includes issues of public debate and controversy about which different groups in society disagree. They disagree and have different viewpoints because of their different social positions, or because of different political or moral values and beliefs; and it is not surprising that, being members of society, social scientists get caught up in these disagreements. So we have to understand the different values and conceptions of society which are involved. You will be doing this when you study the four *traditions of social thought* periodically through the course. However, these matters are not introduced until Unit 5. In Unit 4 we concentrate on basic scientific methods, because they are *shared* by people who have different values and viewpoints and because they are essential for doing social science, irrespective of what overall conceptions of society influence our thinking.

To understand society's influences on social science, or the merits of one viewpoint or explanation over another, you first need to know about some of the basic 'tools of the trade'. However, don't worry if not everything in Unit 4 is completely clear to you. As we review the methods used in the first three units, you may occasionally find it helpful to refer back to them, especially to their periodic 'Summaries'. But how to use the 'tools of the trade' will only become fully apparent when you see how they are used on a variety of topics through the course, and when you practise using them yourself in TMAs and tutorial discussions. Don't be put off by some of the technical terms — they are explained when they are first used, and they will become more familiar as the course progresses. If you need a quick reminder of their meanings, you can always refer to the *Glossary*, which indexes where they are discussed in the course.

All the important points about social science methods are discussed again in more depth in later blocks. Units 4 and 5 are simply a foretaste of what to expect. But — perhaps of more immediate concern — by drawing on Units 1, 2 and 3 for examples, Units 4 and 5 should also help you with TMA 01 in week 5.

In fact, the first three units have covered a lot of ground in demonstrating social science methods, and after studying *food* for three weeks you are already well on the way to *doing* social science. So, to clarify what has been demonstrated, let's summarize (in Section 1.1) the methods which have been used. Then we can outline the general character of social science by differentiating it from 'common sense' and comparing it with natural science (in Section1.2), before discussing its methods in more detail (in Sections 2, 3 and 4).

1.1   A SUMMARY OF METHODS

1   Unit 1 emphasized the need to be clear about the question being addressed (essential when you are answering TMA questions), and the importance of defining key terms or concepts as precisely as possible (as Units 2 and 3 defined concepts such as 'famine', 'poverty', and 'undernourishment'). Good explanations depend on good *conceptualizations*; that is, on the proper definition and use of concepts.

2   Units 1, 2 and 3 demonstrated some of the ways of using the course themes (*representation and reality, public and private, local and global*) in analysing social issues (see Section 2 below).

3   They also showed how putting even familiar things in their social context improves our understanding of them. *Contextualizing* a social event or process simply means relating it to surrounding events and processes and indicating their influences on it (see Section 3 below).

4   Units 1 and 2 introduced the procedures and problems of *classification* when they discussed the UK's world context in terms of 'First', 'Second' and 'Third World' countries. *Classification* (grouping, under a set of headings or categories, things, events or processes which share some common characteristics) is one of the most basic scientific methods (see Section 3).

5   In analysing the causes of famine and the connections between poverty and undernourishment in the UK, Units 2 and 3 used procedures of *abstraction*; that is, they picked out particular social processes and aspects of society for detailed analysis. It's rather like a natural scientist deciding to isolate a particular set of chemicals in a laboratory in order to analyse the interactions between them — excluding other chemicals or 'impurities' which would be present 'in nature' makes it easier to analyse how the isolated chemicals interact (see Section 4 below).

6   Units 2 and 3 also showed how the methods of *conceptualization, classification, contextualization,* and *abstraction* are all used in producing *explanations*. They demonstrated the procedures for constructing explanations which involve combining concepts and theories with factual evidence (see Section 4).

7   Unit 1 indicated that the use and definition of terms and concepts depend on which theory is adopted — different terms can imply different explanations deriving from different theories. For example, saying Europe 'exploited' other parts of the world implies relations of domination and subordination in the world system, whereas saying it 'developed' them could imply a more benign view of mutual interdependence. Unit 1 contained factual evidence to support *both* viewpoints, but we cannot decide between them simply on the basis of 'the facts', because these are always interpreted by theory. Debates about the merits of one explanation rather than another therefore often hinge on the adequacy of the theories, concepts and classifications used to organize and interpret the factual evidence.

8   We saw that 'the facts' themselves depend on how terms are defined. For example, there were no simple answers to the seemingly simple questions: how many starve?; how many are poor? Indeed, there were big differences in the numbers depending on the different ways in which 'famine' and 'poverty' are

defined. Numerical forms of evidence in any science (the apparently 'hard facts') are only as good as the concepts and classification systems on which they are based.

9   Numerical facts are only one form of evidence. Information describing what things are like, their *quality* rather than their *quantity* (the quality of life of the poor for instance — what 'poverty' means, what is associated with it, how people feel about it) often tells us much more than the bare figures can.

10   Facts without theories are blind, while theories without facts are empty, and their necessary interdependence was demonstrated in Units 2 and 3. Combining factual evidence with concepts and theories to produce explanations requires a number of steps, as we saw in the investigations of famine and undernourishment. The sequence isn't rigid or always the same, but typically it involves the following:

(a)   A question or *hypothesis* (a hypothesis is just a question turned into a statement or proposition), which has to be tested against the available evidence (e.g. Unit 3's hypothesis that low personal incomes were the cause of undernourishment in the UK). A hypothesis may be based on an existing theory, or simply a 'hunch', but generating interesting ones, whether in social science or natural science, is essentially an act of the imagination. Science is an exploration which can lead to the discovery of new insights, but there are no 'set rules' guaranteeing success.

(b)   Clarifying the hypothesis by *defining* key terms (e.g. income, undernourishment, famine).

(c)   Collecting and *classifying* evidence about the particular events or processes which have been picked out, or *abstracted*, for detailed analysis.

(d)   Putting the events or processes in their wider social *context* and relating them to surrounding processes.

(e)   Using broad *explanatory frameworks* to help make more sense of particular findings. For example, Unit 2 related explanations of famine to broader frameworks for explaining how the world is organized (in terms of a 'centre' which dominates a 'periphery', or inequalities between 'North' and 'South', or a classification into 'modern' and 'traditional' societies).

(f)   A conclusion, which typically returns to the initial question or hypothesis, sums up the material presented, and reaches a verdict (which is what you should aim to do at the end of your essays). The hypothesis may be proved, disproved, or proved with qualifications which can lead to further investigations.

11   The investigations of famine and undernourishment showed that causes and explanations can be at various 'levels'. The *immediate* cause of a particular famine, what 'triggers' it, may be a drought, a war, or political turmoil, and some explanations remain at this level. But the 'Third World's' continuing *vulnerability* to famines (after all, droughts haven't 'triggered' famines in the 'First World' during this century) stems from more deep-rooted, long-term, or *basic* causes, such as 'the international division of labour' or position in the world economy, the colonial legacy, or international debt. Unit 2 and the first TV programme found that a fuller explanation of a particular famine would have to take into account some of these more basic causes. Similarly, Unit 3 found that while low incomes are generally the most *immediate* cause of undernourishment in the UK, this conclusion had to be qualified: a fuller explanation would have to take more account of particular low-income groups who are especially vulnerable, such as single parents, the elderly, or people who are unemployed, sick or disabled. The effects of poverty are 'filtered' through gender, age, ethnic, regional and other differences, and ultimately (at the most basic level) the causes of poverty itself would have to be explained (e.g. in terms of discrimination of various sorts, or the inadequacies of state welfare, or the class structure of society).

'... SO YOU SEE, THE ENTIRE FUTURE OF THE INTERNATIONAL FINANCIAL SYSTEM HINGES ON YOUR CAPACITY FOR QUICK RECOVERY AND VAST ECONOMIC GROWTH.'

12 Thus, analysis of the various *food* issues has demonstrated some of the hallmarks of good scientific enquiry, pointing to *basic* as well as *immediate* causes and opening up further questions for investigation. For instance, the testing of the seemingly self-evident, even 'commonsensical', hypothesis that low personal incomes cause undernourishment in the UK showed that in general the lower a person's income the higher the proportion of it spent on food, and the lower the food's nutritional value. But it also led to qualifications about vulnerable groups and the nature of poverty which could be the basis for further hypotheses. Besides, higher incomes can sometimes lead to increased consumption of 'junk-food' or alcohol rather than to improved nutrition; and some forms of undernourishment (e.g. anorexia nervosa) are not necessarily connected with poverty at all. Thus, the proper investigation of even a relatively simply hypothesis opens up a number of further avenues for exploration, unlike taken-for-granted 'common sense' which tends to close them off or create blind alleys.

1.2 SCIENCE AND COMMON SENSE

Perhaps the most important lesson to be drawn from the first three units is that social science provides procedures for going beyond 'common sense'. Accepting ideas about society unquestioningly as 'simply common sense' is against the whole spirit of university study which is centrally about the questioning and exploration of ideas. 'Common sense' implies an uncritical acceptance of widely-held views and it tends to stop exploration in its tracks. The objection to 'common sense' is *not* that it is wrong. After all, the term covers all sorts of ideas, ranging from perfectly reasonable ones to 'half-truths', from opinions masquerading as 'facts' to unexamined prejudices and stereotypes which are completely mistaken (indeed 'common sense' is itself a 'common-sense' term, hence the inverted commas). 'Common' sense implies it is shared by everyone (or at least by all 'reasonable people'), or that they ought to agree with it if they don't. But what may be uncritically accepted as 'common sense' and propagated as 'the truth' by one group of people may seem to be 'nonsense' to other groups. There is usually more than one 'common-sense' answer to social questions, and the answers vary widely in their acceptability. However, in doing social science we cannot afford to accept *any* of them uncritically.

Widely held 'common-sense' views can be mistaken; even if they are not they are usually limited and limiting, and their underlying theories and assumptions are often hidden and unexamined. These are the basic objections to so-called 'common sense'.

For instance, social problems and developments are often 'explained' as being due to natural causes or technology, but we need to be very wary of such explanations. Nature is clearly important in food production; so is technology in the way production has been historically transformed. But Unit 1 showed that much more than technological developments was involved in this transformation — technology is in any case a product of society, and its application has to be understood in social terms, such as economic competition and the search for profits. Similarly, Unit 2 demonstrated why 'natural' explanations offer at best a very limited explanation of famine. It was pointed out that nature has been modified by human occupation, and that the effects of natural factors on a society depend on the character of that society and are 'filtered' through social structures. Simply accepting 'common-sense' ideas about natural or technological factors being 'the cause' of social problems or developments would limit investigation before it even got to the *social* causes.

Other 'common-sense' explanations do focus on social causes, but these too have to be questioned, just as Unit 2 questioned 'overpopulation' as the cause of famine. It found world food production has been increasing *faster* than population growth, and that there are famines in countries which are *exporting* food (as happened in Ireland during the Great Famine of the 1840s).

Rather than accepting widely-held 'common-sense' views, social science has to study them because they are socially important, as you will see when we discuss the *representation and reality* theme (in Section 2.1 below). And the challenge to social science is to use its scientific procedures to produce better explanations.

SOCIAL SCIENCE AND NATURAL SCIENCE

Despite big differences in its subject matter, the *basic* procedures of social science are the same as or very similar to those of natural science. Physics, chemistry and biology are what most people in our society take to be 'science' — the image is of laboratories with people in white coats. But the chemist who isolates particular chemicals in the laboratory uses the same sorts of thought-processes as the social scientist who picks out particular social processes for detailed analysis. Both use procedures of *abstraction, conceptualization,* and *classification,* and both have to relate 'the facts' to existing knowledge and broader *explanatory frameworks*.

As the French scientist Henri Poincaré pointed out: 'Science is built of facts the way a house is built of bricks, but an accumulation of facts is no more science than a pile of bricks is a house.' It might be added that 'an accumulation of facts' is about as interesting as a pile of bricks and as meaningful as an overdose of *Mastermind* on TV or an endless game of Trivial Pursuits. To make sense of facts, to make them 'live', we need explanatory frameworks, concepts, and questions. Building a house or constructing an explanation requires a plan or a theoretical viewpoint to help us decide *what* bricks or *which* facts to 'accumulate' in the first place. Putting them together into a construction which stands up requires following certain procedures. And (milking an imperfect analogy a little more) concepts and classifications are the details of the plan and the 'cement' which holds the construction together.

Before going any further it is worth noting the remark of the famous physicist, Albert Einstein, that science is 'a refinement of everyday thinking'. We use rather similar procedures in everyday life. They are not particularly mysterious.

In fact, we couldn't get by without them. Most of us are unaware of it most of the time, but we carry out investigations using concepts and evidence, and we construct explanations, simply to organize our daily lives. Consider, for example, your own thought-processes and procedures when organizing a shopping trip. You are probably not fully aware of them when you go shopping because you have done it so often, but they have a similar structure to scientific procedures.

GOING SHOPPING

To start with you probably make a 'shopping list' of what you are looking for; and you need to have some idea of where to look for the different items. You use *concepts* to describe different types of shops — newsagents, supermarkets, department stores — and you might also *classify* them in terms of the range of choice they offer, the prices they charge, or how easy or difficult they are to get to. From your existing knowledge, or simply on a 'hunch', you might pick out (or *abstract*) certain shops for a detailed investigation and ignore others. And rather than seeing individual shops in isolation, you might put them in *context* in terms of how far apart they are from each other, and on this basis decide to go to a shopping centre which has a variety of shops in close proximity. Even if you are shopping in an unfamiliar town or city, you will be able to *hypothesize* about where you might find the type of shops you are looking for; on the basis of your experience of shopping in similar places you will have a *'theory'* which tells you why the shops you want are likely to be located in a particular part of town.

When 'going shopping' you are continually bringing together factual information, concepts, and explanatory frameworks, to explain to yourself why you should go to certain shops or shopping centres rather than others. Most of the time this comes naturally and you don't even think about it.

But in doing social science you need to 'think about it'. The basic scientific procedures are not very different, but they are less familiar and it is necessary to have a critical awareness of them. Without this we wouldn't get beyond 'common sense'. The procedures, with the explicit treatment of theories and assumptions, are what make natural science and social science a *refinement* of 'everyday thinking'.

However, social science has important differences from natural science. It is sometimes compared unfavourably with natural science, but such comparisons are usually based on caricatures and fail to take account of the fact that in some respects the subject matter of social science is more *complex* and difficult to study.

Basically, it is more complex and difficult because of the differences between atoms, molecules and cells, on the one hand, and people in society on the other. People are less predictable and less reliable! Social science relies on them for its information, but they may not want to give it. They may value their privacy and refuse to talk about their incomes, beliefs, or family histories. To please interviewers they may 'make something up', or lay a trail of false information for motives best known to themselves. Private firms withhold information for commercial reasons, governments and others for political reasons; and for some important social issues the official statistics are either inadequate or non-existent.

Unlike atoms or molecules, people change their minds, or have their minds changed for them by other people or changed circumstances. Modern society is highly dynamic and there are continuing pressures which cause people to change attitudes and behaviour, often in unexpected ways. Predictions, an important feature of some branches of natural science, are therefore usually much more difficult to make in social science. And there is a further reason why they are often unreliable. The predictions themselves can if widely known cause people to *alter* their behaviour. For instance, it is sometimes said (and not just by the losers) that opinion polls predicting the results of an election have affected the actual outcome. Social predictions can become 'self-fulfilling prophesies'; or people, forewarned, can take steps to ensure they *don't* happen. So you won't find many predictions in D103!

Because it deals directly with the activities of thinking human beings, social science is in some respects closer to the arts than to natural science. People attach particular and often different meanings and values to the social events and processes in which they are involved, and social science has to interpret and understand *their* attitudes, beliefs and motives and how *they* see reality. As a social scientist, you have to understand how things appear from *their* viewpoint, irrespective of whether or not you agree with them. 'They', after all, could include all sorts of unsavoury characters or people with whom you have little in common. But to understand their motives and activities it is necessary to *empathize* with them, and this requires an imaginative ability to 'put yourself in the other person's shoes'. This is what writers have to do in creating fictional characters; and in having to interpret other people's attitudes and motives, social science has similarities to the study of literature.

Thus, social science faces problems which are very often different from those faced in natural science, and it has to work out its own methods for overcoming them. The greater familiarity of its subject matter brings particular problems, though it also has advantages. The familiarity can 'breed contempt' (though often this is simply 'common sense' fighting back as best it can!), but it is really a positive bonus as far as learning is concerned. It means that there are relatively few new terms which have to be learned; and studying can be more of a 'dialogue' with the course material than is generally possible when starting natural science. However, it also means that political and moral values, including our own values, impinge more directly than in natural science.

Because of the differences in subject matter, social science cannot be 'scientific' simply by applying the methods and criteria of natural science, attractive as that might seem given the great advances and prestige of the natural sciences. On the other hand, the differences should not be exaggerated as they usually are in common-sense caricatures. Natural science too is influenced by political and moral values, as we shall see in Unit 5. It too has theoretical disagreements; some branches have difficulty getting 'hard facts'; not all are predictive; and indeed the study of complex natural systems, such as the weather or ecology, has problems quite similar to those of social science.

SUMMARY

Units 1 to 3 demonstrated some of the methods and procedures which enable us to get beyond 'common sense'. They are basic for doing social science, irrespective of our different values or conceptions of society (to be discussed in Unit 5). The basic methods will therefore be discussed further (in Sections 2, 3 and 4 below). They are very similar to those of natural science. Although there are important differences, natural science is not as 'hard' nor is social science as 'soft' as popular caricatures suggest.

2 CONCEPTS AND THEMES

We all use concepts to interpret factual evidence; and (as you have seen in the Block Introduction and in Units 1 to 3) the course *themes* consist of pairs of concepts which are used to organize evidence and raise questions about social issues. The themes (*representation and reality, public and private,* and *local and global*) all point to social relationships and tensions in society. Why is some aspect of reality *represented* in such a way by one group and in a different way by another? What is the relationship between … the balance between … the conflict between … the *private* sector and the *public*; or the domain of the *private* household and the *public* outside it; or things which happen *locally* and more *global* processes? The pairing of concepts in the themes enables us to ask a large range of open-ended questions. In this way the themes begin to structure factual evidence but they don't predetermine the answers.

The themes will be used in a variety of ways through the course and they provide links between the different blocks. They can be defined in various ways and applied to different social processes. This exemplifies the more general procedure of *conceptualization* whose importance was emphasized in Unit 1. Social processes don't obviously 'demand' which concepts, or which themes, should be applied to them. The choice is ours and it will depend on *what sorts of questions we want to ask and answer.* As with all important concepts, the choice of which theme to apply has to be made with care, for although each theme is flexible it is only appropriate for certain purposes.

ACTIVITY 1

Pause for a moment. For what purposes were the three themes used in studying *food*? Jot down some examples of how each was used, how the concepts *representation, public, private, local,* and *global* were applied. What issues or questions were raised? (If necessary, you can check back to, for example, Unit 1, Sections 1, 2.1, 2.3 and 3.3; and Unit 2, Sections 3 and 4.4.)

Course theme	Examples of different uses	Issues and questions raised
Representation and reality		
Public and private		
Local and global		

Now you can compare your answers with the examples of each theme in the following sections.

2.1   REPRESENTATION AND REALITY

We saw (in Section 1.2 above) that the social scientist has to *empathize* with how other people think and feel in order to understand what reality means to them. How they see reality, how they interpret or *represent* it to themselves and to each other, is a central concern of social science. Social science is really a *re*interpretation of social events and processes which have already been interpreted by the people involved in them. And it is this fundamental characteristic of social reality which the *representation and reality* theme and the concept of *representations* helps us to analyse.

As individuals, we construct our own *representations* of the social world, partly on the basis of our everyday experiences. But our interpretations have also been formed by our family background, schooling, work and leisure experiences, the books we read, and the television we watch. So doing social science is an opportunity for us to reflect on our own interpretations or *representations* and where they have come from, and an opportunity sometimes for *re*interpretation.

Popular representations in society are often accepted as simply the 'natural' way to think about things; like much of 'common sense' they are unexamined, and the people involved are not always aware of their implications. But such representations are socially constructed, and sometimes for particular purposes; they are shared collectively by social groups, rather than being an individual matter, and they often reflect the particular interests of those groups. They are part of popular culture and are found in the mass media and in advertising. Advertisers, for example, often 'cash in' on popular views about particular products and social situations (a food product may be *represented* as 'homely', 'sophisticated', 'exotic', 'upper class', 'reliable', or 'healthy'), and in many cases they pick up and reinforce *stereotypes* (one-sided, distorted or exaggerated views) which they further exaggerate.

THERE WERE THESE THICK PADDIES........

Representations are contested, particularly the stereotypes which represent certain groups as 'inferior'. Not everyone laughs at 'Irish jokes' no matter how funny, just as Poles or 'Pommies' don't always laugh when the same jokes are told against them in Chicago or Sydney. The jokes and jibes are often funny and harmless; but they are not innocent and in some situations they can be very harmful and not at all funny. It depends partly on the social context and who is telling them. For instance, like other *representations*, they can be a means of trying to undermine the identity of ethnic minorities, 'scapegoating' them for society's problems and mobilizing actions against them.

From these few examples I hope it is clear that social representations are often only a very partial, and sometimes a highly distorted, view of reality, but that they can none the less be very significant socially. A particular *representation* may serve the interests or sense of identity of one group at the expense of others, and can be used to justify its actions. Studying *representations* is thus one way of gaining insights into different groups. Representations compete with one another to persuade and influence people. Some become dominant, some subordinate, and others get censored (e.g. in the media), reflecting the power or influence of different social groups.

Social science studies the social history of representations, as you saw with the picture of 'afternoon tea' in Unit 1. 'Quintessentially' or stereotypically 'English', it certainly did not reflect the 'power and influence' of the people of inner-city Birmingham or the moorlands of Northumberland, never mind inner-city Belfast, the Welsh valleys, or the Highlands of Scotland. We don't have much space for social history in D103, but when you meet different representations in later blocks it will help to remember that they do have interesting and revealing histories.

In Block II you will see that our views on health and illness are not simply individual matters of personal preference and private pain but are socially structured by various popular representations. Block III discusses different representations of the market, and the theme is further developed in Block V's investigation of personal identity and in Block VI's analysis of 'a sense of place' and how different places are represented.

2.2   PUBLIC AND PRIVATE

This theme can be dealt with more briefly. Unlike the concept of *representation*, the 'public–private' distinction is widely used outside of social science, and in several quite different ways. Some are close to 'everyday language' — we talk or read about *private* households, or *private* enterprise, or *private* charity; about *public* meetings, events and affairs, and about the *public* sector. This flexibility — the different usages and distinctions — underlines the point that the concepts are general ideas or 'labels' which for our own purposes we can choose to attach to a variety of aspects of social reality.

What examples did you remember from the study of *food*? What different definitions of *public* and *private* did you note down in the table in Activity 1? In discussing the historical transformation of food production and distribution, Unit 1 (Section 2.1) distinguished between the *private* domain of households producing their own food and the *public* domain of commodity production and the market-place. The *private* domain of the family and unpaid domestic work was differentiated from the *public* world of paid employment.

But Unit 1 (Section 2.3) also used 'public–private' in another quite different way when it discussed sugar production in the West Indies and how *private* multinational companies were nationalized and became part of the *public* sector under *public* control. The issue of *public* control is however much wider than nationalization or economic 'sectors', as you saw in the discussion of 'Free Trade'(Unit 1, Section 3.3). It involves the boundaries and relationships between the *state* (public) and the rest of society, sometimes referred to as *civil society* (private); and it applies to a whole range of economic, social and moral concerns, including, for instance, people's rights to privacy, the protection of young children, and women's 'right to choose' abortion.

As Unit 1 noted, 'Free Trade' was part of the wider social and moral doctrine of *liberalism*. In 1846, import duties were largely abolished after a political struggle by the rising manufacturing classes of industrial capitalism against the then more politically established land-owning and agricultural interests. Broadly speaking, liberalism stands for minimizing state 'interference' in society's affairs, and it will be discussed along with other *traditions of thought* in Unit 5. But here we can note that liberalism's distinction between *public* and *private* (which derives from Roman Law and is reflected in present-day legal distinctions between *public* prosecutions and *civil* proceedings) has long been a major organizing principle of society in the UK. Liberalism's concept of *state interference* can, as Unit 1 pointed out, be countered by views of state action as *protecting* and *enabling*, which are associated with other traditions such as *social reformism*. So issues revolving around the relationships and boundaries between 'state' and 'society' — how they have changed, and disagreements over what the balance *ought* to be — have a long history and feature in a wide range of contemporary concerns.

Blocks III, IV and VI discuss some of these issues in dealing with economics, politics and regional differences. The other main use of the public–private theme, to analyse relations between the *private* domain of personal life and the

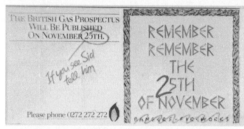

Public or private ownership?

household and the *public* world outside it, is featured in relating the private experience of illness to public health care, unpaid domestic work to paid employment, and personal identities to the wider society, in Blocks II, III and V respectively.

2.3   LOCAL AND GLOBAL

Again the concepts can be defined in different ways, depending on the scope or level of the analysis. Basically, this theme is used in analysing relations between social processes happening in a small (*local*) area and processes in the wider (*global*) society of which it is part. The small area could be very small, your own local neighbourhood perhaps, in which case the wider region, or the UK as a whole, might be considered 'global'. If, however, you were interested in the wider international connections of the small area, you might want to include the European Community, other parts of the world, or even the entire world system in the 'global' level. Conversely, if you were primarily interested in relations between the UK as a whole and its world context, the UK would be 'local', the world 'global'.

The appropriate use and definition of the concepts depends on the processes and interrelationships being studied.

What examples did you note from Units 1, 2 or 3? Unit 3 showed, for example, that shopping in your local supermarket connects you with global processes in the world economy. And Unit 1 showed that 'the making of the world economy' had very different effects at the 'local' level of individual countries. Different countries specialized in different types of production and imported things they had previously produced for themselves. As you saw in Chapter 1 of the Reader, Britain played an important role in the process; and the historical legacy of Empire and being 'the workshop of the world' has shaped the contemporary character of the UK itself — including the different character of its various regions and cities (e.g. port cities), for they too have been affected unevenly by developments at a more global or world level. Unit 2 followed up the question raised in Unit 1 about whether the 'First World' had 'exploited' or 'developed' the 'Third World'. It discussed some of the advantages and disadvantages of colonialism for the colonized countries; and the extent to which the 'First World's' domination of the world economy is a cause of 'Third World' famines. You saw in Unit 1 (Section 2.3) that it was in part the constraints of the global system which led to the failure of local sugar cooperatives in Jamaica; but, as Unit 2 (Section 4.4) indicated, the failures and famines in the 'Third World' are not caused simply by *either* global *or* local factors but by the historical and continuing interplay between them. Local factors such as the indigenous culture or internal strife play an important part, but these factors have in many cases already been shaped by more global processes (such as colonialism). And contemporary global factors such as international commodity prices and international debt continue to exert a crucial influence.

Social scientists specializing in these matters are generally agreed that global *and* local factors are both important, but there is no general agreement about which is the more important or about the ways in which they interact. This theme, like the others, raises lots of open-ended questions but does not predetermine the answers. In summary, it can be used at different levels of analysis for several related purposes:

* comparing local and global differences, to put the local in *context* and understand its particular character
* analysing how local processes are influenced and constrained by their global context

- analysing, conversely, how local processes have wider or more global effects
- seeing local processes as manifestations and part of global processes and how 'globalization' or 'internationalization' reduces local differences
- seeing the interaction between the local and the global as a historical process in which the effects of general global factors vary in different local areas because each local area has a different character to start with.

Social processes occur unevenly over time and space and their effects are uneven because of pre-existing local differences. This point is discussed at length in Block VI. In Block III, the *local and global* theme is applied to analysing the performance of the British economy in its international context; and in Blocks IV and VI it is applied to questions of national sovereignty in the UK and to relations with the rest of the European Community.

2.4 COMBINING THEMES

Between them, the three themes cover most of the important social issues addressed in the course. Mostly they are used 'one at a time', and, as with the study of *food*, each theme will be used heavily in some parts of the course and only marginally or not at all in others. But sometimes two themes can be used together in analysing a particular issue — for instance, the nationalization of multinational sugar companies discussed in Unit 1 can be analysed in terms of *public* and *private* and *local* and *global*. All three themes are rarely used together, but by way of summarizing them, and to suggest how they might be combined in organizing a discussion and raising questions, let's briefly discuss aid for famine relief, the advertising appeals and media coverage.

AID FOR FAMINE RELIEF

As you saw in TV 01, the topic involves questions about *public* aid from the government and charity donations from *private* institutions and individuals; about how famines are *represented* in the media and in appeals for donations; about the *local* situation in the famine areas (e.g. What 'triggered' the famine? Will the aid actually reach those most in need?), and about their position in the wider *global* order which makes them vulnerable to famines. As you saw in Unit 2 (Section 4.4), 'the flow of aid' is one of the links between our society and the 'Third World', and emergency famine relief has to be seen in the context of other forms of aid, not all of which are beneficial or altruistic towards the needy. Moreover, there are inevitably comparisons between poverty at home and abroad, and between competing claims on aid and altruism, while there are some interesting, and perhaps surprising, *local* differences within the UK in donations to *private* charity.

During the 1980s, the balance between *public* and *private* aid for the needy, both at home and abroad, shifted towards greater reliance on the private charity organizations. Their traditional role of *supplementing* state provision was in some cases transformed into one of *replacing* it, in areas where state support had been withdrawn or decreased. As you saw in Unit 3, poverty in the UK increased; and with rising international debts so too did poverty and susceptibility to famine in the 'Third World'. But the amount of *public* aid to overseas countries declined.

In *absolute* terms, the UK gave less in 1984 than in 1960 ($US1,578 million compared to $US1,605 million), despite the country's increased wealth. And as a *proportion* of the total wealth produced annually (its Gross National Product), the UK's overseas aid dropped from 0.56 per cent to 0.34 per cent between

1960 and 1984. In the USA, it dropped from 0.56 per cent to 0.24 per cent; and in Europe only a few countries showed an increase (e.g. Holland up from 0.38 per cent to 0.96 per cent, Sweden up from 0.06 per cent to 0.82 per cent).

With the increased reliance on persuading private citizens and firms to donate to charities there was more popular awareness of aid — through musical spectaculars, the involvement of rock stars and popular comedians, television appeals and the like — but perhaps less actual aid in terms of money. *Private* aid is difficult to measure — it comes from many sources and there are no overall figures available — but after all the appeals for Africa's famine victims in the mid-1980s it appears that the aid received in Africa actually declined. Indeed, there seems to have been a general disparity between increased publicity about and *representations* of people in need, and the amount of financial help which they were given. Some of the 'star' personalities involved, such as the Glaswegian comic Billy Connolly, came to see their voluntary efforts as 'double-edged': helping the needy but providing a 'smoke-screen' for decreases in government support. There was also a growing suspicion that the emphasis on private charity was connected with feelings of guilt in an era which celebrated private greed; but the main issue was whether *private* charity could ever make up for the inadequacies of *public* provision.

On the other hand, as Unit 2 pointed out, the government's overseas aid often comes with 'strings attached', which is less likely with *private* aid. It was questioned whether aid really helped poor countries escape the 'poverty trap', and here distinctions have to be made between: long-term aid which helps the needy to organize their own 'self-help'; short-term measures to deal with an immediate crisis; and loans or grants to 'Third World' governments to buy the donor country's products.

As for *private* charitable donations, *local* differences within the UK and Europe suggest that 'the poor give more'. Northern Ireland is the UK's poorest region according to various regional statistics, yet in some years it gave *twice* as much per person as Britain to the BBC *Children in Need* appeal on TV; and Ireland, one of Europe's poorest countries, far outstripped all others in its per capita

response to the Band Aid famine appeal. The contrasts with rich areas such as South East England were striking, and they hardly support the view that encouraging *private* wealth by reducing taxation for the rich (and reducing *public* resources for provision for the poor) helps the poor because money 'trickles down' to them from the wealthy. 'Trickle' may indeed be the appropriate word. It seems that the poor may get more help from people who are not a great deal better off than themselves.

But how far can we generalize from such regional comparisons? Firstly, not everyone is relatively poor in Northern Ireland just because in overall terms it is the poorest region. Secondly, giving to charity is much more than a matter of income. Short of launching a major research project, we can only speculate — and students and tutors in Ireland may be in a better position to do this than people in Britain — but does Ireland's own history of famine lead to a greater *empathy* with it elsewhere? Aid workers in Ireland report that the most typical individual donor is a middle-aged woman with children. Is the much more central role of religious institutions in Ireland a factor (though by no means all charities are church based)? Perhaps there are more direct *local* or 'grass-roots' links with 'Third World' countries through missionaries and clerics going there and coming back? Is belief in the 'welfare state' — and the idea that providing for the needy is a *public* or state responsibility — weaker than in Britain? Is there a 'culture' of giving to *private* charities which is part of the *local* identity and self-image, something to be 'lived up to'? Is the altruistic side of human nature conditioned by *local* culture?

These may not be the best hypotheses — you may think of others — and certainly they are not answers, but at least the topic of aid for famine relief has illustrated how the course themes can be used to raise questions and organize a discussion.

----------------------------------- ACTIVITY 2 AND SUMMARY! -----------------------------------

This is a 'DIY' summary — you'll learn more by doing it for yourself.

Look back at the notes you made in the table in Activity 1 about how the three themes were used in studying *food* issues in Units 1, 2 and 3. What changes, if any, would you now make to your answers?

(Optional extra: *If* you have been compiling a Resource File of contemporary cuttings on any of the six *food* topics suggested in the Block Introduction (Section 2.1), you could add a few of your own examples.)

3   CONTEXTS AND CLASSIFICATIONS

Putting events or processes in context improves our understanding, whether the context is very immediate or the wider historical and international setting. The first three units of the course demonstrated this by pointing to some of the historical and international influences on contemporary UK society. In beginning to *contextualize* the UK, they also introduced you to the procedure of *classifying* things into categories — the categories 'First', 'Second', and 'Third' Worlds, for example, and some of the problems which this simple classification system presented. Contextualizing various aspects of UK society is a major feature of the course, so we shall focus on it briefly to review the methods and problems which have already been demonstrated.

3.1   HISTORICAL AND INTERNATIONAL CONTEXTS

Unit 1 and Chapter 1 of the Reader pointed to the continuing influence of the UK's history on contemporary attitudes and problems. Some of them have a long history, and many developments since the 1970s, and the UK's multinational and multi-cultural nature, are incomprehensible without a historical awareness.

COMING HOME TO ROOST

The course therefore treats contemporary aspects of society as part of longer historical processes rather than presenting a static 'snapshot'. However, our treatment of history and of the international context is schematic rather than detailed. There is not space for much detail; and it is not history 'for its own sake' that we are interested in, but *contextualizing* today's UK. It will be signalled where that history is contentious — as in the issue of colonialism raised in Units 1 and 2 — but we don't have time in D103 to engage directly with all the historical debates (that is done in other Open University courses — see *After D103*).

The significance of an event or process usually depends on its context. For example, Unit 3 stressed *relative* poverty because the significance of going hungry in the UK rests on being surrounded by well-fed people — being better off on some *absolute* scale of food intake than famine victims in Africa is not very consoling for the undernourished in this country. Much of social science involves *contextualizing*, relating particular events or processes to other processes in the same place and time, but also moving backwards in time and outwards in space.

'What can they know of England who only England know?', to paraphrase Kipling, and for 'England' read 'the United Kingdom'. Comparisons backwards and outwards make us appreciate that what might seem 'natural' in today's UK society is in fact a social and historical construction, and in some respects a very particular one. They did many things differently in the past and they do them differently in other countries.

The international context has always been important — tenth-century Britain, for instance, was in many ways part of the Viking world. But 'internationalization' has proceeded apace in recent times. We are living in a 'shrinking' world and the individual state (certainly the individual state in isolation) is becoming much less satisfactory as a unit or level of analysis because many processes operate at an international or global level (e.g. food commodity marketing, the international debt crisis, the increased concern for the environment, and many aspects of culture and entertainment). In consequence, the boundaries between UK society and 'external' society are becoming much more blurred in all sorts of ways: you see it on TV, you have seen it with the 'British' diet, and you will see it in Block III with the 'British' economy, and in Block VI when you study Japanese factories and offices in Britain. The 'international' is now much more strongly *inside* the UK (and not just in the sense that Welsh, Irish and Scots nationalists consider relations with England 'international'). The traditional use of the term 'inter*national*', meaning relations between distinct and separate states or nations, hardly matches the more complex interlocking of the 'internal' and the 'external', the *local* and the *global*, in a modern society like the UK.

As you will see in Block IV, this has important consequences for the 'sovereignty' of the state, and not only in the sense of formal membership of the European Community. Internationalization means that states such as the UK are experiencing a vulnerability to global forces which once seemed to be confined to weaker 'Third World' countries. And internationalization has also generated counter-tendencies, such as attempts to preserve and revive threatened aspects of local culture, or a growing support for nationalisms. The sovereignty of the UK is under pressure from within as well as from without.

3.2 PROBLEMS OF CLASSIFICATION

In dealing with historical and international contexts, as with any factual evidence, we have to *classify* or group things into different categories. We group countries under various headings depending on their characteristics and we divide history into different periods, but the appropriate *classification system* and what should go in what category is always subject to debate.

In historical classification (or 'periodization') we often use years, decades and centuries as rough categories, but this is inadequate for many purposes. Social processes don't start neatly on New Year's Day, or in 1990; they don't end with the end of a particular decade or century. We have to find the appropriate 'turning points'.

For studying *long-term* changes we classify history in terms of broad eras, such as 'Feudalism', 'Merchant or Commercial Capitalism', 'Industrial Capitalism' (which don't have precise beginning and end points); we focus on 'the long nineteenth century' (1789–1914 — from the French Revolution to the First World War); we refer to the 'inter-war years' (1918–39); or the 'post-war boom' period from the late 1940s to the early 1970s. In discussing 'the making of the world economy', Unit 1 and Chapter 1 of the Reader took the 1760s as the starting point for the Industrial Revolution, because the 1760s saw the start of a period of economic growth, population increase and social transformation in Britain. If, on the other hand, we are dealing with *short-term* changes, the election of a new government (e.g. Mrs Thatcher's in June 1979) might be an appropriate starting point; and for some events and processes (e.g. an election campaign) the appropriate period may be a matter of months or even weeks and days. Furthermore, the same 'periodization' doesn't always apply in different countries or places.

———————————————— ACTIVITY 3 ————————————————

Some important 'turning points' in Welsh, Scottish or Irish history are different for each of these countries and also differ from 'turning points' in England's history. Can you think of examples? If in doubt, you can refer back to the selection of dates in Tables 1.1 and 1.2 of Chapter 1 of the Reader.

Constructing an appropriate classification system depends on our purposes and on our theoretical understanding of the processes involved. But all classifications have their limitations and some can mislead. For example, in the 1980s the government which had been elected in 1979 sometimes took 1981 as the starting point for economic growth figures: this conveniently left out the rapid industrial decline and sharp rise in unemployment in 1979 and 1980 and enabled the government to present its management of the economy in a better light. Whether or not you suspect 'foul play', you should always ask yourself what theories or purposes lie behind a classification system, what are its strengths and limitations. In using official statistics, we often have to work with classifications which are not really adequate for our purposes. Unit 3 noted that the information on the food consumption of different social groups is 'very limited, and very unsophisticated and indiscriminating in its organizing categories'. The categories may not fit our needs (e.g. 'tobacco' gets lumped in with 'food'; 'agriculture' includes non-food products); and in Block II, which is concerned with different aspects and explanations of class structure, you will see that the official Registrar General's 'social classes' are based only on people's occupations and do not take into account the ownership and control of factories and businesses. Classifications also vary for different times and places, which makes comparisons difficult. For example, statistics for Northern Ireland are sometimes presented differently from those for Britain (so the course sometimes only gives figures for the latter rather than the UK as a whole — and before 1921 Northern Ireland did not exist and the UK included the whole of Ireland). Another example is that, between November 1982 and July 1989, twenty-nine changes were made to the way 'unemployment' was officially defined (with the effect of reducing the official numbers). So in using factual evidence it is important to be aware of the definitions involved in classification systems as well as their purposes and theoretical bases.

The simple but useful three-part classification of countries into 'First', 'Second' and 'Third' Worlds in Units 1 and 2 shows clearly both the theoretical element and some of the problems of classification. The category 'Third World' for the world's poorest countries actually includes relatively rich 'newly-industrializing' states such as Singapore, plus oil-rich countries like Libya and Saudi Arabia which have *higher* per capita GNPs than some of the developed market economies of the 'First World' (including the UK, Ireland and Portugal). So it is often necessary to subdivide the 'Third World' into countries which export oil (OPEC) and those which do not (non-OPEC), and into 'newly-industrializing countries' (NICs) and those lagging further behind (sometimes now referred to as the 'Fourth World'). And should 'centrally planned' but 'developing' countries, such as China and Cuba, be classed as 'Third World', or 'Second', or both? It depends on our purposes and underlying theory. If interested in levels of economic development we might put them in the 'Third World' category; if interested in their internal political and social organization we might put them in the 'Second World' along with other centrally planned economies.

In these so-called 'communist' or 'socialist' countries (like China or Cuba) people work for wages as in 'the west', but production has been mainly publicly owned by the state and controlled by state bureaucrats. This is sometimes referred to as 'state socialism', or it is characterized as a form of *state* capitalism' in economic and military competition with 'western capitalism'. How such societies should be characterized and classified is further complicated by the changes in Eastern Europe which started in the late 1980s. The changes significantly altered the UK's 'European context'. 'Privatization' of state-owned enterprises and democratization in countries such as Poland, East Germany and Czechoslovakia mean they have to be *re*classified. Classifications often have to be revised in line with social changes, but how we characterize and classify, and how we choose between alternative classifications, depends on our theoretical viewpoint.

One of the objections to the simple three-part classification of countries, on top of its other limitations, is that it implies three separate 'worlds' when really there is *one interconnected* world. In contextualizing the UK it is the *interconnections* we are interested in, as you saw in Unit 2's discussion of different frameworks for understanding the world system — 'traditional–modern', 'North–South', and 'centre–periphery'.

──────────────────────── ACTIVITY 4 ────────────────────────

There are other ways in which the world is often divided up into major 'blocs'. Can you think of some? They could be political, historical, social, cultural, or economic; and some stress interconnections which might be useful when contextualizing the UK. Any ideas?

For instance, Block IV will use the political–military distinction between NATO and Warsaw Pact countries; and you might have thought of the Cold War classification of 'free' and 'unfree' worlds (*both* of which contain some nasty dictatorships). And there are cultural classifications in terms of religions, or English, French, Spanish, Arabic and other language groupings. In contextualizing the UK, a useful classification, highlighting historical and political interconnections, is based on the 'spheres of influence' of the major world powers (for example, the British Empire, now the Commonwealth), while in terms of dominant economic 'spheres' people now talk of the Japanese, the North American, and the European Community 'spheres'.

Of course, we continue to use rather crude classifications like 'Third World'; and we are often forced to use inadequate ones, like the Registrar General's 'social classes'. But we have to be aware of their limitations (which is why social scientists often put doubtful terms in inverted commas, or twiddle their fingers in the air when talking!).

SUMMARY

- Social processes have to be seen in the *context* of their immediate surroundings and their wider international and historical setting.

- There are different ways of interpreting their historical and international context: the appropriate *concepts* and *classifications* depend on our theoretical understanding of the processes, and on the scope or level of analysis and the detail of our studies.

- International influences have to be seen as *acting* within UK society, not simply as 'external' factors acting on it from the outside.

- Attaching *concepts* or general 'labels' to particular social processes or events and organizing factual evidence in appropriate *classifications*, together with *contextualization* and *abstraction*, are basic procedures in constructing even the simplest of social explanations.

4 CONSTRUCTING EXPLANATIONS

To understand particular processes and explain how they interact we have to *abstract* them from their wider context and analyse them in isolation from other processes. We have to pick out particular aspects of society for specialized or detailed analysis. This is what the five social science disciplines do when they focus on economic, political, psychological or other types of processes, and we can begin to discuss *abstraction* by looking at *disciplinary* specialization. However, as already indicated, the course is *inter*disciplinary and the disciplines are only one basis for deciding *what* to abstract — all five disciplines were involved in the *inter*disciplinary study of *food* in Units 1 to 3 but procedures of *abstraction* were used. You saw (in Section 1.1 above) that constructing explanations (e.g. of famine or undernourishment) involves a series of steps, starting with an initial question or hypothesis, and this is how *abstraction* is best understood. Although abstraction involves isolating processes from their wider context, it is complementary to contextualization because after the detailed analysis the processes have to be 'put back' in context to achieve a deeper understanding. So after looking briefly at disciplinary specialization (in Section 4.1), we shall illustrate some of the steps in constructing explanations (in Sections 4.2 and 4.3). Don't worry if you don't fully grasp what is involved at first. It will become clearer as you study the course, and you might perhaps find it useful to mark any bits you find difficult and return to them later.

4.1 DISCIPLINARY SPECIALIZATION

We can't study 'everything at once' so we focus on some processes and ignore others. We have to specialize, and the separate social science disciplines (described in the *After D103* booklet) are one basis for doing this. Most can trace their roots back to Ancient Greece and Rome and to developments in moral and political philosophy in the seventeenth and eighteenth centuries, but it was only in the early nineteenth century that the term 'social science' came into use, and only towards the end of the century that the different disciplines began to take their present institutionalized form (with university departments, specialist associations, journals and so forth). Basically, the disciplines separated out to provide the detailed knowledge and expertise on social matters which is needed in modern societies, as we shall see in Unit 5. While they continued to have much in common besides their shared 'pre-social science' origins, they also developed particular theories, concepts and methods as they specialized in particular social topics or aspects of society.

That is why Blocks II to VI are 'sponsored' (though not 'monopolized') by sociology, economics, political science, psychology, and geography respectively, unlike Blocks I and VII which are fully *inter*disciplinary. This structure allows us to devote four or five weeks to each discipline's particular set of concepts, methods and interests. But the common concern with understanding UK society means that the disciplines are involved in a cooperative venture and there are no clear-cut boundaries between them. This is illustrated in the table in Activity 5, which matches disciplines to topics. There are few topics which are unambiguously the 'monopoly' of just one discipline (and other disciplines are given in brackets to indicate that more than one discipline can be involved).

─────────────────── ACTIVITY 5 ───────────────────

You'll be studying some of these topics in later blocks. The last four you've already met — try matching disciplines to them.

Topics		Disciplines
1	The experience of black working-class women in the UK	Sociology (or Psychology)
2	State planning and the market	Economics (Political Science or Geography)
3	Democracy and voting systems	Political Science
4	Sexuality and personal relationships	Psychology (Sociology)
5	Global impacts on regional differences in the UK	Geography (Economics, Political Science or Sociology)
6	Internal nationalisms threatening the unity of the UK	Political Science (Geography or Sociology)
7	Poverty in the UK	?
8	The impact of internal wars on food availability	?
9	The advantages of certain countries or regions for producing particular commodities	?
10	How advertisers 'cash in' on people's personalities	?

Clearly there are large areas of overlap in the subject matter of the disciplines, and these will be reflected in overlaps between the blocks. How did you get on with topics 7–10? — fine if your answers were (respectively): sociology or economics; economics or politics; geography or economics; psychology or sociology. But given the overlaps, other answers might be as valid.

D103 is an *interdisciplinary* introduction to social science in general, and Blocks II to VI are *not* fully-fledged introductions to each discipline. There is space for only some of their characteristic concerns. It's not important at this stage to know all about each discipline, but you should look at the *After D103* booklet before embarking on more specialized courses in social science.

More important now is understanding the procedures of *abstraction* which are involved in any specialized analysis. Social reality does not come neatly parcelled up in discipline 'packages', and the procedures have to be 'tailored' to the actual issues being analysed, whether these are picked out on a disciplinary or interdisciplinary basis.

4.2   EXPLAINING BY ABSTRACTION

When 'going shopping' you concentrate on certain goods, pick out certain shops and ignore others. For example, I find that if I'm trying to buy a car my mind is 'full of cars'. I scrutinize them in the street and block out everything else. And if I'm looking for shoes, I see them everywhere and ignore other things. Not very 'scientific' perhaps, but the mental processes of *abstraction* in social science start in a similar fashion.

Even in the most aimless or unplanned 'window-shopping' we have interests and concepts to start with. The activity is rarely completely aimless, and as well as being 'pure entertainment' we pick up information 'by accident' which can be useful in later planned shopping trips. But in doing social science we can't afford the luxury of 'unplanned trips' or learning 'by accident'. To plan our investigations efficiently we need to define our questions precisely, and decide what sorts of facts are most relevant and how they should be *classified*. To come up with answers or explanations we have to follow various steps (and you might find it useful to check back to the summary list of twelve points about methods, and particularly point 10, steps (a) to (f) in Section 1.1).

We have to be aware of the *theoretical viewpoints* underlying different concepts, classifications and questions, because they shape our selection of evidence as well as how we interpret it. We need to keep an 'open mind' about what the answers might be, but that is very different from an 'empty mind'. An 'empty mind' couldn't even 'window-shop', let alone come up with a 'shopping list' of what to look for!

Among all the millions of social facts potentially available, we have to select the ones which are relevant to the question being addressed and ignore others. Social reality as we directly experience it appears to be very tangible or 'concrete', but it is much too complex to be understood as an integrated whole straight away. All sorts of things are 'happening at once'. To understand at least some of them we have to specialize, and, like the chemist in the laboratory, we have to mentally *abstract* some processes and analyse them more or less in isolation from their wider context. We have to 'get below the surface' of social reality and look at the relations between particular processes 'in depth', as Unit 2 did when it analysed the causes of famine. Then, having isolated these processes for analysis, we have to 'put them back together again'. We have to put them back in their context. In a sense, having taken reality apart to analyse how bits of it 'work', we mentally reconstruct it as a more integrated whole, in order to gain a deeper or more 'concrete' understanding of it.

Scientific *abstraction* therefore involves more than just 'picking out' processes. It is a method of analysis which on the basis of some prior theory or hypothesis abstracts particular processes and investigates their interrelationships in order to get a more concrete understanding of them. It involves a series of steps which (ideally at least) move from the 'abstract' to the 'concrete', as we can demonstrate by …

GOING FISHING

Forget for a moment that you are studying social science and imagine that you are a specialist in chemistry trying to catch fish in a beautiful freshwater lake. At first sight the lake is beautiful, but you discover that the fish have been poisoned by chemical pollution. You become a very annoyed chemist; your fishing trip is ruined and there is a serious possibility that people are being poisoned by eating the fish or drinking the polluted water. You decide to investigate the causes of the pollution and to do so you follow a number of steps:

First, you make the general observation that the lake is composed of water, which can be a liquid, a gas or a solid depending on the temperature, and that this may affect the concentration of pollutants. *Second*, you observe that the water in this particular lake comes from rainwater running off surrounding farmland. *Third*, you take samples of water from different parts of the lake and analyse them in your laboratory to discover what the pollutants are, how concentrated they are, and how they interact with each other. *Fourth*, you analyse the rain falling in the area and the water running off the farmland. *Fifth*, you compare the chemical composition of the lake water, the rain, and the run-off water. You find that, although the rain is polluted (it's 'acid rain'), the main source of pollution is the 'run-off' which has heavy concentrations of agricultural fertilizers. You have proved that these are the chemical cause of the lake's pollution.

You object to a local farmer but all you get is a tale of woe. Something about foreign wheat and beef being dumped on the UK, and the Common Market bringing in subsidies for fertilizers. He's not a 'poisoner', in fact he can now produce more food using less land and less labour. There's the wife and kids to support; there's the huge mortgage on the combine harvester; he has to make a living like everyone else. Without fertilizers he'd be bankrupt. He has to pay ridiculous wages since the union stirred up the farm workers — now the kids stay home from school for harvesting and the wife drives the combine harvester — and everyone knows that rents have gone through the roof since the Big Boys in the City started speculating in farmland.

You didn't know this. You are just a simple chemist and it all seems horribly complicated. The pollution clearly has causes which go way beyond chemistry. However, help is at hand. You have some friends who have just started an Open University social science course, and they have been talking about how food is produced. Apparently, a million tons of nitrogen fertilisers are applied to UK farmland every year and farmers have dramatically increased their use of potassium and phosphates. So you ask your friends to investigate the farmer's story and the social causes of the pollution.

Now switch roles and imagine you are one of those friends. How would you analyse the social causes? What might be the equivalent steps or procedures of abstraction to those the chemist used to find the physical causes?

1 First, you could make the general observation that the farmers are producing food in an industrial capitalist system in which capitalists employ labour, compete against each other in the market, and risk going bankrupt if they don't make a profit.

2 Second, you could observe that this is the contemporary UK: while most production is done by employees who work for wages, there are some 'self-employed' people (e.g. our farmer) and also unpaid labour (e.g. members of his family); and people not directly involved in production invest capital in it (e.g. financial institutions which invest in farmland). Production involves relations between different branches of industry (e.g. the fertiliser manufacturers and the farmers); and output is affected by the *public* policies both of the UK and the European Community (e.g. subsidies and quotas for agricultural products), as well as by the market competition of *private* capitalists, both *local* and *global*.

3 Third, having established some of the essential features of this 'mixed economy' (as the chemist established the essentials of the lake), the next steps would involve a detailed analysis of particular processes that are directly related to the increased use of fertilizers. For example, you would want to know how this increased use has affected the productivity and profitability of farming over recent years. You might look at the costs of farm 'inputs' (land, labour and machinery, as well as fertilisers) and the prices for the 'output' (wheat, beef, and so on). And rather than talking to just one farmer you might talk to a sample of them dotted around the lake, perhaps asking all of them a standard set of questions.

4 Fourth (if you had the time and money), you might investigate some of the other processes which relate, directly or indirectly, to the increase in fertilizer use, such as European Community policy on subsidies, the marketing strategy of the fertilizer manufacturers, the shifts in the international wheat and beef markets, the financial investors' interest in farmland, or the wage demands of agricultural workers. And you might analyse how the farmers and the other groups involved each *represent* their 'side of the story'.

5 Fifth, you would bring together your findings on the different processes and groups and reach a conclusion about the main cause of fertiliser increase.

Even if you didn't reach a definite conclusion (the social causes of pollution are much more complex than the chemical causes), you would have achieved a more concrete understanding of the social processes involved. You would have produced useful information for policy makers or environmental campaigners (see Unit 5); and you would have raised interesting questions for further investigation.

4.3 FACTS AND THEORIES

Constructing explanations involves combining concepts and theories with factual evidence. Facts and theories have to be seen as interdependent, as was noted in Section 1.1 of this unit.

Social scientists spend a lot of time accumulating or digging out factual evidence. As you saw in Units 1 to 3, most of the evidence needed in social science is not immediately available from our direct experience. We can directly observe individuals or small groups, although we have to ask them what *they* think they are doing and why, what it means to them and so forth. To understand what is going on we have to *empathize* with them, put ourselves 'in *their* shoes'. But we cannot directly observe larger social groups or classes, or processes in other times and places. We have to rely on other sources and various types of information (such as official statistics and reports, interview surveys, eye-witness accounts, or detailed case studies of particular examples from which we can draw more general conclusions). And we have to deal with some of the problems already mentioned of inadequate sources, or of the information being in a form which does not quite suit our needs.

———————————————— ACTIVITY 6 ————————————————

Quickly look back at 'going fishing', and at the third and fourth 'steps' in your imaginary analysis of why the use of agricultural fertilizers had increased. List some of the sources and types of evidence you might have used; and some of the problems which might be encountered.

In discussing differences between social and natural science (in Section 1.2 above) we noted some of the problems which stem from having to rely on other people for our evidence — they may withhold it or give misleading information. And in Section 3.2 it was pointed out that official statistics often use categories which do not really fit our purposes; and variations in the classification systems used in different periods or places make comparison difficult. There are important aspects of society which official statistics do not cover at all, including things which happen 'unofficially' (such as international trade by smugglers, as in the case of tea discussed in Unit 1).

In your imaginary analysis of the increased use of fertilizers you would undoubtedly have encountered at least some of these problems. They are widespread in social science. So 'getting the facts' is often like detective work, or investigative journalism; it involves sifting out information, piecing together different sorts of evidence, and checking and cross-checking sources which may or may not be reliable.

The 'accumulation of facts is no more science than a pile of bricks is a house', but nor do we find the facts sitting in ready-made piles for our convenience. Knowing what sorts of facts are needed is one thing, getting them another.

We need concepts and theories to know what facts to look for, and clearly there is a *two*-way relationship between 'facts' and 'theories'. The concepts and theories we start with help us to 'formulate' our questions and they suggest *what* facts to look for and how to interpret them. And the factual evidence in turn suggests *either* that the concepts and theories we started with can produce *explanations* which 'stand up', *or* that our concepts and theories are inadequate and need a major overhaul.

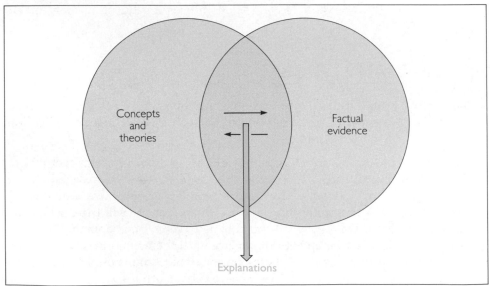

Figure 1 Theories and factual evidence combine to give explanations

The relationship is *not* a linear one where we start with 'the facts' and then develop a theory to explain them, as is suggested in some forms of 'empiricism' (see the *Glossary*). Rather, we start with some concepts deriving from existing explanatory frameworks and some particular question or hypothesis (as you saw in the analysis of the causes of famine), and then we collect factual evidence. The process is one in which theories and evidence 'overlap' and 'interact', and it is from this 'interaction' that explanations are constructed. This is summed up diagrammatically in Figure 1.

The limited areas of overlap in each circle indicate selectivity. Only some of the possible theories and concepts are used (and some of those excluded may have been explicitly rejected — as the theory about 'overpopulation' was largely rejected in the explanation of famine). And the theories and concepts which *are* used lead to selectivity in what evidence is included. Within the (shaded) area of overlap, theory and evidence are combined to produce an explanation of the particular question being addressed (e.g. the causes of undernourishment, the increased use of fertilizer), using the procedures of *abstraction* already described.

The 'interaction' between theory and facts which produces the explanation might appear to be a 'circular argument' — you start with a theory and end up with a theory — but it is much more than simply circular. Firstly, the evidence might disprove or call for major adjustments to the theory and concepts used. Secondly, the evidence may broadly confirm the theory but suggest further avenues for exploration. The investigation of undernourishment, for example, suggested that it was concentrated in certain vulnerable groups. The concept of 'poverty' was questioned, and we can also question the general concept of 'income' for it hides separate *forms* of income: profits and rents, as well as wages, salaries and state benefits. And that could open up the question (prompted by the imaginary investigation of farming) of whether there is significant poverty among small farmers: they have capital but it is 'tied up' in land and machinery; they have a job and they do not show up in the unemployment figures, but in bad years they sometimes show losses rather than profits for their work.

SUMMARY

To construct explanations we have to *abstract* particular processes for detailed analysis and bring together concepts, theories and factual evidence. Concepts and theories shape the evidence, and the evidence in turn may lead to the theory having to be *re*shaped. We start with theoretical ideas but constructing explanations is not a circular return to 'square one'. Our initial hypothesis may be disproved or proved with qualifications which lead to new and perhaps deeper questions. Scientific investigation is 'open-ended'. Disagreements about explanations are 'positive' in that they stimulate scientific enquiry; and our understandings of the social world are deepened by debates over theories, evidence and explanations.

Vulnerable to undernourishment? The investigation of undernourishment in Unit 3 suggested that it is concentrated in certain vulnerable groups.

5   CONCLUSION

We need to know how explanations have been constructed in order to assess their strengths and weaknesses. How do they use *concepts*? What are their underlying theories or *explanatory frameworks*? How appropriately has *factual evidence* been *classified* and how adequate is it? How have particular processes been *abstracted* for detailed investigation, and how have they been 'put back' in *context* to give a deeper and more *concrete* understanding?

We use similar mental procedures in everyday life as you saw in the 'going shopping' example, so there is nothing particularly mysterious about them. But in doing social science we have to be explicit about the 'tools of the trade' and subject them to critical scrutiny. Otherwise we couldn't get beyond 'common sense' and all its limitations. As you saw in the analysis of *food* issues and in the 'going fishing' story, social science employs procedures which are basic for all the sciences. But because of the particular characteristics of its subject matter, it has its own special problems and has had to develop methods for dealing with them.

These procedures and methods — and disagreements about different conceptions of society (see Unit 5) — will become more familiar to you as the course progresses. The review units in later blocks will build on the discussion of methods in this unit, and you yourself will use them in your 'dialogue' with the course material, in tutorial 'debates', and in writing TMAs. They are among the most important things you can learn from D103 for they can be applied to *other* social processes and events, whether in later courses or simply for understanding the world around you.

GOOD STUDY GUIDE

In preparation for writing your first assessed TMA in week 5, you should now turn to *The Good Study Guide* and read Chapter 5, Sections 1 and 2, on essay writing. Reading other students' essays and doing the Activities on them will help you improve your writing skills.

ACKNOWLEDGEMENTS

Grateful acknowledgement is made to the following sources for permission to reproduce material in this unit:

p.159: Oliphant/Copyright © 1990 by Universal Press Syndicate reprinted by permission of Editors Press Service, Inc.; *p.162:* Ian Kellas/*Thin Black Lines* (1988); *p.164:* Starrett/*Thin Black Lines* (1988); *p.166:* (both) John Sturrock/ Network; *pp.169 and 173:* Martyn Turner; *p.171:* Nicholas Garland; *p.178:* Syndication International; *p.182:* Andrew Yeadon.

UNIT 5 SOCIAL SCIENCE IN SOCIETY

Prepared for the Course Team by James Anderson

CONTENTS

1   EXPLANATORY FRAMEWORKS AND SOCIAL VALUES

This short unit continues the discussion of social science begun in Unit 4 and it introduces additional material which you will be studying in more depth from time to time during the course.

In Unit 4 we concentrated on some of the basic 'tools of the trade' for constructing social explanations. They are shared by people who have different viewpoints and values. All use *concepts* and *classifications* to organize and interpret factual evidence, and all use procedures of *abstraction* in picking out particular events and processes for detailed analysis. To gain a fuller understanding of particular processes they *contextualize* or put them in their wider social context and relate them to other processes. We saw that explanations are constructed by bringing together *facts* and *theories,* and that the concepts used to interpret the evidence may be based on different theoretical viewpoints.

But some important ingredients were missing. Unit 4 did not directly address the question of different viewpoints and conflicts in society. It didn't discuss the different conceptions of society as a whole or the broader *explanatory frameworks* which underlie different explanations. It ignored the fact that social issues are often matters of conflict — that people disagree because they are influenced by political beliefs or moral values, by what they think *ought* to happen in society, how they think people ought to behave or how they should be treated.

So now we have to consider how social science is influenced by these *social values* and by different explanatory frameworks or conceptions of society. These are the 'missing ingredients' which *Unit 5* introduces. The social values and conceptions — and the disagreements — emanate from contemporary society and from history, rather than from social science in isolation. Unit 4 for the most part dealt with social science 'in isolation' — we *abstracted* it from its context in society in order to concentrate on its basic methods — but now we have to begin to see it in its wider social and historical setting.

- Section 1.1 summarizes some of the disagreements mentioned in the study of *food,* and suggests how to cope with disagreements as a social scientist;
- Section 1.2 briefly outlines how social values influence explanations and disagreements about them;

- Section 2 gives a preliminary overview of four *traditions of social thought* which provide alternative conceptions of society;

- Section 3 relates their historical development to the history you studied in Unit 1 and Chapter 1 of the Reader; and

- Section 4 outlines the main functions of social science in contemporary society.

We have chosen to concentrate on four traditions — *liberalism, conservatism, marxism,* and *social reformism* — because they cover a broad spectrum of conceptions and viewpoints, and because they are major historical and contemporary influences in society and on social science. They embody and attach varying importance to values or ideals, such as 'equality', 'democracy', 'stability' or 'liberty', which relate to how society *is* organized and how it *ought* to be organized. They provide different conceptions of society and alternative explanatory frameworks which influence how people approach and explain particular social issues.

I.I DISAGREEMENTS IN THE STUDY OF FOOD

From your study of *food* issues it will be clear that social science often has to deal with controversial matters about which groups in society disagree. Being part of society, social science gets caught up in disagreements which typically involve political or moral values about 'what ought to be done', and related differences over the explanatory frameworks being used.

Unit 1 (Section 2.1) pointed out that quite basic concepts are often 'the subject of fierce debate' and are 'rarely neutral for they depend on wider theoretical viewpoints'. There was the choice for instance between seeing government action as state 'interference' *or* state 'protection' (Unit 1: 3.3), and of saying European countries 'developed' *or* 'exploited' other parts of the world. It was concluded that there was 'no simply neutral way' of telling the story of colonialism or of explaining contemporary relations between the 'First' and 'Third Worlds' — should their relations be seen in terms of mutual interdependence or domination and subordination? (Unit 1: 3.2). European governments with a previous history of colonial power and a contemporary priority to represent dominant interests in Europe usually subscribe to the former type of explanatory framework — and to the view that Europe 'developed' other parts of the world. In contrast, 'Third World' governments, and people whose main concern is for those suffering from 'underdevelopment', are more likely to opt for a framework which stresses the subordinate position of the 'Third World' and the continued control if not 'exploitation' by advanced industrial countries. The latter framework implies that the world system *ought* to be substantially reorganized to reduce the unequal position of the 'Third World'.

The adoption of different explanatory frameworks gives rise to disagreements about how particular occurrences, such as famines, are explained. As you saw in Unit 2 (Section 6), famines can only be fully explained in terms of 'broader pictures of the way the world is organized'. But which picture? You were given a choice of three — a world divided into modern societies and traditional ones with local obstacles to modernization; a world of unequal trading partners divided into North and South; or a world of core countries which had actively *under*developed the countries of the periphery. And you may have thought of other pictures: it was questioned whether we can really talk of whole *countries* doing things (except perhaps as 'shorthand') and it was pointed out that other theories would begin with important *social groups* inside the countries, such as British manufacturers, the financial interests in the City of London, the working class and landowners in the case of the UK (Unit 1: 3.2).

From these few examples it is clear that debates about different explanatory frameworks are necessary in social science; and I hope it will become clear that people disagree about explanations partly because they are influenced by social values and different viewpoints about what *ought* to happen in society (they even disagree about what the influence of values *ought* to be! — see Section 3.2, below).

COPING WITH DISAGREEMENTS

We have to analyse different viewpoints carefully — otherwise the disagreements become a barrier to learning and doing social science. We need an awareness of the values and conceptions of society which are embedded in particular explanations, and studying the four *traditions* is one way of developing this awareness. Initially the traditions are presented in relatively 'pure' form. However, as we shall see later, they manifest themselves in various 'mixed' or 'impure' forms and they pervade many areas of social concern, accounting for some of the disagreements within or about these areas (e.g., disagreements about the environment, or the position of women in society, or disputes within religious organizations). So, whether or not we are always aware of it, we have all been influenced by one or more of these *traditions*. Studying them is therefore an opportunity for you to reflect on the values and conceptions which you yourself bring to bear in assessing different explanations.

But it is also important to remember that social science involves much more than values. That is why we dealt first with basic methods in Unit 4. For instance, social scientists analysing undernourishment draw on different *traditions* for their explanatory frameworks, but they all use the same basic 'tools of the trade' for getting and organizing their evidence. And although disagreeing about how evidence should be interpreted, they can have a dialogue and learn from each other. Likewise, you too can learn from *other* viewpoints.

No one tradition or viewpoint has a monopoly on 'truth' or 'falsehood' and all can provide insights. Conversely, you should not necessarily accept an explanation whose values you happen to share — indeed if it seems defective you might be keen to reject it for it could give your position a bad name! You will not be *doing* social science if you simply accept or dismiss explanations because you sympathize, or don't sympathize, with their values. Particular explanations have to be assessed on their merits.

SUMMARY

In doing social science you will often be dealing with controversial issues and disagreements involving *values* and different *explanatory frameworks*. Some of these are embodied in the four major *traditions* and they influence how particular issues are explained. But in assessing different explanations we need to examine their methods and evidence as well as their underlying values and conceptions of society.

1.2   THE INFLUENCE OF VALUES IN EXPLANATIONS

Our views and explanations of existing social reality are inevitably influenced by our values or ideals concerning how things *ought* to be. To understand how values influence explanations, we can make a logical distinction between reality as we see it and the reality we would like. It is a distinction between what *is* and what *ought* to exist. The two things are often confused because they are closely connected, but we need the distinction in order to analyse *how* they are connected. It is a distinction you should remember when writing TMAs. Because explanations of reality are influenced by ideals or values, it is easy to lapse into simply saying what you would like rather than analysing and explaining what actually exists.

The values which we consider most important, what we *value* most — whether for example it's social equality or stability, personal advancement or a sense of community — and how we think they should be achieved, colour how we see the world and explain particular issues. The explanations which we produce, or which we find most acceptable and convincing, depend in part on what relevant things we value *most highly*. For instance, we may be influenced by a strong belief that poverty *ought* to be eliminated, or that taxes *ought* to be lowered, that society's priority *ought* to be protecting the environment, or strengthening 'law and order'. Our explanations may be influenced by how seriously we take various human or civil rights — 'the right to food and shelter', 'the right to work', 'the right to vote', 'the right to privacy'. People may believe in all these 'rights', and they rarely argue *against* ideals such as eliminating poverty or *against* values such as 'a sense of community' or 'social justice'. They value lots of things in principle. However, they do not value them all equally. Some values may be incompatible with others, or they may be consigned to an 'ideal world' which is not expected to arrive or might indeed be actively resisted. So in considering the influence of values on explanations, we are interested in general values which in practice are given *priority*, and particular values which relate directly to the social issues being studied.

For example, people give different explanations of undernourishment partly because they attach different priorities to the ideal of solving this problem. Some give a *higher* priority to other problems or ideals whose solution or achievement may conflict with an immediate solution to undernourishment. They may agree that it is morally wrong for undernourishment to exist when food is available, but they have different ideals about people's responsibility for their own welfare, about the responsibility of other members of the community, or what responsibility the state ought to take. Those who think that the state *ought* to provide a better safety-net of minimum incomes might well see state 'neglect' as part of the explanation for existing poverty and undernourishment. Alternatively, others think that state provision saps individual initiative and distorts the market economy, and that therefore it *ought* to be minimized; and they are more likely to explain problems of poverty as due to state 'interference' rather than 'neglect'. The different priority given to various social values or ideals, such as 'equality' or 'individual initiative', tends to result in different types of explanation. We would not really be surprised if we found, for instance, that people dependent on state assistance and people demanding lower taxes favoured different explanations of poverty.

Assessing how social values have helped to shape particular explanations can, however, be difficult. Firstly, the same general values or ideals are not defined in quite the same way in different *traditions of thought*, as we shall see; and they can mean different things in different social contexts. So we need to assess what is meant by terms such as 'equality' or 'stability' or 'freedom from state interference'. Secondly, the values embedded in explanations may be implicit or unstated and we have to 'dig out' the hidden assumptions about which values or ideals are most important. Thirdly, ideas about what exists and about what *ought* to exist are often very closely interrelated and mutually reinforcing. In debating different explanations we often have to go back to their initial assumptions in order to disentangle the values from their other elements.

Even so the role of values can be represented graphically. We can redraw the diagram 'Theories and factual evidence combine to give explanations' (Unit 4: 4.3, Figure 1) to include the 'missing ingredient' — values. In constructing explanations there are interactions not only between theories and facts: both also interact with values (Figure 1).

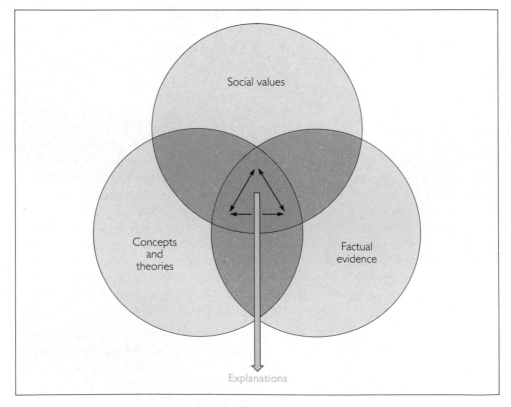

Figure 1   Values, theories and evidence combine to give explanations

The limited (shaded) areas of overlap in each circle indicate selectivity — of values, theories and evidence. The process of selection involves interactions between all three. Any particular explanation will reflect a particular mix of values and exclude or play down others. Their relationships with facts and with theories are *two*-way: values can be either reinforced or undermined by theories and factual evidence; and values influence the choice of theories and evidence included in explanations. The assessments or judgements made about facts and theories are influenced by social values. They are in part *value judgements*.

SUMMARY

Each person's particular mix of social values predisposes them to favour certain theories over others, and to judge some facts more important than others or to interpret them differently. Value judgements have to be made about facts and theories when constructing our own explanations and assessing those of other people. Explanations of existing reality are inevitably coloured by social values concerning how things *ought* to be and how they should be achieved. We need to study social values in their own right and understand where they have come from.

---

2 TRADITIONS OF SOCIAL THOUGHT

At one level our social values and conceptions of society are a personal matter. Our values reflect our particular personalities, backgrounds, education, interests, position in society, and so forth. But they also fall into certain broad patterns. Various social groups which share the same backgrounds or positions in society, for instance, tend to have similar viewpoints and make similar value judgements. More generally our values and conceptions have roots in earlier historical periods. There are very few contemporary moral, social or political issues which are entirely new. The issues may arise in new social contexts but most of the important questions about society — about how it *is* organized and how it *ought* to be organized — have been thoroughly dissected and debated in the past. A wealth of different ideals and conceptions of society has been handed down to us by the world's great religions, by a stream of philosophical writings since ancient times, by storytellers oral and literary, by travellers, politicians, historians and others, and by social science itself. It is an amazingly rich heritage of views about the human condition.

Some of this heritage is encapsulated in the traditions of *liberalism, conservatism, marxism* and *social reformism*. They contain influential assumptions about human nature and the individual's place in society, about how human society develops and how social order should be maintained. While sharing some values, each tradition gives them different emphases, or defines them in different ways, and integrates them into different explanatory frameworks. The values are broadly social and moral rather than narrowly political. We are primarily interested in the traditions as *intellectual* traditions which social science can and does draw on to help make sense of society. They provide us with alternative conceptions of society and a range of ideas about how best to study and understand it.

Each *tradition* is fully discussed in the chapter which forms Part 2 of the Reader. But this long chapter is meant to be studied in easy stages, a section at a time over the first five blocks of the course. Therefore we will briefly introduce all four traditions here in a preliminary overview which describes their main charcteristics, before you embark on a more detailed study of each of them.

—————————— ACTIVITY 1 ——————————

As you read the description of each *tradition* in the preliminary overview you can reflect on your own viewpoint. Note down your responses to the material as you read it (e.g., note where you 'agree' or 'disagree' with each tradition's conceptions and emphasis on particular values). Doing this will help you to clarify your own values and conceptions, and also prepare you for the next Activity.

2.1 LIBERALISM

Accounts of society in the *liberal* tradition (for brevity referred to collectively as liberal*ism*) take as their starting point a conception of society which sees it as composed of self-interested individuals. Human nature is generally assumed to be constant, though different writers vary in their estimations of the selfishness or altruism of the individual. The *liberty* or freedom of the individual from state 'interference' in the market place is one of liberalism's central values, as you saw in the discussion of 'Free Trade' (Unit 1: 3.3); and the emphasis on liberty from what it sees as arbitrary action by the state, the church, and other established institutions or collective groups, is applied to other *freedoms* and *rights*, such as freedom of religion, or of the press, rights to privacy, and equal rights in law irrespective of religious or political beliefs (see Gray, 1986).

John Locke, 1632–1704: English philosopher and one of the founders of the liberal tradition, he wrote *Two Treatises on Government* (1690)

In economic matters, liberalism sees market competition between individual private companies and reliance on the price mechanism as the best way of allocating material resources and ensuring prosperity and *progress*. Conversely, 'interference' from the state, or from the actions of collective groups such as trade unions, or 'price-fixing' cartels of companies, are generally seen as the cause of economic problems. Where state intervention is required (e.g. to provide 'public goods' such as transport systems or education which would not otherwise be available), it should be based on general and impersonal rules, rather than the discretion of politicians or bureaucrats, because this is open to corruption and also means that all the individual decision makers in society cannot 'know the rules' in advance.

Liberalism generally believes that individuals know their own interests best and that collective institutions (particularly the state and trades unions) hamper individual initiative. Individuals should get rewards for initiative and suffer penalties for failure. Liberalism prefers the minimum of state involvement (except in defence and 'law and order' which ensure the freedoms of the market), and it tends to favour regional and local levels of government rather than a strongly centralized state (Hallett, 1973, p.16).

While liberalism recognizes that society is divided into various groups and classes, its explanations focus on individual decision makers. With this distinctive approach (sometimes referred to as 'methodological individualism') liberalism explains social issues in terms of the decisions and actions of individuals, or of groups and institutions treated as if they were 'individuals' (e.g. individual companies, or individual pressure-groups).

2.2 CONSERVATISM

This tradition also sees people's human nature as constant, innate or 'God-given', but stresses its imperfectability and its variability from person to person. Conservatism therefore concludes that inequalities and a hierarchical order are inevitable in human society. It does not share liberalism's enthusiasm for *progress*, stressing instead the importance of social continuity and stability. It does not have such a well-developed methodology; and, although it does not have such a strong aversion to state involvement in the economy, it now gets most of its economic views from liberalism.

Edmund Burke 1729–97: Irish politician who supported the American War of Independence (1776) but developed some of the basic principles of conservatism in opposition to the French Revolution.

However, conservatism starts with a very different conception of society as a whole, seeing it as a historically evolved 'organism' made up of different social orders or classes. The 'organism' is delicate and social stability has to be maintained by leadership and discipline, and by long-established (or apparently long-established) social institutions such as constitutional monarchy, the church and the family. Conservatism emphasizes the need to *conserve* the social 'organism' and to oppose the disruptions of rapid or large-scale changes.

Initially it opposed the disruptive advent of industrial capitalism which liberalism had embraced. It was first codified in opposition to the French Revolution of 1789 — Edmund Burke's *Reflections on the Revolution in France*, 1790 — though it had earlier roots in 'The "old moral order" of traditional deference in small communities where the old classes lived close together and everyone, supposedly, knew their place...' (Unit 1: 2.2).

Thus conservatism cherishes the values of social continuity and established custom; of reciprocal duties and obligations between the different social orders — respect for authority, the higher orders helping the lower; a sense of community, patriotism and nationhood (see Nisbet, 1986). Social problems therefore tend to be explained in terms of the erosion of these values, and the undermining of institutions such as the church and the family by subversive ideas or disruptive social changes.

2.3   MARXISM

In contrast, thinkers in the marxist tradition generally explain social problems as an outcome of the way existing society is organized into social classes which have different and conflicting interests. Marxism sees disruptive social changes as inevitable in capitalist society because of its dynamic and conflict-ridden nature.

It defines social classes in terms of people's different relationships in the production system (e.g. owners and controllers of capital, the employed workforce, intermediate groups such as managerial staff). Capitalism (like other class-divided societies) is seen as based on the exploitation and oppression of subordinate classes and groups. They constitute the great majority of the population and produce most of society's wealth. But employed workers have no democratic control over what they produce; production priorities are determined by the profit motives of employers rather than democratically according to the human needs in society; and there are built-in tendencies towards economic and political crisis. Genuine democracy simply is not poss-

Karl Marx, 1818–83:
his writings include
The Communist Manifesto
(with Engels, 1848) and
Das Capital (1867)

ible in a society divided into exploited and exploiting classes. The state acts mainly on behalf of the dominant or 'ruling' classes and is an essential institution for maintaining the class system and the exploitation of workers (see Callinicos, 1983).

Exploitation, and the competitive rivalries between different capitalist interests, are seen as continually recreating or preventing any real solution to a whole range of social problems (e.g., poverty in the midst of plenty, racism and women's oppression, mass unemployment, the waste associated with war). Marxism therefore concentrates on the need for workers to end their own exploitation. For Marx, socialism meant 'the self-emancipation of the working class' and a class*less* society in which it would be possible for people to achieve their full human potential — an ideal which no modern society has (yet?) come anywhere near to realizing in practice.

Marx assumed that people's human nature is shaped by their experiences and circumstances, and that it is therefore improvable by the people themselves changing their circumstances. Like liberalism, marxism has a well-developed methodology (sometimes called 'historical materialism'). It stresses that historical developments involve conflicts between different classes and that human actions are constrained by pre-existing social structures. To paraphrase Marx, 'People make their own history but not in circumstances of their own choosing'.

2.4   SOCIAL REFORMISM

Social reformism tends to see society as composed of a multiplicity of different institutions and 'interest groups' with the state acting essentially as a 'referee' to manage the conflicts which arise. It tends to explain social problems in terms of the complex and changing nature of modern industrial society, inadequacies in state policy and other institutional arrangements, and the need for social reform (see Kavanagh and Morris, 1989).

John Maynard Keynes, 1883-1946: wrote *The General Theory of Employment, Interest and Money* (1936) which supported state regulation of the economy and justified 'full employment' policies after the Second World War.

Unlike marxism and liberalism, social reformism does not have a strongly developed and unified methodology of its own, and it draws on the other traditions in widely varying proportions. Like marxism, it assumes that human nature varies with social circumstances and that it can be improved by better social conditions and education; but many of its explanations are constructed using liberalism's 'methodological individualism' (see Section 2.1 above). However, unlike liberalism, it believes that state intervention can be very beneficial. Capitalist society can and should be improved by reforms instituted by the state. Private enterprise has to be publicly controlled by state regulations and supplemented by state welfare provision, and the state may have to own and manage some parts of industry in the collective interests of society as a whole.

Many of the values cherished in social reformism, particularly those relating to the political and legal rights of individuals, are taken from liberalism; but social reformists (especially those influenced by marxism) also emphasize economic rights and the need to reduce economic inequality. They believe that the 'mixed economy' of state regulated private capitalism, and partial progress through gradual reform, offers the best hope for society. Liberals, however, would retort that state 'interference' is a cause of economic problems rather than a solution to them; and marxists, while supporting reforms which benefit the working class, would criticize gradual reform as merely tinkering with the symptoms rather than removing the basic cause of social problems.

2.5   USING THE TRADITIONS

In using these *intellectual* traditions as explanatory frameworks it is important not to confuse them with political parties or regimes which adopt similar 'labels'. Political organizations often propagate views or act in ways which have little or nothing in common with the traditions they claim to represent. For example, the ideals and methodology of Marx should not be confused with political regimes whose official state ideology has proclaimed them to be 'marxist'. Most contemporary marxists do not accept that the legacy of Stalin's Russia has much in common with what Marx advocated or with the original ideals of the Russian Revolution. They disagree about why the ideals were subverted and how to classify authoritarian centrally planned economies ('state socialist' or 'state capitalist'? — Unit 4: 3.2). But as we shall see (Section 3.1, below), Marx wanted the state to 'wither away' whereas under Stalinism the exact opposite happened. Some of the economic and democratic reforms introduced since the late 1980s are seen as having more in common with *social reformism* or *liberalism* than with marxist ideals of democracy and how the economy should be controlled by the people who actually produce the goods and services. Political regimes and parties often distort traditions or involve a mixture of different ones. In the UK, for example, the post-war Conservative Party combined *conservatism* and *social reformism* until the latter was largely displaced by *liberalism* under Margaret Thatcher's leadership in the 1970s — the so-called 'New Right' (sometimes referred to as 'Thatcherism' and discussed later in the course) is an uneasy combination of *liberalism* and *conservatism*.

To appreciate the traditions as explanatory frameworks for understanding particular social problems, we have to ignore the mixing and distortions of them in the realm of party politics and concentrate on their basic conceptions of society. These are summarized in Table 1 so that you can refer back to them easily.

Which conception of society did you find most convincing? To get a preliminary feel for how the *traditions* influence explanations, consider again the general problem of *poverty and undernourishment in the United Kingdom*. How might the different traditions go about explaining it? Take the tradition which you find provides the best explanatory framework and note down what sort of explanation it leads to. Concentrate on the *causes* which might explain the problem (rather than on solutions to it), referring to the rows on 'human nature', 'society' and 'economy' in Table 1.

SUMMARY

Table 1 Four Traditions: A summary of characteristic views and values

Traditions	Liberalism	Conservatism	Marxism	Social Reformism
Human Nature	Generally seen as constant, though different writers put more stress on the selfishness or altruism of individuals.	Human nature imperfect and varies from person to person. Inequalities are innate, and hence inevitable in society.	People can change their nature depending on social circumstances and their own activities.	Human nature varies with social circumstances and can be improved by better social conditions and education.
State and Society	Society composed of individuals born with rights which the state should protect, but also respect by keeping its interference in social life to a minimum. Stress on freedoms of speech, religion, the press, etc; and on 'state interference' as a cause of social problems.	Society a historically evolved organism held together by leadership and discipline, institutions such as the state, the church and the family, and by the shared customs and traditions of 'community' and 'nation'. Social problems are due to the erosion of these institutions and traditions, and the undermining of mutual obligations and duties.	Capitalist society is inherently unstable because of the conflicting interests of its different social classes. As in previous class-divided societies the state is an organization for the control of society by the dominant class. Social problems are due to class domination and conflict.	Society composed of a variety of institutions and social groups. They pursue their own interests with the state acting essentially as a 'referee' to manage conflicts which arise. Social problems are due to the complex and changing nature of modern society and inadequate institutional arrangements.
State and Economy	Competitive markets with minimal involvement by the state and other collective groupings such as cartels and trade unions, are the best means of allocating resources and ensuring economic growth.	Similar views to liberalism, though with less opposition generally to state involvement.	Production in capitalism is for profit; it ought to be according to people's needs. Workers who produce society's wealth ought to have democratic control over what to produce.	Private enterprise has to be publicly controlled by state regulations; and supplemented by state welfare provision and, where necessary, by state-run industry.
Social Change	Markets ought to be liberalized if distorted by collective institutions such as the state. Individual initiative should be rewarded and failure penalised.	Continuity is more important than change. Change where necessary ought to be managed by strong leadership.	Radical changes required to achieve the ultimate goal of a classless society in which the oppressive state is no longer necessary. Class struggle by workers and other subordinate groups.	Change ought to be gradual and managed by the democratic state.

To assess particular explanations we would have to examine their methods and evidence. But, prior to that detailed examination, we would probably form some judgements on the general framework or approach adopted. A *conservative* approach to explaining poverty and undernourishment in the UK would typically focus on the undermining of traditional institutions and values, such as the family, religion, or a sense of mutual obligation between the members of the community; it might also focus on the 'inevitability' of social inequalities because of innate differences in human nature. *Marxist* explanations would focus on the direct and indirect effects of class exploitation and oppression; on production being for profit rather than need; on capitalism's tendency toward economic crisis, and on members of the working class being the main sufferers.

Social reformists typically would explain undernourishment in terms of the safety-net of state assistance not being adequate to counter the inequalities of the market; and they might focus on the breakdown of various institutional arrangements, such as the non-take up of benefits to which the poor are entitled. *Liberal* explanations, on the other hand, would focus on state interference, seeing it as distorting the workings of the market, sapping individual initiative and leading to lower levels of prosperity; and they might also blame collective action by trade unions for interfering in the labour market, forcing up wage levels and leading to people being 'priced out' of work.

3   SOCIAL THOUGHT IN HISTORICAL CONTEXT

The *traditions* developed historically in response to developments in society as well as in competition and interaction with each other (Section 3.1). They are part of the 'pre-history' of institutionalized social science as well as contemporary influences on it, though some social scientists have sought to minimize their influence (Section 3.2).

3.1   THE DEVELOPMENT OF THE TRADITIONS

Their development can be related to the revolutionizing of society with the rise of merchant capitalism and then of industrial capitalism which you studied in Unit 1 and Chapter 1 of the Reader (referring to Tables 1.1 and 1.2 in Chapter 1 will help you to locate the traditions historically).

Liberalism, with its revolutionary ideal of *individual liberty* from the religious and political controls of feudalism and all-powerful monarchs, developed along with merchant capitalism. It was part of the European *Enlightenment* which rejected the largely religious interpretations of society and nature dominant up

Adam Smith 1723–90: wrote
*An Inquiry into the Nature and
Causes of the Wealth of
Nations* (1776)

to the *Renaissance* and *Reformation*. The *Enlightenment* stressed rational thought over superstition and religious dogma, and it saw human history as a story of *progress*, in contrast to earlier notions of society as 'static' or social change as merely 'circular'.

The emphasis on the individual raised questions about *human nature*, and in seventeenth and eighteenth century *liberalism* we can see the beginnings of modern psychology, politics and economics. For instance, the English philosopher, John Locke, argued that people were born with *individual rights* rather than being granted them by church or state — the state's role *ought* to be the protection of individual rights and liberties. The Scottish philosopher and political economist, Adam Smith developed a powerful argument that state involvement in the economy *ought* to be kept to a minimum and that private individuals trading in the market without state 'interference' was the best way of ensuring 'the wealth of nations'.

As we saw in Chapter 1 of the Reader, the development of industrial capitalism transformed the structures of power as it transformed the system of production. With the 'Repeal of the Corn Laws' (1846) the rising manufacturing classes of the cities won an important victory for *liberalism* and 'Free Trade' over the old-established landed classes (Unit 1, Section 3.3).

Marxism developed in this context, as a response to industrialization, to *liberalism* and to the French Revolution of 1789. Karl Marx and Friedrich Engels, both Germans living in England, took up the *Enlightenment* belief in *progress* even more enthusiastically than liberalism.

According to them, the French Revolution's promise of 'liberty, equality and fraternity' could not be delivered in a class-divided society based on exploitation. Whereas *liberalism* saw the state as protecting the rights of individual property-owners and employers, Marx and Engels saw it as an oppressive organization set above society to maintain class rule — 'the dictatorship of the bourgeoisie' — but an oppressive organization which *ought* to 'wither away' with the development of an egalitarian and democratic socialist society. They

Friedrich Engels, 1820–95: close collaborator with Marx, in 1844 he published *The Condition of the Working Class in England* (based on Manchester where his family were cotton manufacturers).

accused *liberalism* of accepting gross economic inequalities in the sphere of employment and material *production*, and of being concerned only with *legal* equalities, especially those relating to contractual relationships of *exchange* in the market.

However, they drew on *liberalism* for their analysis of capitalism. This exemplifies the important point that we can often learn from *traditions* and explanations with which we disagree. It was Adam Smith who had introduced the concept of *social classes* into British political economy; it was he and other *liberals* who developed the 'labour theory of value'. Smith's concept and theory were taken up by Marx and Engels and transformed into central elements of their analysis (Roll, 1973, pp.154–64). The *liberals* had established that human labour (rather than land or trade) was the basic source of wealth (or 'value') in society, the relative prices of different goods in the market place being basically determined by how much labour it took to make them. But this *solution* to the problem of how prices were determined was for Marx and Engels the central *problem* of capitalism: workers produce more in value than they are paid in wages (the price of their labour), and this results in the exploitation of 'surplus value' from workers (the difference between the value of their wages or salaries and the value of what they produce). This was the means by which capitalists expropriated the wealth collectively produced by the working class (the 'surplus value' appearing in the form of profits, rents on property used in production, and the interest payments). Marx and Engels concluded that workers had a direct material interest in ending their own exploitation. Their slogan should be: 'Expropriate the expropriators'. With industrialization they now produced most of society's wealth and by establishing collective and democratic control of production the working class could unlock, for the good of humanity, the tremendous wealth-creating potential which industrial capitalism had made possible.

John Stuart Mill (1806–73): philosopher, economist and active political reformer, his writings included *Representative Government* (1861)

However, while *marxism* presented a strong intellectual challenge to *liberalism*, it was itself to face a strong practical challenge for workers' support from *social reformism*. This tradition emerged from the 'crisis of liberalism' and a more interventionist 'new liberalism' in the latter part of the nineteenth century which drew on the ideas of John Stuart Mill. There were growing doubts about 'Free Trade' from the 1870s as Britain's supremacy in world markets was increasingly challenged by new industrial powers. Other states such as Germany gave more assistance to industry and protected it from foreign (most notably British) competition. A split developed in *liberalism*, the financial interests in the City of London wanting to retain 'Free Trade' while the 'Tariff Reformers' in manufacturing centres like Birmingham wanted state protection (Unit 1: 3.3).

Support for non-intervention was also weakened in the field of social welfare. *Liberalism's* doctrine of not 'interfering' in the market had already meant that during the Irish Famine in the 1840s grain continued to be exported from Ireland rather than being used to feed the starving population — the 'fetish of free trade' tied the British government's hands (Edwards and Williams, 1956, pp.256–7). The appalling squalor in working class areas of the large cities had been publicized in various surveys, and belief in leaving the provision of work-ers' housing and water supply to private enterprise and the market was tem-pered by middle class fears that the squalor would lead to epidemic diseases and to social upheaval. From workers themselves there were growing demands for state welfare provision and these became more effective when most male workers achieved the right to vote in 1884. The 'liberal' state was transformed into the 'liberal democratic' state, and mass political parties were created, based or drawing substantially on workers' support (Chapter 1 of the Reader). There was a struggle for their allegiance between *marxism* and *social reform-ism* which the latter won decisively in the case of the British Labour Party. Its *social reformist* policies owed most to two 'new liberals': John Maynard Keynes, the main 'architect' of the state-regulated 'mixed economy' which characterized the UK after the Second World War; and William Beveridge who prepared the ground for the 'welfare state'.

William Beveridge, 1879–1963: wrote *Social Insurance and Allied Services* (1942), a basis of the post-war welfare state.

=== READER ===

To see in more detail how the fourth tradition, *conservatism*, developed, turn to section 2.4 of the Traditions chapter of the Reader.

You will see how *conservatism* emerged as a reaction against the social turmoil and class conflict unleashed by industrialization. Class conflict was dramatized in the French Revolution against which Edmund Burke established the conservative position. You will also meet Benjamin Disraeli who established 'One Nation' conservatism in an industrialized society, and you will see how conservatism was subsequently developed.

Benjamin Disraeli (1804–81): novelist and British Prime Minister, he helped establish the 'One Nation' conservative tradition in a society already industrialized.

This is an opportunity to practice your note-taking skills. As you read, note down the characteristic views and values of conservatism. You can then compare your notes with the brief summary of conservatism in Table 1 — and see what you can add to it.

3.2   'VALUE FREE' SOCIAL SCIENCE?

The *traditions* are part of the 'pre-history' of institutionalized social science and they continue to have profound though uneven influences on it, as you will see when you study other sections of the Traditions chapter with later blocks. However, some social scientists have been unhappy about the continuing influence of these traditions, and with the viewpoint (expressed in Unit 1: 3.2) that it is impossible to explain contentious social issues in a 'simply neutral way'.

The contrary viewpoint, that social science could and should be 'neutrally objective' or 'value free', developed with the emergence of social science disciplines in their present institutionalized form towards the end of the nineteenth century (Unit 4: 4.1). Some people saw social values as intrusions which should be minimized or excluded from 'scientific' enquiry. They hoped that excluding values — excluding questions about how society *ought* to be organized which concerned the earlier moral and political philosophers, and which are now encapsulated in the *traditions* — would give social science the authority and social standing of natural science (which was assumed to be 'value free', having been, since the time of Galileo, slowly disentangling itself from religious interpretations of nature). Social science should study 'the facts' of existing society. Possibly dangerous speculation about how society *ought* to operate could be 'ruled out of court' as not 'scientific'. And as social science became more involved in policy-related research for powerful institutions, the idea that its findings were 'scientific' (i.e., like natural science) lent them (and the institutions) the authority of 'objectivity'. It implied that they were above moral and political questioning and had to be accepted as 'the truth'.

The advocacy of 'value free' social science, and the exhortation that scientists should study 'the facts' and exclude value judgements, is sometimes referred to as 'positivism'. Its development can be looked at favourably as part of the effort to establish a modern social science firmly based on factual evidence. It was a reaction against 'over-opinionated' (or 'under-evidenced') accounts of society, and the danger that strong moral or political values can make us blind to evidence which does not fit in with them — a real danger we all need to guard against. However, as has been emphasized in this block, 'the facts don't speak for themselves', they are selected and interpreted in the light of theories and explanatory frameworks, and this involves making value judgements (see Section 1.2, above). The unfavourable view of positivism is that it has a very narrow and limiting idea of what it means to be 'scientific', an idea often based on a caricature of natural science.

Many natural scientists do not accept that science can be 'value free'. For instance, Michael Polanyi (who was unusual in being a Professor of Chemistry *and* a Professor of Social Studies) argued that it is impossible to be 'value free' in social or natural science (Polanyi, 1978, pp.15–17, 371–3). Attempts to exclude values typically involve limiting studies to narrow technical questions, but these are inevitably embedded in larger questions or assumptions about society and nature where values are unavoidable. Positivists who think values have been excluded may simply be blind to their own values.

Natural scientists in fact have major disagreements about social values. Decisions about research priorities and investment — what gets researched and what does not — are *social* decisions, and they shape the character of the natural science which is produced. There are disagreements about the social 'use' or 'misuse' of natural science; and in some of its most fundamental areas, disagreements involving social values (including religious views) which go right to the heart of the conceptions which natural scientists have of the natural world. Einstein believed the physics of the universe were predictable, and faced with Heisenberg's 'uncertainty principle' about the unpredictability of sub-atomic particles, he declared that 'God does not play dice'. Some physicists now speculate about God's role in the origin of the universe. Many questions about the historical development of nature (like most questions in social science) cannot be settled by replicable laboratory experiments, and one in particular — the question of how biological species evolved — clearly exemplifies the influence of social ideas on the interpretation of nature. Darwin's 'theory of evolution' was one of the most influential 'models' of natural science in the late nineteenth century, which is rather ironic because the theory's central causal mechanism — the notion of the 'survival of the fittest' — was derived from political and economic philosophy and the prevalent Victorian *social* theory of how human society operated. It is doubly ironic because this conception was then relayed back into social science (as 'social Darwinism') invested with all the 'objectivity' and prestige of natural science!

However, while rejecting the characterization of natural science as 'value free', it has to be acknowledged that social values usually impinge much more directly on social science because of its subject matter (Unit 4: 1.2). Short of inventing a whole new technical jargon, we have to use terms from everyday life which are already 'loaded' with social meanings and values. (Even seemingly innocent place-names. I once got into a spot of bother for referring in Open University material to 'Derry', which is what locals of all political persuasions call it in ordinary conversation, not least because 'Londonderry' is a bit of a mouthful. But someone objected that it might offend some students. So I used both words which may not have pleased everyone but at least showed that the term was politically contested.) Where people's values and disagreements are central to the subject-matter, it is difficult if not impossible to be completely 'neutral'. But that is all the more reason to acknowledge and be aware of values, rather than artificially trying to exclude them. Indeed some social scientists argue that it is *essential* to have a value position in order to be able to produce insights, and that it is morally wrong to try and exclude value judgements — to assume a position of 'neutrality' about, for instance, racial assaults or battered wives. It has been pointed out that a 'neutral' or 'value free' explanation of the Jewish 'Holocaust' would itself be an obscenity.

SUMMARY

- We have to be alert to the danger that our values may blind us to evidence which does not fit in with them, but the attempt to exclude values from social science can limit studies to narrow technical questions and may result in the values merely being 'hidden'.

- The four *traditions* developed in response to changes in society and through a mixture of competition and partial agreements with each other, as you saw in *marxism's* relationship with *liberalism* and *social reformism's* widespread 'borrowing'.

- The *traditions* are a major source of values in social science, but they have to be differentiated from any particular political parties or regimes which adopt similar 'labels'. As 'grand theories' of society they provide explanatory frameworks within which we can study particular social problems. However, the adoption of an 'acceptable' framework and 'acceptable' values is not a substitute for specific explanations, adequate evidence and proper methods of analysis.

---

4   SOCIAL ROLES OF SOCIAL SCIENCE

As well as being influenced by the *traditions*, social science gets its values more immediately from the varied roles it performs in contemporary society and the different social contexts within which social scientists work. Social science provides critical commentaries on society and detailed analysis of particular issues and problems. It is a force facilitating and shaping the ways society operates. Modern societies could not operate without it. It helps to clarify and solve problems, though curing, or not curing, them is in the broadest sense a matter of political decisions for the whole of society.

Social scientists work in educational institutions and specialized research centres, in central and local government, in private corporations, trade unions, charities and other types of organizations. How they approach their work and the values they bring to it are influenced by these different contexts. Where they are employed to do 'applied' research on topics specified by private or government institutions (e.g., economists working in financial institutions, psychologists in the personnel departments of large corporations, geographers in regional development agencies), the values involved may largely be determined by others — 'they who pay the piper call the tune' — and the work can lose its critical and exploratory edge by accepting the institution's 'official' definition of the problems being addressed. However, in most cases social scientists do not simply produce results 'to order' — not least because the results of research cannot be specified precisely in advance. In the case of 'pure' research, which is produced in universities and research institutes for general public consumption rather than for particular 'customers', the various discipline and interdisciplinary groups set their own agendas. In this type of institutional setting there is less direct external control over research topics and approaches. Nonetheless, even here, there are continuing tensions between performing roles specified by society — or rather by powerful groups and institutions — and the role of critic, saying things which people in society do not always want to hear.

You would probably have faced some of these tensions in the imaginary 'Going fishing' investigation of the polluted lake (Unit 4: 4.2). The initial motives for the research involved values — the values of a clean environment, opposition to pollution — and you would have had to make value judgements about who or what to blame — the farmers, the fertilizer manufacturers, European Community policy, or the capitalist organization of agriculture. But what — and this question also involves values — would you have done with your research findings? Given them to the local authority, or a political party, or an environmental pressure group? Gone fishing in another lake and left the whole messy business to someone else, or become actively involved in campaigning yourself? What might that have meant for the farming families whose livelihood, at least in the short term, depended on using the polluting fertilizers? And how might your intentions of what to do with the findings have influenced the actual research itself? There are no easy, happy-ever-after answers. It is people in society who make the decisions about which problems to solve and how to solve them. But social science, in providing explanations on which these decisions may be based, often involves 'taking sides', whether we are dealing with problems in the UK or more global problems such as international debt.

However, all 'sides' need reliable information, and values on their own do not provide it. In 1885 a survey by a *marxist* political group, the Social Democratic Federation, reported that a quarter of Londoners lived in abject poverty. Charles Booth, a wealthy supporter of *liberalism* determined to disprove this 'incendiary claim' which 'grossly overstated the case'. A scientific enquiry would expose the marxist exaggeration. But his massive survey of Londoners established that, contrary to his initial hypothesis, the marxists had actually *under*estimated the extent of poverty (see Booth 1903).

Research does not always bear out the values we start with, and social science has a role and influence in society by virtue of its scientific procedures rather than its values as such. It has to produce evidence and properly constructed explanations. But if it has socially relevant things to say it is unlikely to please everyone. It has many roles in society not all of them comfortable ones.

SUMMARY

The values in social science come from the immediate context in which it is produced as well as from intellectual traditions. Social science is produced in many different contexts, and there are tensions between its role as critic of society and producing results for powerful institutions and groups.

5 CONCLUSION

In this unit you have seen that *doing* social science involves thinking about alternative *explanatory frameworks* and the influence of *social values* on explanations. Explanations of existing social reality are coloured by values concerning how things *ought* to be. Values given a high priority — whether 'individual liberty', 'social stability', 'economic and social equality' or other values — predispose people to favour certain theories over others, and to judge some facts more important than others or to interpret them differently. The four intellectual *traditions* (summarized in Table 1) embody social values, and their overall conceptions of society provide alternative frameworks for explaining particular social issues or problems.

You may favour one tradition and be inclined to dismiss others, but it is important to remember that all four can provide insights. Particular explanations have to be assessed on their merits, rather than being dismissed because you don't sympathize with the values embedded in them. As Unit 4 emphasized, it is necessary to examine how explanations are constructed, their methods and evidence, as well as their underlying values and conceptions of society.

All these points will become clearer as the course progresses and you get more practice in *doing* social science. Some new or unfamiliar ideas may still be unclear but the important ones will be returned to again.

Block I was intended to whet your appetite. With its associated audio-visual material, chapters in the Reader and *The Good Study Guide*, the block has provided plenty of 'food for thought' about society, social science and how to study. There has been plenty to think about. You have been introduced to the three course themes — *Representation and Reality, Public and Private, Local and Global* — and to the different *traditions* of thought which you will be studying throughout the course. You have had a preliminary look at contemporary UK society seen in its historical and international setting. The first three units were a demonstration of social science in action, the last two a review of the methods used and a reflection on the nature of social science. You've covered a lot in five weeks. I hope you enjoyed it and that you'll enjoy the rest of the course.

REFERENCES

Booth, C. (1903) *Life and Labour of the People of London*, (Selected edition: *Charles Booth's London,* A. Fried, R. Elman (eds) (1971), Harmondsworth, Penguin.)

Callincos, A. (1983) *The Revolutionary Ideas of Karl Marx*, London, Bookmarks.

Edwards, R.D. and Williams, T.D. (eds) (1956) *The Great Famine: Studies in Irish History 1845-52*, Dublin, Browne and Nolan.

Gray, J. (1986) *Liberalism*, Milton Keynes, Open University Press.

Hallett, G. (1973) 'The political economy of regional policy', in Hallett, G. Randall, P. and West, E. (eds) *Regional Policy for Ever?*, London, Institute of Economic Affairs.

Kavanagh, D. and Morris, P. (1989) *Consensus Politics from Attlee to Thatcher*, Oxford, Basil Blackwell.

Nisbet, R. (1986) *Conservatism: Dream and Reality*, Milton Keynes, Open University Press.

Polanyi, M. (1978) *Personal Knowledge: Towards a Post-Critical Philosophy*, London, Routledge and Kegan Paul.

Roll, E. (1973) *A History of Economic Thought*, London, Faber and Faber.

ACKNOWLEDGEMENTS

Grateful acknowledgement is made to the following sources for permission to reproduce material in this unit:

p.186: Michael Heath; *p.188:* McKale/*Thin Black Lines*; *p.192:* National Portrait Gallery; *pp.193 and 202:* Mary Evans Picture Library; *pp.194, 199 and 200:* Mansell Collection; *p.195:* Ramsey & Muspratt Archive; *p.198:* Scottish National Portrait Gallery; *p.201:* Hulton Deutsch Collection; *p.205:* MacNelly/ *Thin Black Lines/Chicago Tribune/*Universal Press Syndicate.

STUDY SKILLS SECTION: WRITING TMA 01

Prepared for the Course Team by Elaine Storkey

By now you will probably be thinking about that first assessed assignment which you will be writing on this block. I hope that the practice run proved a help and that the essays in Chapter 5 of *The Good Study Guide* gave you some thoughts about the different ways of constructing an essay. What I want to do now is just to pull some points together to help you focus on the task coming up. You might have come across some of this advice before, but it will bear repeating! You should also refer to the audio-cassette for Block I which contains some general comments on writing TMA 01. It is always a good idea to have a few rules of thumb close at hand before you settle down to write this first TMA.

I   WHAT IS EXPECTED FROM YOU IN A D103 ASSIGNMENT

In the past you may have been set essays which were particularly designed to exercise your *imagination*. For example you might have been told 'Write a story which begins: "The twilight threw the Big Top into dark relief against the subdued sky …"' Or alternatively, you may have been given titles which asked especially for your *opinion*: 'Write 1,000 words on "Capital punishment is the scourge of civilized society"'. Or again, there may have been essays designed to test your *memory*: 'Write a detailed account of the Battle of Bannockburn'. So it is sometimes difficult for students new to the Social Sciences to learn that in D103 we are not primarily testing imagination, opinion or memory.

Instead, the TMAs are designed to give you practice at developing your own responses to the course material; and to assess how competent you are becoming in grasping some ideas, arguments and issues which are important in the Social Sciences. They are there to find out if you have understood the course material, and, eventually, whether you are able to apply the concepts and analyses of the course to other examples and situations. This does not mean of course that you must write dull prose, never give your 'opinions', nor recall some other relevant points from memory. But it does mean that whatever views you offer they must be backed up with arguments, reasons and evidence which relate closely to the material and to the question set.

So the TMAs are set on different units in the course, and the notes you have made on the units will be very important in helping you to prepare for the writing, which is one reason why we laid such stress on note-taking earlier in the block.

2   GIVE YOURSELF ENOUGH TIME

You will have noticed that the students who wrote those short essays in *The Good Study Guide* took quite a long time over it. Very few people, even professional writers, can make notes, plan and write a polished essay in one complete sitting. For most of us (including me), the subject has to be around in our head for days or even weeks before we can get down to committing that first sentence to paper. Even then, the chances are that the sentence will be scrapped by the end! So don't try to short-cut on the thinking process. But don't panic either if you have done some thinking and you still find you're sitting in front of a blank sheet of paper and nothing seems to be coming. It just means there are endless possibilities yet to be realized! A few systematic steps might help you in the process.

3   THINK ABOUT THE ESSAY QUESTION

It is a good idea to have the essay question in mind as you go through a piece of reading, even if you are not intending to write the essay for several days. That way, you are already asking questions from the text which will be relevant when you come to write. It is important therefore that you understand the question, and don't feel thrown by it. So what are the key words in the TMA questions? Underline them, and ring any that you're not quite sure about. You could try putting the question into your own words. Then go back to the original wording. Is there anything you haven't understood? Reading it out loud several times, emphasizing the key words can make even a difficult-looking question become much clearer.

So what kind of question is it? Is it asking you to list, to discuss, describe, compare, or is it a mixture of these? How many parts are there to the question? If there is more than one, do you understand what each part is looking for?

Let's take as an example a TMA question you might have been given for this block:

Discuss the view that foreign aid is of no long-term advantage in alleviating famine.

This is a *discuss* question: it is asking you to identify the issue, to look at some pros and cons, perhaps mentioning what different people have to say on the subject and then draw some conclusion. When you 'discuss the view that ...' you can also bring in another view which says something different as part of your discussion.

So picking out the other key words would give you 'foreign aid', 'no long-term advantage', and 'alleviating famine'. You might rewrite the question for yourself; it could be something like: 'In the long-run, giving famine-stricken countries aid won't make their situation better. — Is this true?'

4   LOOK OVER YOUR NOTES IN THE LIGHT OF THE TMA QUESTIONS

The essay questions are designed to get you to think over what you have been studying. Most of the material you need for the essay may be in your notes, but they may not be in the form you want. You might have summarized the argument well and got many important factors down but perhaps there are missing points which now seem more important. You may also have to select from your notes or restructure them to the emphasis in the TMA questions. If you don't feel you have what you need there, look at the most relevant sections of the unit and go through them again. You are not being asked to simply repeat the material, so don't get into a habit of copying out large sections of the unit into your essay. But if you find a really succinct sentence, which you think you might like to quote later, jot it down. Remember to make a note of where it came from: a reference to the unit is important both for you and for your tutor reading your assignment.

5   NOTE DOWN SOME IDEAS

Many students find that when they have an essay question in front of them the most productive way to start is by 'brainstorming' — writing down everything that comes to mind which is relevant to the question. Initially, you don't need to put these down in any order, or even in clear sentences. They may be very random, haphazard ideas, bits of recall from the unit, or any odd point you can just remember. Just jot down the ideas as they occur to you. If you are the sort of person who thinks quickly and can make a lot of connections this will be a time when you cover a lot of paper. You may of course end up with far too many ideas for the space allowed. With a later reading, some of what you've written might be off the subject. So you will have to prune your jottings, order them, work out which belong together, and perhaps reject some. But you have made a start.

However, even with this method some students may find that nothing comes readily to mind at all. In that case, it's a good idea to re-read your notes, look over those unit sections and Summaries again, and lift out anything which seems relevant. The TMA is based on the unit, don't forget, so all the relevant points will be there. Just think of yourself as having to do a little detective work.

With the 'discuss' title on foreign aid and famine, my brainstorming produced the following:

> 'emergency relief vital', 'stops starvation short-term'. 'Long-term could help sustain projects', 'redistribution', 'aid helps development', 'dependency created — reinforces power of developed countries', 'home-grown technology possible', 'what about trade?', 'better to stop exploitation than give aid?' 'What does it mean by advantage?', 'where does political control come in?' 'interdependence?' 'where's the catch?'

You can see that my jottings were a mixture of ideas and questions. The ideas came to mind as I recalled Unit 2, and the questions were those I might need to resolve in the answer. Of course I have an advantage over you since I have read Unit 2 on several occasions. You might have found the ideas did not come so quickly and you needed to look up Section 4.4 and read the part on 'The flow of aid'. Don't worry. That is what it is there for!

6   ARRANGE YOUR IDEAS AROUND THE QUESTION

At some stage your collection of ideas will have to be assembled into an essay which has a beginning, a middle, and an end. This means that you will need to make a plan to help you place all your jottings in the right slot in your answer. All you are doing here is mapping out how your essay might develop and what its overall structure will be. And you can try several plans (as you would if you were planning a new layout for part of your home), before you decide that one of them offers you the greatest scope for putting your ideas together into a coherent answer to the question.

Back to my example TMA: *'Discuss the view that foreign aid is of no long-term advantage in alleviating famine.'* When I look again at this question, and at the sections in the unit, and my own notes and jottings, I can see that several headings emerge. Obviously, I need an introduction. Then there are arguments *for* the view, and arguments *against* the view. (Which way round should I put them?) Finally, I need a short conclusion.

My plan might look like this:

1 *Introduction:*
   what the essay is about:
   what is foreign aid? — some definition
   Who is involved   • public agencies
                       • private citizens

Where does aid go? • Third World countries
                    • Development programmes.
                    • Emergency relief.

Set question up for rest of essay to answer — short term it is obviously vital in terms of emergency — stops people starving to death. But long-term?

Effectiveness of foreign aid in long-term alleviation of famine?

2 *Arguments for:*

*   Funds new development projects, sanitation, roads, better health service, education.

*   Brings in new technology: which helps grow crops, develops irrigation systems, prevents future droughts.

*   Raises consciousness (and conscience) of rich countries and keeps them involved.

*   Brings experience and expertise of rich countries to poorer countries.

*   Even emergency relief helps people through a time of famine and builds up their resources for the future.

*   Helps poor countries to become self-sustaining.

3 *Arguments against:*

*   Aid creates dependency, making poor countries dependent on affluent countries and therefore politically vulnerable. Aid can be used as a weapon against them.

*   Opens poor countries up to more exploitation and gives them a weaker bargaining position, especially in trading.

*   Countries don't become strong or self-sufficient when dependent on aid. Famine will remain a potential problem.

*   Aid in the end favours the rich of the world, not the poor.

4 *Conclusion:*

*   Which side do I come down on?

*   Pick out the most significant point 'for and against'.

7   WRITING A FIRST DRAFT

It is at this stage that you can now take up another clean sheet of paper and actually start to put down some of those ideas, shaped and developed according to the plan you have made. But even now, unless you are a practised writer, you may need several attempts before you have produced an essay you are satisfied with. That's why it is a good idea to think of this initial writing stage as a first draft. You are trying out your ideas and your plan to see if they work.

But before you start you do need to think about your audience. Who are you writing for? Well, that seems easy enough: you are writing for your tutor. But in fact it is not quite that simple, for if you were writing only for your tutor you would probably not bother to say half the things you are going to say in this essay, because they would already be very familiar to him or her. So, although the tutor marks it, the essay is really aimed at some interested lay-person who does not yet have all the information you want to offer, and who would enjoy having your ideas spelled out. But you also need to assume that this person would be fairly alert and possibly even critical — he or she might ask questions and will need to be convinced!

The important thing about a first draft is probably simply to make a start in writing to this interested person 'out there' and get down as many of your ideas in as structured a form as you can.

At the end of your draft, or as far as you have managed to get on the first attempt it is a good idea to put it away, rather than struggling on for hours more trying to get it right. It would be better to come back next day and look at it again. The trouble is that something which seemed to be written very clearly the night before might turn out next day to be incomprehensible! But it is also true that thoughts which just would not go down on paper at one time can come quickly and clearly after a break.

8   WRITING A FINAL VERSION

In reading and correcting the first draft it is good to have a few questions in your mind. First, are the sentences clear; are there any verbs missing; do the sentences get over your points well? Second, are the steps of your essay easy to follow; do you carefully lead the reader from one point to the next? Third, have you linked up some of the ideas which go together and have you separated ideas by using new paragraphs or *link words*? Fourth, what about *signposting* — have you put in words or sentences which give your reader some directions, indicating where you have been and where you are going next? Fifth, have you included examples to help your reader get the point more easily? Finally, is there an obvious conclusion, rather than a sudden end? Have you rounded off what you have said, perhaps leaving a particular point or set of points for the reader to take away?

If you have time, it is often a very good idea to read your whole finished essay out loud, imagining yourself trying to communicate to this imaginary person, and seeing how convincing you sound! Better still, find a real person who will sit and listen with a sympathetic ear, and tell you what works best and what did not come over so clearly.

It is important to get the TMA in on time: even if you are not happy with it, feel completely discouraged, wish you had never started, and are already drafting your letter resigning from the course! Just hand the TMA in! Your tutor is there to give you advice and help, and may well see ways in which you can improve quite painlessly. What's more, that's one assignment down and only six more to go.